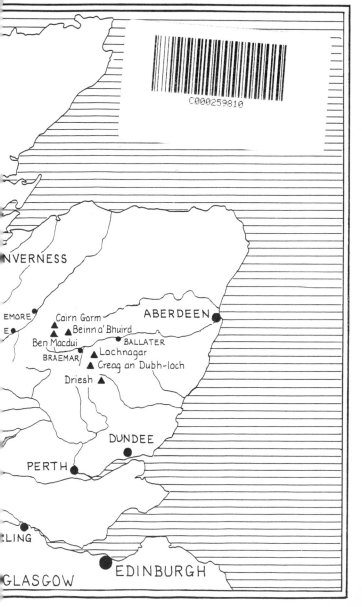

SCOTTISH
WINTER CLIMBS

SCOTTISH MOUNTAINEERING CLUB

Scottish Winter Climbs

Classic Routes from An Teallach to The Cobbler

Compiled by
Andy Nisbet
Rab Anderson

Series Editor: Roger Everett

SCOTTISH MOUNTAINEERING CLUB
CLIMBERS GUIDE

Published in Great Britain by the Scottish Mountaineering Trust, 1996
Copyright © The Scottish Mountaineering Club

British Library Cataloguing in Publication Data
ISBN 0-907521-47-9

A catalogue record for this book is available from
the British Library

Illustrations
Front Cover: The Shield Direct, Ben Nevis
                 (Climber, Andy Forsyth) *Bruce Goodlad*
Pretitle page: Liathach   *John Bennet*
Frontispiece: On the Forcan Ridge of The Saddle   *Gill Nisbet*
Back Cover: In Coire an Lochain, Aonach Mor   *Roger Everett*

Maps drawn by Jim Renny and Noel Williams
Diagrams drawn by Jeremy Ashcroft, Donald Bennet, Mary Benstead,
   Davy Gardner and Kevin Howett
Production by Scottish Mountaineering Trust (Publications) Ltd
Typeset by Westec, North Connel
Colour separations by Arneg Ltd, Glasgow
Printed by M and M Press, Glasgow; White Crescent Press, Luton
   and St Edmundsbury Press, Bury St Edmunds
Bound by Hunter and Foulis, Edinburgh

Distributed by Cordee, 3a DeMontfort Street, Leicester, LE1 7HD

Contents

Introduction   1
The Northern Highlands   15
 Beinn Dearg   16
 An Teallach   22
  A' Ghlas Thuill   24
  Toll an Lochain   26
 Sgurr Mor   29
 Sgurr nan Clach Geala   30
 Liathach   34
  Coireag Dubh Beag   38
  Coireag Dubh Mor   40
  Coire na Caime   45
  The South Side of Liathach   54
 Beinn Eighe   55
  Coire Mhic Fhearchair   55
 Sail Mhor   62
 Beinn Alligin   63
 Fuar Tholl   65
  South-East Cliff   66
 Sgorr Ruadh   72
 Beinn Bhan   75
  Coire na Feola   77
  Coire na Poite   78
  Coire nan Fhamhair   82
 Sgurr a' Chaorachain   83
 Meall Gorm   83
 The Saddle   85

The Cairngorms   86
 The Northern Corries of Cairn Gorm   87
  Coire an t-Sneachda   87
  Coire an Lochain   103
 Loch Avon Basin   112
  Carn Etchachan   113
  Shelter Stone Crag   118
  Hell's Lum Crag   122
  Stag Rocks   127
 Creagan a' Choire Etchachan   130
 Beinn a' Bhuird   135

Lochnagar	139
Creag an Dubh-loch	150
Eagles Rock	158
Glen Clova	159
Driesh	159
Corrie Fee	160
Ben Nevis and Lochaber	165
Ben Nevis	166
Coire Leis	176
The Little Brenva Face	177
North-East Buttress	178
Observatory Gully	180
The Minus Face	180
The Orion Face	181
Observatory Buttress	187
Indicator Wall	188
Tower Ridge	192
The Douglas Boulder	193
Secondary Tower Ridge	193
Garadh na Ciste	196
Coire na Ciste	197
Number Two Gully Buttress	197
Comb Gully Buttress	198
Number Three Gully Buttress	200
Creag Coire na Ciste	203
Trident Buttresses	204
Carn Dearg	207
Carn Dearg Buttress	208
Raeburn's Buttress	212
The Castle	212
Castle Ridge	213
North Wall of Castle Ridge	214
Aonach Mor	215
Coire an Lochain	217
West Face	224
Aonach Beag	225
North Face	225
West Face	229
Creag Meagaidh	231
Bellevue Buttress	233
Pinnacle Buttress	233
The Post Face	236

The Inner Corrie 240

Glen Coe 243
Buachaille Etive Mor 244
  North and North-West Faces 247
  North-East Face 250
  East and South-East Faces 253
The Bidean nam Bian Massif 255
Coire Gabhail (The Lost Valley) 256
  Lost Valley Minor Buttress 257
  Lost Valley Buttress 258
  East Face of Gearr Aonach 262
Stob Coire nan Lochan 267
  Coire nan Lochan 267
  North-West Face of Gearr Aonach 275
  East Face of Aonach Dubh 275
  North Face of Aonach Dubh 276
Coire nam Beithach 278
  West Face of Aonach Dubh 279
Stob Coire nam Beith 283
Bidean nam Bian 288
  Diamond Buttress 289
  Church Door Buttress 289
  West Top 292
Aonach Eagach 293

The Southern Highlands 295
The Bridge of Orchy Hills 296
Stob Ghabhar 296
Beinn an Dothaidh 299
  North-East Corrie 299
  Creag Coire an Dothaidh 304
Beinn Dorain 307
  Creag an Socach 307
Beinn Udlaidh 311
  Coire Daimh 311
Ben Lui 316
Beinn Chuirn 317
The Arrochar Alps 317
The Cobbler 318
  North Face of The South Peak 320
  Centre Peak Buttress 322
  South Face of The North Peak 323

List of Diagrams and Maps

Northern Highlands, Ullapool to Loch Fannich (Map) 17
Beinn Dearg, Gleann na Sguaib 19
Beinn Dearg, West Buttress 21
An Teallach, A'Ghlas Thuill 25
An Teallach, Toll an Lochain 27
Sgurr nan Clach Geala, East Face 33
Northern Highlands, Torridon to Applecross (Map) 35
Liathach, Coireag Dubh Beag 37
Liathach, Coireag Dubh Mor 43
Liathach, Coire na Caime (east) 49
Liathach, Coire na Caime (west) 51
Beinn Eighe, Coire Mhic Fhearchair 59
Fuar Tholl, South-East Cliff 69
Sgorr Ruadh, Raeburn's Buttress 73
Beinn Bhan, Coire na Feola 79
Beinn Bhan, Coire na Poite 81
The Cairngorms (Map) 88-89
Coire an t-Sneachda, The Mess of Pottage 93
Coire an t-Sneachda, Aladdin's and Fluted Buttresses 95
Coire an t-Sneachda, Fiacaill Ridge 101
Coire an Lochain (left) 105
Coire an Lochain (right) 109
Carn Etchachan 117
Shelter Stone Crag 121
Hell's Lum Crag 125
Stag Rocks 129
Creagan a' Choire Etchachan 133
Beinn a' Bhuird, Garbh Choire 137
Lochnagar 143
Creag an Dubh-loch 153
Driesh, Winter Corrie 161
Corrie Fee, South Face 163
Ben Nevis and Lochaber (Map) 169
Ben Nevis, The North-East Face 172-173
Ben Nevis Summit (Map) 175
Ben Nevis, North-East Buttress to Tower Gully 179
Ben Nevis, Observatory Ridge and Buttress 185
Ben Nevis, West Face of Tower Ridge 195
Ben Nevis, Number Three Gully Buttress 201

Ben Nevis, Creag Coire na Ciste	205
Carn Dearg	211
Aonach Mor, Coire an Lochain	218-219
Aonach Beag, North Face	227
Creag Meagaidh, Coire Ardair	237
Creag Meagaidh, The Inner Corrie	241
Glen Coe (Map)	245
Buachaille Etive Mor, North Face	249
The Lost Valley Buttresses	259
East Face of Gearr Aonach	265
Stob Coire nan Lochan, Summit Buttress	269
Stob Coire nan Lochan, South, Central and North Buttresses	273
Aonach Dubh, North Face	277
Aonach Dubh, West Face	281
Stob Coire nam Beith	285
Bidean nam Bian, Diamond and Church Door Buttresses	291
The Southern Highlands (Map)	297
Beinn an Dothaidh, North-East Corrie	301
Beinn an Dothaidh, Creag Coire an Dothaidh	305
Beinn Dorain, Creag an Socach	309
Beinn Udlaidh, Coire Daimh (east)	312-313
Beinn Udlaidh, Coire Daimh (west)	315
The Cobbler	319
The Cobbler, North Face of the South Peak	321
The Cobbler, South Face of the North Peak	325

The Climber and the Mountain Environment

.With increasing numbers of walkers and climbers going to the Scottish hills, it is important that all of us who do so should recognise our responsibilities to the mountain environment in which we find our pleasure and recreation, to our fellow climbers, and to those who live and work on the land.

The Scottish Mountaineering Club and Trust, who jointly produce this and other guidebooks, wish to point out to all who avail themselves of the information in these books that it is in everyone's interest that good relations are maintained between visitors and landowners, particularly when there might be conflicts of interest, for example during the stalking season. The description of a climbing, walking or skiing route in any of these books does not imply that a right of way exists, and it is the responsibility of all climbers to ascertain the position before setting out. In cases of doubt it is best to enquire locally.

During stalking and shooting seasons in particular, much harm can be done in deer forests and on grouse moors by people walking through them. Normally the deer stalking season is from 1st July to 20th October, when stag shooting ends. Hinds may continue to be culled until 15th February. The grouse shooting season is from 12th August until 10th December. These activities are important for the economy of many Highland estates. During these seasons, therefore, consideration should be given to consulting the local landowner, factor or keeper before taking to the hills.

Climbers and hill walkers are recommended to consult the book HEADING FOR THE SCOTTISH HILLS, published by the Scottish Mountaineering Trust on behalf of the Mountaineering Council of Scotland and the Scottish Landowners Federation, which gives the names and addresses of factors and keepers who may be contacted for information regarding access to the hills.

It is important to avoid disturbance to sheep, particularly during the lambing season between March and May. Dogs should not be taken onto the hills at this time, and at all times should be kept under close control.

Always try to follow a path or track through cultivated land and forests, and avoid causing damage to fences, dykes and gates by climbing over them carelessly. Do not leave litter anywhere, but take it down from the hill in your rucksack.

The number of walkers and climbers on the hills is leading to increased, and in some cases very unsightly erosion of footpaths and hillsides. Some of the revenue from the sale of this and other SMC guidebooks is used by the Trust to assist financially the work being carried out to repair and maintain hill paths in Scotland. However, it is important for all of us to recognise our responsibility to minimise the erosive effect of our passage over the hills so that the enjoyment of future climbers shall not be spoiled by landscape damage caused by ourselves.

As a general rule, where a path exists walkers should follow it and even where it is wet and muddy should avoid walking along its edges, the effect of which is to extend erosion sideways. Do not take short-cuts at the corners of zigzag paths. Remember that the worst effects of erosion are likely to be caused during or soon after prolonged wet weather when the ground is soft and waterlogged. A route on stony or rocky hillside is likely to cause less erosion than on a grassy one at such times.

Although the use of bicycles can often be very helpful for reaching remote crags and hills, the erosion damage that can be caused by them when used 'off road' on soft footpaths and open hillsides is such that their use on such terrain must cause concern. It is the editorial policy of the Scottish Mountaineering Club that the use of bicycles in hill country may be recommended on hard tracks such as forest roads or private roads following rights of way, but it is not recommended on footpaths or open hillsides where the environmental damage that they cause may be considerable. Readers are asked to bear these points in mind, particularly in conditions when the ground is wet and soft after rain.

The proliferation of cairns on hills detracts from the feeling of wildness, and may be confusing rather than helpful as regards route-finding. The indiscriminate building of cairns on the hills is therefore to be discouraged.

Climbers are reminded that they should not drive along private estate roads without permission, and when parking their cars should avoid blocking access to private roads and land, and should avoid causing any hazard to other road users.

Finally, the Scottish Mountaineering Club and the Scottish Mountaineering Trust can accept no liability for damage to property nor for personal injury resulting from the use of any route described in their publications.

Acknowledgements

The production of this guide has been the result of the efforts of many people. In particular, we are indebted to the authors of the comprehensive guidebooks of the SMC Climbers Guides Series, whose work formed the basis of much of the content of this book. Among these authors are Geoff Cohen, Ken Crocket, Simon Richardson and Allen Fyffe.

The quality of the text was further improved by those who made constructive comments, among whom are Dave Broadhead, Dave Cuthbertson, Graeme Ettle, John Lyall, Martin Moran, Tom Prentice and Martin Welch.

We would also like to thank everyone who supplied photographs for consideration. The illustrations that were selected came from a total of more than 500 that were viewed during a session that lasted long into the night. The diagrams and maps were drawn by a team of artists — Kev Howett, Mary Benstead, Donald Bennet, Davy Gardner, Jeremy Ashcroft, Jim Renny and Noel Williams. We thank them all.

The production of the book would not have been possible without the support and encouragement of members of the SMC Publications Sub-Committee. In particular, thanks are due to Roger Everett for preparation of the text on disc prior to our work as authors and for editing the final versions, and to Donald Bennet for meticulous proof-reading and comments on the text, and his work on the design and production of the book.

Andy Nisbet and Rab Anderson
November 1995

Introduction

Scottish winter climbing is now an activity of international importance, with visitors arriving from not only south of the border and from all corners of Europe, but also from the other side of the Atlantic. This huge rise in popularity is easily explained by the very special climbing conditions that are readily produced by the alternation of the influences of moist maritime and cold polar air masses. The frequent freeze-thaw cycles and high precipitation creates snow, ice and 'mixed' conditions which can be a joy to climb, often in remote and impressive surroundings. However, the very factors which produce these unique climbing conditions are themselves a problem for the climber; the weather may be poor, even hostile, and the rapidly changing conditions may make one crag a bad choice, while another nearby is excellent. For a first-time or occasional visitor these problems can be frustrating, even dangerous. This book aims to overcome the frustrations by describing a selection of the best winter climbs throughout mainland Scotland, with notes on how to judge weather and climbing conditions to select the best option for the day. We have also expanded the repertoire from that of other selected guides in the hope that this may encourage climbers to venture from the well known climbing areas (excellent though they are) so that they may discover the wealth of opportunity that lies elsewhere. Finally, the leading activists suggest that success depends as much on tactics as on sheer ability, so we have included a section on hints of how to get the most out of your visit. The routes that we have selected are spread throughout the grades, but any selection is bound to be open to argument. Suffice to say that there are many other excellent climbs and crags in Scotland that have not been described in this book, so if your appetite has been whetted you can obtain fully comprehensive coverage in the SMC Climbers' Guides series.

CHOICE OF VENUE

Scottish weather and conditions are very variable, so flexible plans are the key to success. The ideal is to decide the destination area a day or two before departure, and the particular cliff the day before, reviewed in the morning. Any plans made several days ahead of a weather forecast are a gamble to be avoided if possible. Those who can go climbing midweek at short notice have a big advantage. The general weather rule is to let the wind cross as much land as possible to find the least snowfall and mist. If the weather is cold (and has been for a few days), stay low; if mild, go high. Avoid visiting a cliff for the first time in mist. If it is thawing at all levels, perhaps go home. If there is a blizzard, go home. Going home should make you keen not to miss the next spell of good weather. It is crucial to be keen, but don't push your luck in deteriorating weather or on potential avalanche slopes.

Prediction of good conditions is harder, particularly in relation to the thickness of ice which is determined by the weather during the previous weeks. Years of experience will help accurate prediction, but the word from someone who's been there recently will always be better. Generally speaking, a long spell of cold weather without thaws means thicker ice, although not on Ben Nevis and parts of the Cairngorms, where thaws are required. Conditions for turf and rock mixed climbing are less critical, but try to avoid deep powder or unfrozen turf. Remember that the turf will freeze more rapidly early in the winter if it is not insulated by a thick layer of fresh snow.

THE NORTHERN HIGHLANDS
Conditions can be good even into April, especially with easterly or northerly winds, but showery polar maritime (heavy snow) or tropical maritime winds (quick thaw) often bring poor conditions. There is a wide variety of options if it is cold enough. Note that it is further to drive, information on conditions may be harder to obtain, and the weather can be different to everywhere else.

THE CAIRNGORMS
The best climbing is usually early or late season, as deep powder or thick rime cause problems in the middle. The mixed climbing is reliable. The weather is drier and colder than the west during the prevailing westerly winds, but prone to wind and spindrift. Northerly or easterly winds often cause poor conditions.

BEN NEVIS
This is the best venue for snow-ice, which can be wonderful or awful. Go mid to late season, after thaws and a re-freeze. The Ben is useless and dangerous under deep powder, and mixed climbing is very limited. Early season and mixed climbing alternatives can be found on the nearby Aonachs.

CREAG MEAGAIDH

Ice climbing predominates here, which requires good conditions, both for safety on the routes and the long approach. It is a place to avoid under powder or spindrift, and February or March are usually best.

GLEN COE

There is a wide variety of options here. Cold conditions are required for good ice, which can be quickly stripped by thaw, so it is not a good late season venue. Northerly or easterly winds bode well.

THE SOUTHERN HIGHLANDS AND ARROCHAR

The climbing here is mostly turfy, but some ice forms if it is cold. Many of the cliffs are relatively low, and so they are very prone to thaw in tropical maritime winds. Avoid in late season, but turf conditions can be excellent after heavy frosts and light snow in early winter.

SUMMARY OF BEST SEASON:

Nov to Dec: Cairngorms, Aonach Mor
Jan: Southern Highlands and Arrochar; low areas of Glen Coe; Northern Highlands
Feb: Creag Meagaidh, Glen Coe, Northern Highlands
March: Cairngorms, Ben Nevis, high areas of Glen Coe and Northern Highlands
April: Ben Nevis, Cairngorms

WEATHER FORECASTS

The weather forecast is one of the key factors in choice of venue. Obviously it may not be correct, especially for more than two days ahead, although better than your best guess. Once committed (i.e. after arrival), the best information is found by looking out the window. The other problem is interpreting a ground level forecast into a mountain forecast, particularly one relevant to your intended route. This takes much practice; cliff altitude, aspect and location, and wind strength and direction are all important factors. Obviously the temperature is crucial, but this is not always easily predicted from the valley. While it is true that it usually gets colder the higher one goes, the rate at which this happens (the lapse rate) depends on the origin and humidity of the air mass. As a general rule, the lapse rate is lower in moist maritime air than in showery polar air. Hence, if it is mild and drizzly (say 8 to 10 degrees C) in the valley it will probably be soggy on most cliffs, while the same valley temperature in a north-westerly airflow may cause crisp and sparkling neve high up. Another exception is in periods of settled high pressure, when temperature inversions keep the valleys cold (and sometimes dull) while the crags may be basking in sunshine above a blanket of cloud. Those climbing for one or two days can obtain the forecast before leaving home; those with a longer time in the hills are advised to update their information. The four choices are radio, TV, newspaper or telephone recorded messages.

Radio

Radio 4 gives the most concise forecasts, although often lacking detail for Scotland. Radio Scotland forecasts are quite good. The best combination is the Shipping Forecast on Radio 4 (5.50 pm) giving sea winds which are relevant to mountain winds, followed by the weather forecast (5.55 pm) with other details, particularly rain, snow and timing of fronts. On the Shipping Forecast, Mallin (south-west), Hebrides (north-west) and Cromarty (east) are relevant.

Newspapers

A synoptic chart, from which mountain weather can be interpreted, is important. The Scottish national papers, *The Scotsman* and *The Herald*, include a chart and Scottish detail. The tabloids are useless.

Television

The BBC offers a better and more detailed chart than ITV. The forecast after Reporting Scotland (between 6.50 and 7.00 pm) is perhaps the best. Current weather readings from Cairngorm summit (temperature and wind) are on the Ceefax ski report service. This is particularly useful to monitor the pattern of thaw and freeze during the week prior to the trip, and it also gives a short-term freezing level, wind and weather forecast for the Cairngorm, Lecht, Aonach Mor and Glen Coe areas.

Telephone

There are two recorded message sources which give good mountain forecasts, but it is expensive to obtain all the necessary information, especially from a public phone booth. Both give similar information including a two-day forecast of weather and mountain conditions, including summit winds and freezing levels, followed by a three-day outlook forecast and lastly the Scottish Avalanche Information Service report.

Climbline: East Highlands (Cairngorms): 0891 654 668
West Highlands (Lochaber, Glen Coe): 0891 654 669

There is also a FAX service: 0336 413 075
Mountaincall: Scotland West: 0891 500 441
　　　　　　　　Scotland East: 0891 500 442

AVALANCHE FORECASTS

The Scottish Avalanche Information Service provides avalanche forecasts throughout the winter. These are available through the telephone services (detailed above) and also by e-mail (just send any message to AVALANCHE@DCS.GLA.AC.UK and the latest forecast will be sent in reply). These forecasts are based on actual observation, so they apply only to the most popular climbing areas. Climbers in the Northern Highlands will have to make their own assessments. The forecasts are often posted in outdoor shops or at strategic positions in the climbing areas.

However, it should be stressed that climbers must use this information intelligently; local avalanches may occur despite a low risk level forecast, and conversely, a high risk forecast does not necessarily mean a day restricted to the valley. However, climbers venturing into known avalanche territory in periods of high risk are definitely asking for trouble.

RISKS

Scottish winter climbing is a potentially dangerous sport, but part of the challenge is reduction of the risk to an acceptable level. The following are common causes of accidents:

DETERIORATING WEATHER

The number of fine days in the winter is small, so you must climb in poor weather if you want to get anything done! But there is a big difference between poor and stormy weather. Stormy weather in the morning is less of a problem, because a change of plans is obvious. A fine start with a rapid deterioration to wind and blowing snow can be a trap. It is hard for the inexperienced to realise just how bad the weather can get; ferocious winds with blowing snow can make walking and navigation almost impossible, preventing descent. This can and does prove fatal; it happens every year. The only answer is to have flexible plans when the forecast is poor. A quick easy route ahead of the bad weather is still fun, but have the courage to turn back if it seems prudent. Remember that the weather on top is likely to be much worse than in the relative shelter of the cliff or gully.

BASIC MOUNTAINEERING SKILLS

The importance of proficiency in ice axe braking, walking in crampons and navigation, and sufficient fitness, can be underestimated by those who are climbers instead of hillwalkers. In fact, of those in their first winter season, the experienced winter hillwalker is perhaps more likely to be a safe winter climber than a technical rock climber, who has much to learn. These skills apply to the unroped part of the day, but this is normally the longer part. Don't relax at the top of the route; maintain concentration and a sense of urgency until the road is reached. Many of Scotland's best winter climbers started with an instructional course, and this can only be recommended.

AVALANCHES

The possibility of avalanches should always be considered unless all the snow is hard or there is only a dusting. An awareness that avalanches are common coupled with some knowledge of how they occur is half the battle. Be flexible in your route choice, because normally there are safe options, even if the grade is easier than planned (including bagging a peak instead of a Grade I climb). The other half of the battle, deciding whether a potential risk is real, is anything but easy and even experienced climbers get avalanched, although excessive enthusiasm in poor conditions is usually their problem.

By far the commonest cause of avalanches in Scotland is windslab, which is wind-blown snow settling in an unstable layer, usually on lee slopes. Any freshly deposited snow should be treated as highly suspicious, whether freshly fallen or powder blown onto a lee slope. The greater the depth, the greater the risk. If you can see spindrift, then it is likely there will be dangerous slopes where snow is settling. The steeper the angle of slope, the greater the force on any layer; but snow does not settle above 60 degrees and tends to slough down above 45 degrees. 35-45 degrees is therefore the worst angle. Continuous wind will maintain the risk but if the direction changes, new slopes will accumulate snow and become dangerous, whereas freshly scoured slopes will become safe. Any top layer of soft snow (if you sink in as you walk) should be tested before entering the "danger zone". The test is to determine how well the top layer is bonded to layers below. The method is to excavate a vertical wall exposing the layers of snow, then a quick examination followed by a practical test of increasing pressure to see how easily the top layer will slide off. If you've never seen a "snow pit", get someone to show you. It normally takes one to two minutes. Literature is useful, but nothing beats practical experience. Consider the following questions and principles:

1. Before leaving your accommodation, before leaving the road and as you approach the cliff, consider whether the choice of cliff is sensible in terms of windslab accumulation. Is snow being blown (or has it been recently) and collecting above, on, or below the cliff? Unfortunately for the climber's comfort, snow collects in sheltered spots, normally on cliffs or slopes facing away from the wind.

2. Having looked at conditions and thought of a route, is it possible to reach the route safely? Winter cliffs have a snow slope below them which normally steepens up to about 45 degrees, the worst angle for avalanches. Also, the base of a cliff is where snow accumulates at its deepest. Is there a fresh layer of snow (as against isolated patches) of sufficient depth to avalanche (about 15cm)? If in doubt, dig a pit but remember that any dangerous layer will deepen approaching the cliff base. So assess the depth of the top layer as you proceed. Other factors are often observed and can aid decision. Convex slopes seem more dangerous (the snow below is less supported from below). Protruding rocks help to anchor a slope. Even a thin crust (starting to freeze after a thaw) stabilises a slope.

3. Having reached it, is the route safe? Ridges are much safer than gullies, but only assuming they continue as ridges to the top.

4. Is the finish, particularly the cornice, safe? Snow, freshly blown over a cliff top, tends to accumulate on the cornice itself and the slope immediately below. On a big cliff it is easy to underestimate the amount of snow collecting so far away. While the slope below a cliff tends to avalanche when triggered by a climber, cornice slopes tend to avalanche spontaneously and funnel down gullies. The consequences of an avalanche at the top of a climb are more serious.

5. Once you are on or below the slope, you are committed!

6. However much you know, no-one knows everything. Even the Scottish Avalanche Information Service are continually modifying their ideas, following an unpredicted event or snow formation. So there will be many exceptions to the above generalisations. For example, windslab has been known to become more dangerous with time (instead of the normal consolidation) due to vapourisation inside the snowpack.

7. Avalanche reports are informative, but slopes can stabilise or become more dangerous even before the tester reaches the foot of the climb. Your own assessment at the cliff is crucial.

8. Other avalanche types also occur. Old wet snow (crystalline) is usually safe, with rare exceptions where the snow is lying on a smooth ground layer. Fresh wet snow is not safe, nor are wet cornices. Fresh snow in the sun can avalanche from a single point spreading out, but this is rarely serious unless on steep ground (but it is extremely dangerous in the Alps).

If avalanched, try to jump free or ice axe brake. The chances of escaping may be quite good if the avalanche is a small volume, or you are near the edge or top. If swept down in a large volume on a slope, try to stay on the surface. Keep your mouth closed, especially in powder, and as the snow slows down try to create a breathing space in front of your mouth. Wet snow avalanches harden rapidly on settling, so try to break free just before the debris stops. If trapped, try to stay calm, which will reduce oxygen demand.

If you are an uninjured companion or witness to an avalanche, it is vital to start a search immediately; don't go immediately for help. Remember, the same slope will not avalanche again. Sometimes there is an arm, leg or piece of equipment visible even if the head is under the snow. If buried, victims will often be alive at first but their chances of survival lessen rapidly. Unless severely injured, some 80% may live if found immediately, but only 10% after a three-hour delay (the minimum time for a rescue team to arrive). Listen for any sound, look carefully for any visual clue and mark the burial site if it can be guessed, or at least the line of fall. Search for a considerable time, ideally until rescue arrives (if someone else has summoned them). A working knowledge of First Aid is important, as many victims may have stopped breathing.

PROTECTION

In most cases, protection on winter pitches is poorer than on summer ones. Even mixed routes classified as safe involve more risk of injury after a fall than the average rock climb. The consequences of a fall in winter, particularly in a remote place in poor weather, are more serious. Ice routes are more serious again and on some, particularly the thinly iced slabs of Ben Nevis, a fall might be fatal. Impatience in the searching for runners and belays has to be resisted. Their quality may still be poorer, in particular camming devices in icy cracks are close to useless, as are dead men in shallow snow. Despite recent disapproval of pegs placed on good rock climbs, pegs should always be carried in case icy cracks make them the only safe option. Most winter climbs follow vegetated or gully lines and scarring by pegs will not offend. On good rock climbs, one should try to limit their use, remembering that a nut is quicker to place and remove.

DESCENTS

Some of the descents described involve snow slopes of up to 45 degrees (Grade I). At this angle of icy snow, there is no guarantee that an ice-axe brake will be effective, especially after some speed has been built up. Choose your route carefully, remove clogged snow from your crampons as necessary and don't trip up.

WINTER TACTICS

Having decided where to climb, a number of other factors must be considered to produce a successful day.

ACCOMMODATION

The early starts required for the normal winter day mean that convenience takes precedence over comfortable accommodation, although for longer trips the latter is also a necessity. Those lucky enough to live in Scotland can often climb for a single day by leaving home very early in the morning, which avoids the problem. However, for longer trips in terms of both time and distance, somewhere to spend the night must be found. To maximise use of daylight, it is best to stay as close as possible to the point of departure from the road. Many have found that sleeping in their car or van is best for one or two nights, especially if cooking breakfast inside can be done safely. Short-term camping is also a possiblity, but putting a tent up in the dark in a blizzard after a long drive is not something that many people take pleasure in. Except for the most remote cliffs, camping above valley level is rarely advantageous and many tents have been destroyed by wind. In some instances there may be bothies which can be used, but most climbs in this book can be done in a day from the valley.

These temporary accommodation tactics must be modified for longer trips. Clothing and equipment are likely to be wet after a day on the hill, and unless drying facilities are available, a complete second set of clothes is a good precaution for the second day of a weekend. Similarly, because frozen ropes are difficult to handle and possibly dangerous, a spare is worth considering. So, after a day or two on the hill many teams will welcome somewhere warm to spend the evening, have a comfortable night, and dry clothes and equipment.

There are many club huts scattered throughout the climbing regions of Scotland, and most are open to bookings; a list can be obtained from the Mountaineering Council of Scotland (Offices at 4a St Catherine's Road, Perth. tel. 01738 638 229. Fax 01738 442 095). There are at least as many establishments which offer bunkhouse accommodation and which generally advertise in the specialist climbing magazines. Caravans or chalets offer a good option for slightly larger groups, and information on these is available either through the climbing magazines or the local Tourist Information Office.

Finally, although more expensive, bed and breakfast accommodation is worth considering as it can be more convenient at short notice. However, not many proprietors can be expected to provide breakfast at the required hour for an early start. All these options of comfortable indoor accommodation reduce flexibility because of the pre-booking that may be required, and the fixed location. Therefore, a willingness to drive to other areas from these bases is important.

STARTING TIMES

Early starts are more or less essential in winter, especially in December and January when limited daylight means that it is sometimes necessary to be at the foot of a long climb at first light. Accordingly, except for the most convenient cliffs, be prepared to start the approach walk in the dark. The longer climbs are probably best climbed later in the season if possible, when the days become luxuriously longer. It is best to aim to get to the top of the cliff or past the most awkward part of the descent before darkness falls, as once it becomes dark, anything technical will take at least twice as long (half an hour in the morning can save two hours or more at the end of the day). Therefore try to calculate your starting time by estimating the timing backwards from this point. Although some famous heroes of the past seemed to thrive on late starts and climbing through the night, do not attempt to emulate them unless you enjoy being frightened and uncomfortable.

EQUIPMENT

A basic knowledge of winter hillwalking is assumed, indeed it is a prerequisite for winter climbing. The following notes may be found helpful by those starting the winter climbing game.

Helmet: This is absolutely essential; put it on below the approach slopes. It should be big enough to go over a balaclava.

Harness: It should be possible to put your harness on while wearing crampons, so a nappy-style design is better than one with leg loops. Holsters are useful, particularly for mixed routes.

Axe and hammer: Banana pick axes are better for ice or technical routes, while curved picks are equally good for easier routes and better for ice-axe braking. Some of the axes that are designed specifically for thick water ice may not be suitable for general Scottish use as contact with rock may ruin them. Sharp axes work immeasurably better than blunt ones on ice.

Crampons: Step-in crampons are by far the most convenient if your boots will take them; otherwise choose a model with a buckling system as simple as possible. Pure steep ice routes are easier and safer if a specialist crampon, such as 'Footfangs', are used; keep them sharp. While it used to be held that a flexible crampon was better for mixed climbing, many people now favour rigid or semi-rigid crampons as they give greater precision and security on small holds.

Rucksack: This should be quite big, 50-60 litres, so that all clothing and equipment can be stowed inside to be kept dry during the approach.

Boots: Plastic double boots are undoubtedly the best, since they will keep your feet warmer and drier, and they fit crampons more easily. Have them loosely laced for the approach, then tighten them up at the foot of the climb.

Hardware: This will vary according to the climb being attempted. Hard mixed routes will require a plentiful supply of rock gear. Remember that drive-in ice-screws are good for both ice and turf. Deadmen may be required for the easier gullies, or harder ones with long easy sections, but rarely for mixed climbs. Always take a supply of rock pegs. Wide-bore tubular ice-screws are best for ice.

Waterproofs and principal clothing: It should be possible to put over-trousers on over crampons, but they can be constricting so try not to wear them while climbing. Alternatively, a tight garter fitted just below the knee can maintain enough material around the knee to allow flexibility. A good quality waterproof jacket is essential. Salopettes are better than breeches as they avoid cold spots at waist and knee.

Gloves: The problem here is maintaining both warmth and utility. Large insulated mitts can be clumsy, but if they are large enough and have restaining straps, thin fingered gloves may be worn underneath to allow removal of the mitt when necessary. Dachsteins are good for warmth, but sometimes difficult to get back on over wet hands. For harder routes, some have experimented with rubberised working gloves, insulated gardening gloves or fingered ski gloves. While these allow greater dexterity, they are not as warm and a high pain tolerance is required. It would be wise to have a warm pair of gloves in reserve.

Headtorch: Another absolutely essential piece of equipment. Get a good one with long-life batteries and a spare bulb. One of the authors can confirm that it is very cold sitting on a ledge throughout the night because of a forgotten headtorch.

Spare clothing: While sound mountaineering principle requires a spare jacket (or duvet) to be carried, in practice the climber needs to wear sufficient clothing to remain warm while belaying in cold and windy conditions for perhaps hours at a stretch. Therefore, additional clothing is not really required. However, a bivouac sac is a good precaution.

Food and drink: A thermos flask is probably not worth the extra weight, but this is a matter of personal preference. However, take plenty of liquid to replace that lost during the sweaty approach, and take enough calories to keep you going. Don't overdo it – those who take enough for the unexpected night out are more likely to need it than less heavily laden climbers.

Other items: A map and a compass for both climbers (what happens if your mate falls through a cornice with the only set?), a small First Aid kit, and spare gloves. An increasing number of people take mobile phones. While they have undoubtedly been of great use in some cases, they have also been abused and may give a false sense of security. In addition, they will only work in a limited number of climbing locations.

WINTER GRADES

The new two-tier system has been used. This gives an overall grade based on an extended version of the previous I to V system, at present reaching VIII. Technical grades, with an arabic numeral, apply to the hardest move or short section on the route. The same technical grade (e.g. V,5) is given to routes of average technical difficulty for their overall grade and average seriousness (for winter, more serious than rock climbs). One higher technical grade (e.g. V,6) is allowed for safe routes (usually mixed) or two grades (e.g. V,7) for routes with a short, very safe section. A serious route normally has one lower technical grade (e.g. V,4). In addition, a long sustained route is likely to have lower technical difficulty. To distinguish whether a lower technical grade is due to seriousness or sustainedness, one must refer to the description. Only technical grades 4 and above have been used, usually applying to IV and above. The extension of the grading system has meant the elimination of split grades for indecision, though they may still occur for variability due to conditions, generally the easier grade for more ice.

Even this has been discouraged, preferring to specify the conditions for which the grade applies.

The following is an approximate definition of the overall grades, but remember that the grade may vary with conditions so the route description is no guarantee of what one will find.

Grade I: Climbs for which only one axe is required, either snow gullies around 45 degrees or easy ridges.

Grade II: Axe and hammer are required because of steep snow, a difficult cornice, or a short ice pitch. Difficulties are usually short. The ridges are more difficult but usually still summer scrambles.

Grade III: Similarly technical but more sustained than Grade II. Sometimes short and technical, particularly for mixed ascents of Moderate rock climbs.

Grade IV: Steep ice requiring some arm strength, from short vertical steps to long pitches of 60-70 degrees. The mixed climbs require more advanced techniques such as torquing moves.

Grade V: Sustained steep ice at 70-80 degrees. Mixed climbs requiring linked hard moves.

Grade VI: Vertical ice. Mixed routes either long and sustained, or if short, sufficiently technical to require careful calculation.

Grade VII: Multi-pitch routes with long sections of vertical or thin ice. Mixed routes requiring fitness and experience to link many technical moves. There are very few Grade VII climbs in this book.

Grade VIII: The hardest few routes in Scotland, at present.

Technical grades on ice:
As a rough guideline, 3=60 degrees, 4=70 degrees, 5=80 degrees or vertical steps, 6=vertical.

RECOMMENDED ROUTES

The star system has been used to assist route choice; the more stars, the greater the recommendation. Factors such as sustained climbing and a well-defined continuous line would tend to attract more stars. In winter, however, the enjoyment of a route varies with conditions so the star rating should be taken as even less reliable than for summer routes. Routes which are rarely in good condition have been given reduced stars, however good they occasionally are. Rather than copying stars from existing guides, routes have been reassessed to give a range of stars and provide consistency throughout Scotland. In addition, stars have been spread throughout the grades; the lower the grade, the less that technical interest affects the recommendation until at Grade I the cliff scenery becomes perhaps the most important factor, and the stars become even more subjective. For a route to be given three stars, it must be one of the best at its grade in Scotland. Two star routes are still excellent in a local context whilst the routes without stars in this guide are still good enough to have been selected.

ROUTE DESCRIPTIONS

Only certain routes, and usually harder ones, have been described pitch by pitch. This is largely for the convenience of reading longer descriptions and usually indicates where the first ascensionist belayed, rather than any necessity to belay at the same place. The easier the route, the deeper snow it may hold and the less likely it is for parties to use the same belays. Well defined lines normally have short descriptions without describing individual pitches. Some climbs have been given only very brief descriptions, either because they follow prominent landmarks, or because they provide easily followed worthwhile alternatives to those described in more detail. In some cases, climbs have been left undescribed but their line and grade are indicated on a diagram in relation to the described climbs.

RESCUE PROCEDURE

Despite the utmost care, winter climbing has its dangers and you may be faced with looking after an injured partner. The key decision for the standard climbing party of two is whether you should stay with the casualty, leave them and go for help, or struggle to assist them down towards shelter and safety. Clearly, the decision depends on circumstances, of which there are endless variations. Remember that a helicopter might arrive one or two hours after your call for help, but in bad weather when helicopters cannot operate, it might be over four hours before a rescue team can arrive on the scene. If the decision is to go down, then the aim is to reach a phone as soon as possible and dial 999 for the Police, who coordinate mountain rescue. Public phones are marked on the OS maps. Minutes spent making decisions and longer making your partner comfortable are time well spent when the arrival of a rescue may take hours.

The Northern Highlands

This huge area of mountains offers a lifetime of exploration, but many folk have yet to start. This guide can only offer a selection of the cliffs with good climbing, as we have preferred to include a range of routes in each described area. Most of the routes have only been climbed in the last 25 years and the harder ones in the last 15, and many are unrepeated. The visitor should savour the atmosphere of exploration, and not simply choose a route and follow it. Consider carefully the choice of mountain, lines of approach and descent, and whether there are other routes in better condition.

All styles of climbing and grades are available in the Northern Highlands, although there is rarely a free choice. All the venues offer fine ice climbing, and the season starts earlier than on Ben Nevis. In terms of conditions, the area should be considered as an average of the rest of Scotland. Its northerly position makes it less susceptible to thaw than Glen Coe and the south, but due to lower altitude and the proximity of the sea the climbing conditions in the north are less reliable than those of Ben Nevis or the Cairngorms. A January to March season is the average. It can be ideal if you get it right, but with the West Coast unpredictability, you can end up chasing conditions in circles round the area; all part of the challenge! At present the chances of finding someone else on your route, apart from the classic mountain traverses, are close to nil.

With the exception of the classic Forcan Ridge on the Saddle in Kintail, the chosen cliffs are grouped into three areas, all within 1½ hours drive of each other and about the same from Inverness. The many excellent cliffs north of Ullapool have not been included, but they are fully described in the SMC Climbers' Guide to the Northern Highlands, Volume 2. The southerly group, based around Glen Carron, is composed of Fuar Tholl, Sgorr Ruadh and the Applecross hills. Fuar Tholl and Beinn Bhan form big ice routes but require cold weather; Sgorr Ruadh is more varied and less fussy. The Torridon hills are in the next glen north; Beinn Alligin, Liathach and Beinn Eighe are well known and the climbing here is gaining a reputation. The sandstone of Beinn Alligin and Liathach provides big icefalls and gullies while the quartzite of Beinn Eighe has a unique mixed style of torquing and hooking without ice or turf. Further north, although all three areas are equidistant from Inverness, are the Fannaichs, Beinn Dearg and An Teallach. This last group is further away from a mild sea, offers a wide range of routes, but involves more committing approaches if the weather is doubtful.

The crags are described proceeding in general from north to south.

Maps
The following sheets of the Ordnance Survey 1:50,000 Landranger Series cover the areas described in this chapter:
Sheet 19 for An Teallach and parts of Beinn Eighe and Beinn Alligin.
Sheet 20 for Beinn Dearg, Sgurr Mor and Sgurr nan Clach Geala.
Sheet 24 for Beinn Alligin, Beinn Bhan and the other Applecross hills.
Sheet 25 for Liathach, Sgorr Ruadh and Fuar Tholl.
Sheet 33 for The Saddle.
The Ordnance Survey 1:25,000 Outdoor Leisure Map *The Cuillin and Torridon Hills* is particularly useful for Beinn Alligin, Liathach and Beinn Eighe.

BEINN DEARG
1048m   (Map Ref 259 812)

This massive mountain offers excellent winter climbing in three different corries. The climbs described here are approached from the west up Gleann na Sguaib, leaving the more remote Cadha Dearg and Coire Ghranda to the adventurous.

Weather and Conditions
The gullies give the best climbs as the buttress routes usually lack good lines. The West Buttress is higher and Penguin Gully is very reliable. The Diollaid a' Mhill Bhric gullies are less reliable, but one can always continue to the West Buttress. Fenian Gully, however, is normally good.

Access
From the A835 Braemore to Ullapool road, at the head of Loch Broom, a forestry road runs up Gleann na Sguaib to the upper limit of the Inverlael Forest. A good path then leads up to the Bealach Coire Ghranda, passing first below the cliffs of Diollaid a' Mhill Bhric, the long sloping north-west shoulder of Beinn Dearg, and then below the large West Buttress of the mountain. In heavy snow the path drifts badly, but in normal conditions it gives a relatively short and fast approach to the lower climbs (2 hours).

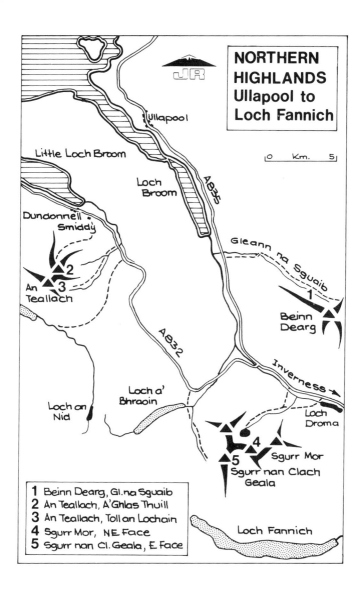

NORTHERN
HIGHLANDS
Ullapool to
Loch Fannich

0   Km.   5

1 Beinn Dearg, Gl. na Sguaib
2 An Teallach, A'Ghlas Thuill
3 An Teallach, Toll an Lochain
4 Sgurr Mor, NE Face
5 Sgurr nan Cl. Geala, E Face

Layout and Descent

The climbs are described from right to left, as one approaches up the glen. Between Diollaid a' Mhill Bhric and the West Buttress is a broad gully, the Cadha Amadan, or Fool's Pass, which provides a convenient descent from many of the climbs. Alternatively, in poor conditions, return along the ridge above the glen until the cliffs fade and allow a descent down heather slopes back to the path. The problem with this option is that the river may be hard to cross. There are six well defined gullies on the line of cliffs under the Diollaid a' Mhill Bhric.

WhatawaytospendEaster   120m   I
W. Sproul, A. McKeith   25th March 1967
The first gully provides a straightforward snow climb.

Rev. Ian Paisley Memorial Gully   150m   I
W. Sproul, A. McKeith   25th March 1967
The second gully is also straightforward, uncompromisingly direct, not to be taken too lightly and prematurely named.

Orangeman's Gully   150m   III *
T.W. Patey   10th March 1968
The third gully is narrow, twisting and bow-shaped. The first pitch, which can be hard, starts up a chimney and goes left under an overhang on iced slabs. Continue up two more ice pitches to easy snow.

Emerald Gully   150m   IV,4 **
B. Fuller, P. Nunn, A. Riley   March 1970
The fourth gully provides a highly recommended climb that can be hard in lean conditions. It usually has at least two big ice pitches.

Jewel in the Crown   160m   VI,6 **
S.M. Richardson, C. Cartwright   6th January 1991
The impressive icy corner on the left wall of Emerald Gully presents a good line which is quite often in condition during a hard winter, particularly after a heavy snowfall followed by a sustained period of frost. Start 20m below the first steep step in Emerald Gully. Move left across mixed ground, climb a steep icy corner for 10m to a terrace below the corner (25m). Climb a frieze of icicles to enter the corner which leads to a good stance on the left (20m). Move right and climb a steep ice wall, then continue up mixed ground to a small cave in a terrace (45m). Continue up ice, snow and mixed ground to the top.

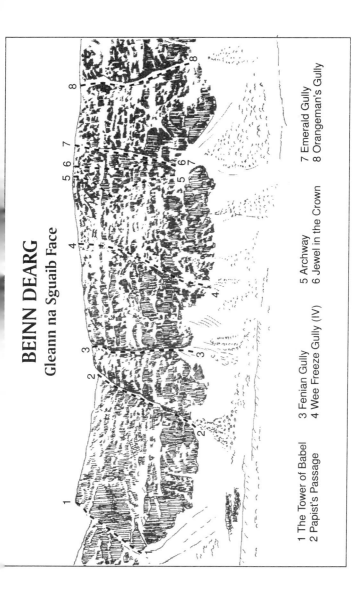

BEINN DEARG
Gleann na Sguaib Face

1 The Tower of Babel
2 Papist's Passage

3 Fenian Gully
4 Wee Freeze Gully (IV)

5 Archway
6 Jewel in the Crown

7 Emerald Gully
8 Orangeman's Gully

Archway   250m   IV,4 *
R.D. Everett, S.M. Richardson   7th February 1988
This is an entertaining route which weaves through some impressive scenery. Start at the lowest point of the buttress left of Emerald Gully.
1 , 2 and 3. 150m   Follow open grooves just left of the steepest rocks to reach a prominent cave-like depression beneath huge roofs.
4. 40m   Climb up right through the roof of the cave.
5 and 6. 60m   Follow an interesting gully and groove system up right to finish.

Fenian Gully   170m   IV,4 **
T.W. Patey   11th March 1968
The fifth of the main gullies provides quite a sustained climb but with no particular crux. It is recommended as it is often well iced.

Papist's Passage   180m   II
T.W. Patey   10th March 1968
The sixth gully, just left of Fenian Gully. The main obstacle is a huge chockstone above a cave at 75m, which is climbed by the right-hand corner. Depending on the build-up, it can be Grade I or III.

The Tower of Babel   160m   IV,6 **
S. Aisthorpe, J. Lyall   22nd February 1989
This is the imposing tower to the right of the Cadha Amadan, the wide gully separating the climbs described above from the West Buttress. The route is often well frozen but seldom snowy enough to look really wintry. For best effects, it should be climbed during a blizzard! Start on the easy shelf leading out of the gully. Climb the crest of the tower as directly as possible for 60m, then take a slabby ramp on the left side of the crest (20m). A steep recess on the left leads to a promontory below a short vicious wall which is taken direct to a higher ledge (40m). Climb the final wall by a diagonal crack on the slabby left side and finish by a step left into a square-cut recess (40m).

THE WEST BUTTRESS

Beyond the Cadha Amadan the cliffs rise up to their greatest height in the so-called West Buttress. In fact the cliffs have a north-west facet (well seen as one approaches up the glen), then bend round to face

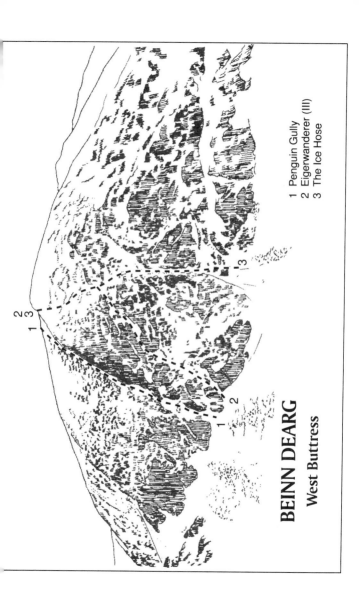

BEINN DEARG
West Buttress

1 Penguin Gully
2 Eigerwanderer (III)
3 The Ice Hose

north and finally face north-north-east above a small lochan below the col between Beinn Dearg and Meall nan Ceapraichan. There are a couple of well defined classic lines and large areas of buttress with rather ill defined routes and many variations.

The Ice Hose   350m   V,4 **
I. Dalley, D.M. Nichols, G.S. Strange   7th April 1979
A recommended route which is rarely in condition. Climb the prominent ice ribbon directly for 140m. From its top, either follow the shallow gully easily leftwards or, better, gain the buttress on the right (with a downward-pointing toe), get onto the crest and follow it to the top.

Penguin Gully   350m   III,4 ***
T.W. Patey, W.H. Murray, N.S. Tennent   29th March 1964
This classic climb, concealed during the approach, provides one of the longest climbs on the mountain. It is probably one of the few ice routes where consistent conditions prevail from January to April. A steep icefall at the start can be avoided by a dog-leg gully trending right then left (the start of Eigerwanderer) to join the main gully about 75m above the start. The main gully contains several ice pitches and may occasionally have a through route behind a chockstone. In lean conditions it can offer continuous ice (Grade IV,4); well worth doing.

AN TEALLACH
1062m   (Map Ref 069 843)

This majestic mountain is one of the most sought-after in the Northern Highlands. The winter traverse of its tops ranks with Liathach as the finest in the area, although it does not equal its Torridonian rivals for the quality of its snow and ice climbs.

The main ridge runs in an east-facing crescent from Sail Liath in the south over the main tops of Sgurr Fiona and Bidein a' Ghlas Thuill to Glas Mheall Mor. A ridge running east from Bidein a' Ghlas Thuill separates two large east-facing corries, Toll an Lochain and A' Ghlas Thuill. Both have climbs of interest, and Toll an Lochain in particular is a magnificent sight even when winter climbing conditions are poor.

The main ridge of An Teallach between Sgurr Fiona (right) and Corrag Bhuidhe (centre) with the dark tower of Lord Berkeley's Seat between them
Photo: Donald Bennet

Access

The approach leaves the road (A832) through thickets of overgrown rhododendrons near a bridge at a point opposite Dundonnell House. The best line is about 200 metres on the Dundonnell side of the burn. Head diagonally towards the burn to join the path which climbs up on its north side. For A'Ghlas Thuill, branch off up the hillside to the west after about half an hour, at a big waterfall. For Toll an Lochain, continue up Coir' a' Ghiubhsachain following a cairned path, then climb the slabby hillside into the corrie. It is equally convenient to go to Toll an Lochain by the Shenavall path, starting from the A832 at Corrie Hallie.

Descent

Descents can be made at a number of places. After climbing in A'Ghlas Thuill, the easiest is to go to the summit, Bidein a' Ghlas Thuill. From here, follow the ridge north, then drop down the west flanks of Glas Mheall Mor to join a footpath leading to Dundonnell. Alternatively, descend into A'Ghlas Thuill from the col below Glas Mheall Mor.

The descent is longer after climbing in Toll an Lochain. It is possible to descend very steeply back into the corrie from the col between Sgurr Fiona and Bidein a' Ghlas Thuill. Going in the opposite direction along the ridge towards Sail Liath, the descent from the first col south-east of Corrag Bhuidhe South Buttress (Map Ref 068 829) is also steep. Going further along the ridge to the Cadha Gobhlach pass (Map Ref 070 825), there is a less steep descent down the wide gully to Loch Toll an Lochain. All these routes are Grade I and may be harder if icy.

Conditions and Weather

The mountain is high and holds snow well. Toll an Lochain is a more committing day, both in terms of longer approach and difficult descent.

An Teallach Ridge   II ***

A long and intricate expedition with some sections of Grade II. The 'Pinnacles first' direction is easier but the 'Munros first' direction, as described, provides a good day even if discretion wins at the Corrag Bhuidhe pinnacles. The highest top, Bidein a' Ghlas Thuill, is easily reached. From here to Sgurr Fiona is steep but the route finding is easy (as long as one is not tricked by the more obvious east ridge towards Glas Mheall Liath). The hardest section follows, all of which is very

Destitution Road on the East Face of Sgurr nan Clach Geala
Climber: Kevin Murphy
                                    Photo: Dougie Dinwoodie

exposed and a slip could be disastrous unless roped. There is a lot of scrambling over Lord Berkeley's Seat to the Corrag Bhuidhe pinnacles. The easiest line is initially about 10m below the crest on the west (a path in summer). Fairly soon (actually about halfway along the pinnacles) there is a shallow descent gully. Go down this and traverse below the steepest rocks to bypass 'the bad step', which is the descent off the fourth pinnacle (the crest direct will require an abseil). Continuing the traverse beyond the descent gully is easier than following the crest, but this route will still probably require an abseil. This option is also reached by descending from the ridge further along (beyond the easy descent gully). This whole section can be bypassed by traversing low on the west side, but it is still very exposed. Once on Corrag Bhuidhe South Buttress, the going towards Sail Liath is relatively straightforward.

A'GHLAS THUILL

A prominent feature of the south side of the corrie is the bold buttress of Major Rib, with Minor Rib to the right and the clean line of The Alley in between. To the left of Major Rib is a series of parallel gullies known as the Prongs, and to the right of Minor Rib is the big Hayfork Gully leading up to an obvious notch. Right again is North Gully which leads up to the last notch left of the summit of Bidein a' Ghlas Thuill. Below and immediately right of the summit is a rather indistinct area of buttress and snowfield, but further right are a number of more definite lines, the most obvious of which is Checkmate Chimney. The climbs are described from right to left.

Checkmate Chimney   250m   IV,5 **
T.W. Patey, C.J.S. Bonington   3rd March 1969
This superb route is unfortunately not often in condition. It is the first obvious line, a long narrow chimney, left of the easy slopes at the back of the corrie. Climb a 10m step, then 60m of snow to a fierce 30m icefall. This can be climbed on the left by a groove (thin ice and mixed, but protected). From here on the climbing is Grade III. Climb a long enclosed chimney section with a number of short ice pitches, and finish up an easy 60m snow channel.

North Gully   300m   I **
The gully running up to the first notch left (east) of the summit of Bidein a' Ghlas Thuill is also known as Murdo's Gully, and is better seen on the approach than is Hayfork Gully.

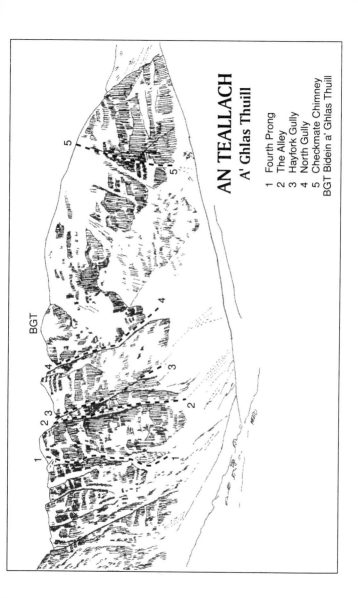

AN TEALLACH
A' Ghlas Thuill

1 Fourth Prong
2 The Alley
3 Hayfork Gully
4 North Gully
5 Checkmate Chimney
BGT Bidein a' Ghlas Thuill

Hayfork Gully   300m   I *
G. Sang, W.A. Morrison   26th March 1910
This is the deep and straightforward gully left of North Gully and right of Major and Minor Ribs. It runs up to the second notch on the east ridge of Bidein a' Ghlas Thuill.

The Alley   300m   II *
R. Baker, A. McCord   18th December 1978
The gully between Minor Rib and Major Rib gives an attractive climb, usually with some small ice pitches in the lower section. With a good build-up, these disappear completely. After about 150m the gully becomes less distinct and the natural way is out right over broken rocks to the crest of Minor Rib. Continuing in the line of the gully is less interesting and can be harder.

Fourth Prong   300m   II
T.M. Lawson, R.J. Tanton, J. Clarkson   15th February 1959
This good climb is immediately left of Main Rib. There is a short pitch in the lower section. Higher up, climb a narrow chimney, then trend right over rocks below a large buttress. Finish rightwards up easy snow. It can bank out to Grade I after heavy snow.

TOLL AN LOCHAIN

Starting with the steep north-facing crags of Sail Liath on the extreme left of the corrie, to the right are easy snow slopes which lead up to the pass of Cadha Gobhlach. Right again is the rounded Cadha Gobhlach Buttress, then another col, before the South Buttress of Corrag Bhuidhe whose rocks drop straight into the loch. The first route described takes a long shallow couloir which separates the South Buttress from the main crags of Corrag Bhuidhe.

Constabulary Couloir   360m   II
The couloir may have an avoidable icefall near the bottom, and the rest is straightforward snow.

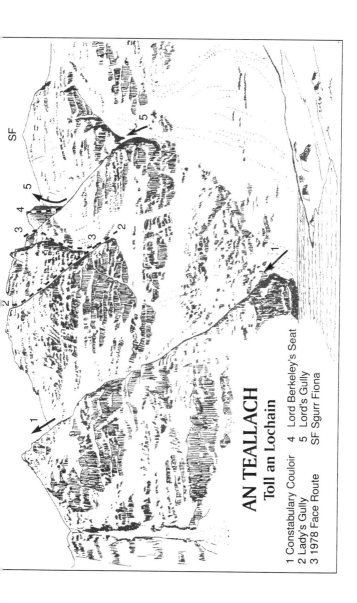

AN TEALLACH
Toll an Lochain

1 Constabulary Couloir   4 Lord Berkeley's Seat
2 Lady's Gully
3 1978 Face Route

5 Lord's Gully
SF Sgurr Fiona

The main face of Corrag Bhuidhe has near its base a large triangular snowfield above a short rock barrier. This may be used to locate the next climbs.

Lady's Gully   240m   II
F. Fotheringham, J.R.R. Fowler   30th December 1974
Gain the triangular snowfield at its lower left corner and go up to the apex. Follow the left-trending gully on steep snow to the top.

1978 Face Route   250m   IV,4 **
M. Freeman, N.D. Keir   19th February 1978
This atmospheric route finds a way through serious open terrain. Gain the triangular snowfield and from its apex go past Lady's Gully and continue under the wall to gain (crux) and follow a right-sloping ramp which approaches the crest of the buttress overlooking Lord's Gully. Either finish up a steep gully or follow the crest to the top.

Lord's Gully   400m   II (Right) III (Left) **
J.H.B. Bell, E.E. Roberts   Easter 1923 (Right Branch)
A. Borthwick, F. Fotheringham   17th February 1973 (Left Branch)
This is the long left-slanting gully between Corrag Bhuidhe and Sgurr Fiona. The long initial section is usually straightforward snow. At its top it has two branches going either side of the huge tower of Lord Berkeley's Seat. The left branch is better defined with more interest but harder climbing. Difficulties in the right branch are often circumvented by a deviation right onto the face of Sgurr Fiona which involves some low-angled ice.

Lord Berkeley's Seat   130m   VI,6 *
S. Jenkins, A. Nisbet   28th January 1991
This spectacular route up the face of the Seat is not as hard as it looks. Favourable conditions are well frozen turf and not too much snow. Start just left of the toe of the buttress.
1. 45m   Climb the crest, trending slightly right until stopped by a barrier wall.
2. 35m   Traverse right and climb a short slab overlooking the right branch of Lord's Gully. A series of walls leads to another barrier.
3. 25m   Traverse left and climb corners just right of the crest.
4. 25m   A short turfy ramp leads diagonally right to the final wall, which is finished to the right of the summit.

SGURR MOR
1110m   (Map Ref 203 718)

The impressive north-east face of Sgurr Mor, the highest peak of the Fannaichs, holds snow well and can offer a winter route into April, or even May were it to freeze.

Weather and Conditions
This is a big serious face, so choose good weather and beware of windslab, cornices and warm early morning sunshine. The better the quality of snow and ice, the easier the routes are.

Access
Park on the A835 (there is a good place at Map Ref 235 759) about 3km south-east of the Braemore Junction where a small ruined building is seen down by the river. This is the start of the path to Loch a' Mhadaidh, which is not obvious at first but it is easily found at the second stream crossing after 400 metres, where there is a bridge. Follow the path until just short of Loch a' Mhadaidh, then head up a vague spur and traverse to the foot of the cliff. Allow about 2½ hours.

Descent
The most pleasant descent is to head south-east then north-east along the ridge to Beinn Liath Mhor Fannaich; either bag the summit or traverse below it on the left. Go north-east down to Loch Sgeireach and north from there to the small dam on the Allt a' Mhadaidh.

Easter Gully   240m   II
B. Brand, O. Bruskeland   10th April 1967
This straightforward snow gully on the left (south) corner of the face often has a big cornice. In leaner conditions it may have an ice pitch low down but perhaps the cornice will be easier.

The Resurrection   320m   III ***
J.R. Mackenzie, D. Butterfield   14th March 1980
This central route on the face provides a serious climb with a great Alpine atmosphere. The last belay is the summit cairn of Sgurr Mor, the highest point in the North-West Highlands. With a big build-up, the route has no rock protection or belays, so expect to use snow belays and ice screws and a warthog or two for turf, particularly at the top.

Start towards the left side of the face, at the right side of a dead-end gully right of Easter Gully. There is a large icefall, although it may have thawed away towards the end of the season. Climb the icefall, normally 45-50m, but it could be longer early in the season and steep at the bottom (Grade IV), to reach the base of a big snowfield. Climb 45-50 degree snow for two or three pitches, then a short icefall to reach a steeper snow field, climbed in one or two pitches to a scoop below the steep capping wall (no rock belay here). Go diagonally right, then continue straight up to the top (55m). This pitch is not difficult but the only protection is warthogs in the turf, the rope is too short, there may be a big cornice and it's a long way to retreat.

Easy Start   I

Start by a shallow runnel just left of East Face route but go left onto the lower snowfield of Resurrection. In ideal conditions this can reduce the overall grade to II.

East Face   300m   III *
R. Graham, R. Warrack   11th April 1967

A fine route, often high in its grade, and not always in condition. Climb a shallow gully in the face right of The Resurrection. It is initially Grade I snow, but higher up there are several ice pitches.

SGURR NAN CLACH GEALA
1093m   (Map Ref 184 715)

The fine crags on the east face of this mountain (at about Map Ref 191 717) are not marked on the OS map. It is however an impressively steep crag, one of Scotland's best, and not nearly as remote as rumour might have you believe. In fact, the approach is fairly easy and the descent is fast and convenient.

Weather and Conditions

The approach requires a short descent past a possibly large cornice, so good visibility is essential. In addition, wildslab can build readily below the cornice on the sheltered east-facing slopes. However, if the weather is too good the sun will warm the climbs as rapidly as the initially grateful climber! The cliff is often in good condition although the buttresses are very steep and stripped of snow quickly in a thaw or in strong sun. The gullies reliably hold sufficient ice. The cliff base is at 650m.

Access

There are several possible approaches. By far the best and shortest is from the east end of Loch a' Bhraoin, reached from a track starting at Map Ref 163 763 on the Braemore Junction to Dundonnell road. Follow the path south along an unnamed glen and after about 3km cross the burn and strike up east to the col between Carn na Criche and Sgurr nan Clach Geala. In good conditions this takes about 2½ hours. The descent from the col requires care as the slope may be corniced.

A longer approach is to leave the Garve to Ullapool road as described for Sgurr Mor and follow the track towards Loch a' Mhadaidh. Skirt round the east side of the loch, climb up to the col between Sgurr Mor and Carn na Criche and make a diagonal descent into the corrie.

Descent

From the top of the climbs, descend the slopes northwards back to the col and reverse the line of ascent to Loch a' Bhraoin. This is very straightforward and it has been known for a party to get back to Glasgow in about 5 hours from the col (without speeding too much, honest officer!).

Layout

The main cliffs comprise a wedge-like cluster of six narrow buttresses, numbered 1 to 6 from left to right, separated by five gullies, Alpha to Epsilon. From the top of these cliffs a graceful ridge leads south-west to the summit of the mountain, beneath which there is a more broken buttress. Access to the base of the cliffs is by a rock step and a steep apron of snow. The rock step is most easily passed at its right by a slanting rake running up to buttresses 5 and 6.

Alpha Gully   240m   II
P. Baker, D.S.B. Wright   6th March 1965
The leftmost gully may contain two or three small ice pitches or it may be only steep snow. Take the left fork 15m below the top of the gully. The gully finishes after 120m on the crest of No.2 Buttress which gives a further 120m of good climbing.

Sunrise Buttress (No.2 Buttress)   150m   IV,5
P.R. Baines, D.M. Nichols   18th February 1978
This route follows a line in the centre of the buttress. Start at the foot of Beta Gully and climb ice bulges for three pitches, then an obvious gully system. Turn the overhang at the top on the left and continue up the arete to the top.

Beta Gully   270m   III
P.F. Macdonald, J. Porteous (Centre Fork)
I.G. Rowe, W. Sproul (Right Fork)   28th February 1970
An icefall gives access to the gully, which is straightforward up to a trifurcation. Here a short left fork goes out to No.2 Buttress, the Centre Fork contains a steep pitch, and the Right Fork avoids this pitch and rejoins the Centre Fork above.

Destitution Road   200m   VI,5 *
D. Dinwoodie, K. Murphy   19th February 1986
This takes the central icefall of Cuileag Buttress (No.3 Buttress). It may not often be in condition, but **Cuileag Corner**, the line of corners to the right, is V,5. Climb directly up the middle of the buttress using the general line of a shallow corner to gain the icefall. Climb this direct past a jutting nose of rock, then traverse right to gain a blocky corner cutting through the overhangs. Climb this to the easier crest of the buttress.

Gamma Gully   210m   IV,5 **
P.N.L. Tranter, I.G. Rowe   6th March 1965
This is perhaps the best of the gullies on the crag. Climb up for 30m to enter and climb a deep narrow 30m slot. Some 20m higher is the crux, a steep 10m ice pitch with smooth rock walls on either side. Another 10m ice pitch follows, then climb steep snow and occasional rock steps to gain the large scoop above Beta Gully.

Skyscraper Buttress Direct   240m   VI,6 ***
R.J. Archbold, M. Freeman, J.C. Higham, R.A. Smith   18th February 1978 (Original Route)
D. Dinwoodie, C. Jamieson, K. Murphy   9th February 1986 (Direct Start)
R. Everett, S.M. Richardson   13th February 1994 (Empire State Variation)
This magnificent sustained mixed climb is one of the finest expeditions in the Northern Highlands. The best line takes the icefall at the base of the buttress, The Direct Start. Climb the icefall and move across left at the top to belay under a roof. Pull up right into a shallow undercut groove which leads up and left to a traverse line beneath the steep central section of the buttress. The Original Route reaches this point by following Gamma Gully to the slot, then traversing easily right. It will be necessary to go this way if conditions are lean. From the traverse ledge, move right for 20m to the foot of a steep corner. This provides

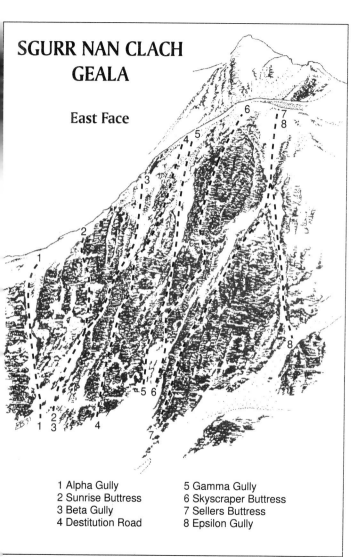

SGURR NAN CLACH GEALA

East Face

1 Alpha Gully
2 Sunrise Buttress
3 Beta Gully
4 Destitution Road

5 Gamma Gully
6 Skyscraper Buttress
7 Sellers Buttress
8 Epsilon Gully

an airy crux. The Original Route now follows the obvious series of cracks on the right side of the buttress but, if time allows, the exposed Empire State Variation should not be missed. From the top of the crux corner, follow the Original Route up and right for 15m to a huge flake on the left. Move left around the edge above the flake to gain a small hanging snowfield, and climb a left-slanting, shallow turfy groove which cuts into the headwall looming above (50m). Climb straight up *via* cracks and grooves to reach a ledge and niche overlooking Gamma Gully on the left (45m). Continue up the steep groove above to ledges, then take a turfy corner leading into the centre of the final overhanging wall. Step right into a second groove, then trend up and left in a spectacular position to the top (45m). These final three pitches are very steep, but protection is excellent and the turf is very accommodating. Finish easily along the horizontal ridge to the plateau.

Delta Gully   240m   IV,4 **
D. Dinwoodie, M. Freeman   March 1972
After two pleasant steep pitches the gully widens and is followed more easily with impressive rock scenery on the two enclosing buttresses.

Sellers Buttress (No.5 Buttress)   240m   IV,5 *
G.S. Strange, D. Stuart   19th February 1972
Start at the lowest rocks and climb by grooves and shallow corners always to the left of the crest. Near the top move up right to finish up the crest. About 130m of easy snow common to Delta and Epsilon Gullies leads to the plateau.

Epsilon Gully (140m, Grade III) starts higher up the snowy ramp on the right of Sellers Buttress. It is straightforward after a hard start.

LIATHACH
1054m   (Map Ref 929 579)

Liathach comprises a range of seven tops forming an 8km chain running east to west on the north side of Glen Torridon, towering directly above the road. The highest point on Liathach is Spidean a' Choire Leith at 1054m, midway between Stuc a' Choire Dhuibh Bhig, 913m, guarding the east end of the chain, and Mullach an Rathain, 1023m, at the west end above Torridon village. A broad ridge extends west for 2km from Mullach an Rathain rising slightly to Sgorr a' Chadail before dropping down to Coire Mhic Nobuil.

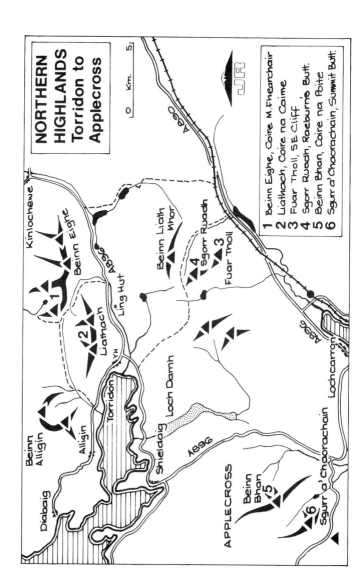

NORTHERN HIGHLANDS
Torridon to Applecross

0   Km.   5

1 Beinn Eighe, Coire M.Fhearchair
2 Liathach, Coire na Caime
3 Fuar Tholl, SE Cliff
4 Sgorr Ruadh, Raeburns Butt.
5 Beinn Bhan, Coire na Poite
6 Sgurr a'Chaorachain, Summit Butt.

Kinlochewe
Beinn Eighe
Liathach
Ling Hut
A896
YH
Torridon
Shieldaig
Loch Damh
A896
Beinn Liath Mhor
Sgorr Ruadh
Fuar Tholl
A890
Lochcarron
A896
APPLECROSS
Beinn Bhan
Sgurr a'Chaorachain
Diabaig
Alligin
Beinn Alligin

In winter the mountain is transformed to produce some of the best icefall climbing in Britain. The traverse of the mountain gives one of the classic ridge expeditions of the mainland, with sensationally exposed views onto the surrounding prehistoric hills of the Torridon area.

In the past, winter climbing conditions on Liathach were renowned for being rather fickle. However, with more information available from recent activity, it seems that good ice forms regularly every season at any time between January and April. A warm weather system may strip the buttresses and their icefalls, but the ice will re-form quickly on a return to colder conditions. The most reliable climbs will be found in Coireag Dubh Mor and high up in Coire na Caime. With heavy snowfalls, or late in the season, many of the bigger, easier gullies will bank out with snow.

Liathach Main Ridge Traverse   II ***

A superb expedition with continuously interesting walking and spectacular mountain scenery. It is usually done from east to west. Ascend Stuc a' Choire Dhuibh Bhig by its north-east ridge (although there are several Grade I or II gullies as alternatives). The hardest part is the traverse of the Fasarinen Pinnacles which warrants Grade II, but all sections of the traverse involve Grade I up, down and traversing. A low traverse of Am Fasarinen on the south side, a path in summer but steeply banked out in winter, is often more difficult than the crest, especially in bad snow conditions. Usually a mixture of traversing and the crest will be taken, with route-finding and judgement of line more important than technical skills. The recommended route is to traverse initially (at the eastern end) round The Pinnacles, but follow the crest over Am Fasarinen. Most people who claim to have "done the Pinnacles" have followed this logical route. The main ridge finishes at Mullach an Rathain.

Access

The climbs on the north side of Liathach are described from east to west, approaching *via* the Coire Dubh footpath from the National Trust carpark in Glen Torridon (Map Ref 958 568). The path rises under the east buttress of Stuc a' Choire Dhuibh Bhig and round the back to give access to the three northern corries of Coireag Dubh Beag, Coireag Dubh Mor (the north-east corrie of Spidean) and the larger spectacular Coire na Caime. Access from the footpath to each corrie, and also the descents, are described for each one individually.

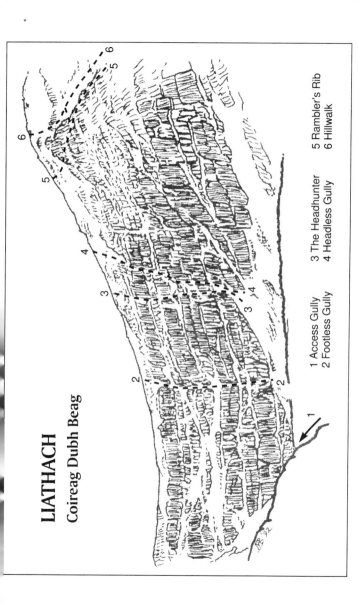

LIATHACH
Coireag Dubh Beag

1 Access Gully
2 Footless Gully
3 The Headhunter
4 Headless Gully
5 Rambler's Rib
6 Hillwalk

COIREAG DUBH BEAG

This is the first of the northern corries. It is a classic bowl with an easy snow gully in its left corner (Access Gully) and broad steep terraces sweeping round to the right into the climbing area. From a distance, the cascades of ice look discontinuous, but the lines become more apparent on closer inspection.

The best approach is to follow the burn draining from the corrie. The quickest descent is to go down Access Gully and return by the approach route. Alternatively, continue along the ridge east beyond Access Gully to traverse Stuc a' Choire Dhuibh Bhig and descend off the east end of the ridge. The third option is to descend the opposite side of Access Gully (i.e. southwards) or from a point just to its west, then turn right (west) to traverse into Coire Liath Mhor.

The Snotter   40m   VI,6
A. Cunningham, A. Nisbet   25th February 1986
Left of the base of Access Gully is an obvious short deep cleft. This route climbs the one-pitch vertical icefall on the left wall of the cleft.

Beag Pardon   200m   III
Climb the cleft, chimneying on steep ice, to finish above or by a more obvious easy gully on the right.

Access Gully   120m   I
The obvious snow gully on the left side at the back of the corrie gives a pleasant route onto the main ridge and, being a less steep Grade I which does not usually have a cornice, it may also be used as a descent.

Footless Gully   150m   IV,5 *
C. Rowland, A.S. Rowland   February 1977
This is the obvious line on the back wall where it bends round into the east-facing wall. The first 10m is the crux, an awkward narrow vertical chimney slow to fill with ice, and the climb is often only Grade III after the first pitch. Although there are many terraces, the direct line feels natural.

Opposite: Poacher's Fall, Coireag Dubh Mor, Liathach
       Climber: Grahame Nicoll   *Photo: Rab Anderson*

Next page: Brain Drain, Coireag Dubh Mor, Liathach
       Climber: Andy Nisbet   *Photo: Andy Cunningham*

The Headhunter   200m   V,5 **
N. Kekus, S. Anderson   7th February 1994
Left of Headless Gully (which has the thickest ice) a prominent chimney-groove diverges leftwards due to the change in aspect of the face. The first ascensionists climbed it in mistake for Headless, as others may have done before; arguably, it is more of a gully. The route starts up a steep icefall, the leftmost of several, to gain the first terrace. From here, climb a short awkward corner to the bottom of the chimney. Climb the chimney (50m, can be split). Continue straight up the fault by steep iced slabs, then a steep icy corner.

Headless Gully   150m   V,5 **
S. Kennedy, A. Nisbet   February 1984
This is the main line on the right (east-facing) wall and the route most likely to form regularly. Start by the highest point of snow under the middle of the wall. Climb an initial short steep icefall to the first terrace. Move left into the main icefall which is steep for 25m (crux) before easing onto more terraced ground. Finish *via* an ice-filled corner through the top tier onto the summit snowfield. The main icefall forms down a chimney line and on the first ascent, after a long thaw, the gap between ice and rock was chimneyed at Grade IV. Subsequent ascents were grade V.

Rambler's Rib   350m   II
D. Broadhead, S. Sillars   15th February 1987
The left rib of Hillwalk, starting just inside the gully, is not a safe option in avalanche conditions because even though one can start safely by traversing right from the lip of Coireag Dubh Beag, the route finishes on open slopes. Climb the rib direct, with short technical walls above big ledges; a contrast in style to the following route. Avoid the big final tier on either side.

Hillwalk   300m   II *
The long gully between the two corries gives several short pitches, but in late season it often banks out to a steep Grade I. It opens into a bowl after its narrow section. Beware of avalanches, which may funnel down the route.

*Previous page: Andes Couloir, Coire na Caime, Liathach
          Climber: Andy Cunningham   Photo: Andy Nisbet*

*Opposite: East Buttress, Coire Mhic Fhearchair, Beinn Eighe
          Climber: Rab Anderson   Photo: Grahame Nicoll*

COIREAG DUBH MOR

This corrie is topped by Spidean a' Choire Leith, the highest peak of Liathach, and provides top quality icefall climbing, the equal of anywhere in Scotland and lacking only the length of season of Ben Nevis.

Conditions and Weather

This corrie is the most reliable option in Torridon, since the thicker icefalls form readily and last well, throughout January to March, and survive most thaws. The normal absence of cornices means that these icefalls can sometimes be climbed during a thaw, accepting slushy ice and possible rockfall. The thinner icefalls require good conditions and tend to lose their first pitches during a thaw. Conditions are often good when the south (road-facing) side of the mountain is bare, common in the second half of the season. The corrie is very exposed to a northerly wind, but somewhat sheltered from a south to west wind, although this often swirls around the corrie. The slope above the routes can avalanche, particularly down Poacher's Fall.

Layout

The corrie faces north, with huge rambling buttresses on the left cut by two gullies, West Gully and Spidean Way, followed by a deep snow gully, Way Up, which borders the left end of the steep back wall. Way Up leads to a bealach on the main ridge, from where the commonest descent leads down the opposite side of the ridge. The 200m back wall extends rightwards to a left-slanting gash, George, before merging into the north ridge of Spidean. In the centre of the back wall, and obvious from a great distance, is the magnificent ice cascade of Poacher's Fall, the line that forms most readily.

Access

Access into the corrie is from the Coire Dubh footpath, leaving it just before the watershed and angling up to join the burn draining from the corrie itself. The routes are described from left to right.

Descent

1. For the main face, the quickest descent is to make a rising traverse left to join and descend the east ridge of Spidean to the above mentioned col. From the col, Way Up can be descended northwards back into the corrie, but it is quicker to descend in the opposite direction

(south) down a shallow gully (Grade I) to a flat area. Go straight on from the base of the gully to the south rim and descend another gully. Continue in the same direction down a shallow continuation to cross the stream and gain the footpath. In favourable conditions much of this can be glissaded.

2. If the summit of Liathach has been visited, either as an option or after George, one can still descend the east ridge to the col but it is less steep to descend the south ridge (a notorious dead end) until it becomes level, then turn left (east) and descend diagonally leftwards to gain the descent gully from the col not far above the flat area.

3. From West Gully or Spidean Way, one can either go west or east and descend as above or as for Coireag Dubh Beag.

West Gully   300m   I
C. Rowland, R. McHardy   Winter 1978
The first obvious gully in the mouth of the corrie, with a steep right wall and bounding the left side of a rambling terraced buttress. It is normally banked up, but it can form an ice pitch at the narrows.

Spidean Way   250m   III *
C. Rowland, B. Griffiths   Winter 1977
The next gully line is left-slanting and bounds the right side of the terraced buttress. One ice pitch low down is always present, but it can bank up in heavy snow to reduce the climb to Grade II.

Way Up   250m   I *
This straightforward snow gully leads to the bealach on the main ridge. It is also a way down! The grade does not vary with build-up, nor does it form a significant cornice.

Over Sixties Icefall   100m   III
M. Johnston, A. Nisbet, D. Thompson   7th March 1994
On the right wall of Way Up after about 100m is a low-angled icefall which is excellent when formed, but poor in some years. It provides a shorter and quicker route than others in the corrie. The steeper sections can be taken direct if wished. It leads in two or three pitches of continuous ice to a big terrace from where a horizontal traverse leads left to the descent col. It can also be started by traversing left along the terrace from the base of Poacher's Fall, or more directly on ice just right of Way Up, then following turfy grooves slanting left.

Hooded Claw   150m   IV,5
A. Nisbet, A. Cunningham   13th January 1987
The icefall towards the left edge of the main face gives a good climb.

Umbrella Fall   230m   IV,5 **
M. Fowler, P. Butler   1st April 1984
The thick icefall on the face between Way Up and Poacher's Fall
provides continuous ice but only one pitch of 5. The length includes an
optional first ice pitch up the lowest tier next to Way Up. The main icefall
steepens to its crux pitch. Often this forms a deep groove on the right
which can be eased by bridging, or even chimneying, but it could be
V,5 if not. It contained an ice umbrella on the first ascent.

Snow Goose   230m   IV,5
A. Cunningham, A. Nisbet   25th February 1986
Between Umbrella Fall and Salmon Leap are three thinner icefalls
whose lines are obvious, although slower to form than the classics
either side. This is the left-hand icefall; the crux is an icicle high up.

The Deer Hunter   200m   V,6 *
A. Cunningham, A. Nisbet   24th February 1986
The middle of the thinner icefalls has a strenuous chimney with a
difficult exit through the last bare tier.

White Tiger   220m   VI,6
A. Cunningham, A. Nisbet   14th January 1987
The right icefall, next to The Salmon Leap, is slow to form at the base,
but the first tier can be avoided on the left. Avoid the last tier on the right
by a traverse into The Salmon Leap, or by mixed climbing direct (crux).

The Salmon Leap   180m   VI,6 ***
A. Cunningham, A. Nisbet   23rd February 1986
This is the left side of Poacher's Fall, separated in the top half by a rock
rib. It forms quickly and lasts well, so it is usually climbable, but it has
a steeper section than Poacher's Fall which, with average ice quantity
or less, has short vertical sections. In very good conditions, there are
grooves past the vertical sections and it can be easier than Poacher's
Fall (and with better rock belays). Start at the centre of the icefall but
move left as soon as possible and climb ice close to the left wall.
Thereafter, chose the best line through steep ice, with rock belays on

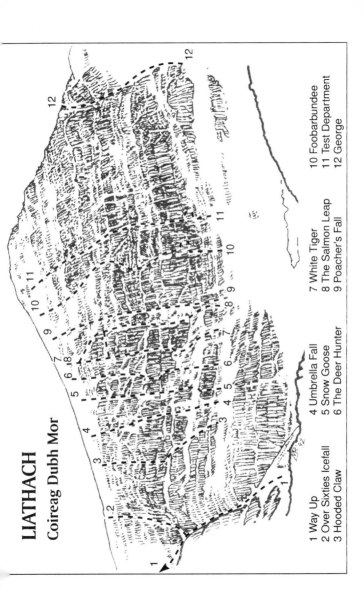

LIATHACH
Coireag Dubh Mor

1 Way Up	7 White Tiger
2 Over Sixties Icefall	8 The Salmon Leap
3 Hooded Claw	9 Poacher's Fall
4 Umbrella Fall	10 Foobarbundee
5 Snow Goose	11 Test Department
6 The Deer Hunter	12 George

the left wall. The line finishes naturally up a left-slanting chimney-crack, but if the ice in this has thawed, finish on the right, possibly as for Poacher's Fall. An optional start follows Poacher's Fall to the cave, then moves left.

Poacher's Fall   160m   V,5 ***
R. McHardy, A. Nisbet   11th February 1978
This classic route follows the right side of the obvious steep, wide icefall draining the middle of the back wall. It is harder than Point Five Gully, being more sustained on steep ice. The top section is in a deep groove right of the separating rib and is partially hidden on the approach to the corrie. It is normally easier than Salmon Leap, particularly in thin conditions, and it comes into condition quickly. The most obvious belay is at the right end of a ledge between the two steepest sections and about 15m below the groove. This is 60m above the start. Sometimes a sheltered ice cave with a good rock belay forms in the centre of the fall at about 50m. The top groove is steep but helpful and can be climbed even when the ice is thin. Expect ice screw belays (although not consecutive) in prime conditions.

Foobarbundee   200m   VIII,7
C. Cartwright, D. Hesleden   22nd February 1994
The long-eyed (and previously tried) icefall first right of Poacher's usually has a break at a big overhang in the first major tier. In 1993 and 1994 it changed course and formed down the steep slab right of the overhang and provided arguably the hardest thin ice pitch in Scotland (although the ice was thicker at times in both years). Icy grooves led to a left-facing corner right of the ice line. This was climbed for 6m, then a tension-traverse left was made onto the thinly iced hanging slab, which was climbed trending left. Above this is a thicker but still impressive icefall.

Test Department   185m   VII,7
M. Fowler, C. Watts   11th January 1987
The next ice line to the right looks superb, but has a fragile icicle low down and is yet to be freed (2 pegs for aid). Exceptional conditions or insanity are required.

Brain Strain   180m   V,5
D. Wills, M. Fowler   17th February 1991
This is a thinner ice line, which starts up a shallow chimney.

Brain Drain   180m   IV,5
A. Nisbet, A. Cunningham   13th January 1987
The next ice line is thicker, but rarely forms down the first tier, which was climbed as for Brain Strain.

The Temptress   220m   IV,5
A. Cunningham, A. Nisbet   16th February 1988
This is the last icefall before George, finishing up Brain Drain.

George   200m   III,4 **
I.G. Rowe, M. Kelsey   February 1967
Sinister Prong   III,5 **
J. Grant, J.R. Mackenzie   12th February 1978
The steep back wall of the corrie finishes at a big gully, the next feature left of the north ridge of Spidean. The gully gives the best Grade III in the corrie, with short but technical difficulties, although Over Sixties Icefall can have more ice. It is almost always in condition, even when lean. It is not prominent on the approach to the corrie partly because it slants left out of sight and partly because its start is shallower than the deep upper section. Initially the gully is easy, but the snow gradually steepens to an easy ice pitch at about half-height. Another ice pitch in a steepening groove ends at a wall. Here is the fork, the more obvious chimney on the left being the harder Sinister Prong. For the normal route, climb rightwards out of the groove on steepish ice. This is the crux in lean conditions, because one can now crawl under a big chockstone to a narrow exit. In full conditions, one must continue on ice over the chockstone. The route finishes over an awkward bulge of jammed blocks, then goes up a shallow groove (turf and ice) to the crest of the north ridge.

  For the Sinister Prong, move left from the groove to the base of a chimney. The chimney has two difficult bulging sections (both well protected). A right traverse joins the normal route for its final groove. The summit of Liathach is easily visited. A left traverse across the top of the corrie is steep, exposed and only saves a few minutes.

COIRE NA CAIME

Walking west along the Coire Dubh path, this is the third, the most scenic and largest of the northern corries. Its relative remoteness ensures that it is less popular than the others and it will appeal to those who wish a day with a mountaineering atmosphere and an element of exploration. There is a bigger selection of lower grade ice routes, but it lacks the steep icefalls of Coireag Dubh Mor. The routes have had few ascents; the stars are based on limited experience so a choice based on conditions on the day is important. Even the routes briefly mentioned have been seen with continuous ice (or with none).

Access
1. Leave the Coire Dubh path near the watershed as for Coireag Dubh Mor and skirt round under the north ridge of Spidean into the corrie. The exact height of approach depends on destination, but all are bouldery unless there is hard snow. This takes 2 hours in perfect conditions but 3 hours or more is more normal. This is the easiest approach but returning to the car is longer.
2. Recommended for Bell's Buttress and the upper corrie is an approach over the top. Follow the path up the Allt a' Tuill Bhan, as if heading for Mullach an Rathain, but leave it and climb direct up a shallow gully which leads towards a small top formed by Bell's Buttress. For Bell's Buttress, descend the gully immediately to the west (this can be corniced) and turn right. For the Trinity Gullies, turn left as soon as possible into the base of Coireag Cham. Alternatively, or if approaching from Mullach an Rathain, descend the gully from the small col just east of Mullach. Both gullies are Grade I and descending the wrong one means only some easy traversing.
3. Useful for Am Fasarinen and the east end of the corrie, this is similar to the second option but trends further right on the approach (further right than appearances might suggest), then goes further east along the main ridge to the west end of Am Fasarinen. Traverse the ridge eastwards, descending gently on easy ground. Gully 8 is at the main col. The broad Gully 7 (easy Grade I and the cornice passed easily on the right) is less obvious on the approach but lies at a flat section soon after Gully 8, before a 5m rise to a bump. After this the ridge starts to narrow and gently drops to another col (the top of Twisting Gully) before a steep rise to Am Fasarinen. If this steep rise is reached, you have gone 100 metres past Gully 7.

Descent
Descent from the east end of this corrie can be serious and as hard as the easier routes. The choice of direction may depend on the location of your transport. It may be best to traverse the ridge eastwards *via* the Fasarinen pinnacles and go to the summit of Spidean. Descend from there as described for Coireag Dubh Mor. The last 30m below the summit can be traversed on the right to the top of Pyramid

Buttress. For the centre and western end of the corrie, traverse the ridge westwards and reverse approach 3 or 2 (the gully described in 2 descends directly from the top of Bell's Buttress and in ideal conditions provides a long glissade).

Layout

As the name may suggest, 'crooked corrie', it is more complicated than the typical bowl shape. Loch Coire na Caime lurks at the entrance, with Meall Dearg on the west and Spidean towering above to the east. The broad ridge of P.C. Buttress divides Coire na Caime leaving a small hanging bowl on the left enclosed by the Fasarinen Pinnacles and Am Fasarinen, and a larger three-stepped corrie reaching high to the right, finishing in upper Coireag Cham overshadowed by Bell's Buttress, Mullach an Rathain and the Northern Pinnacles.

The routes are described from left to right, starting with the Fasarinen pinnacles and Am Fasarinen. The first two pinnacles have slabby faces which can hold ice and are flanked by easy gullies, Grade I or II. The Dru is the third pinnacle, impressive when seen from the ridge or the corrie. It is the tower high up on the left (south-east) from the loch. With a bit of imagination, it might seem similar to the slightly bigger Chamonix mountain of the same name.

Dru Couloir   150m   V,6 *
R. Anderson, M. Hamilton   23rd February 1986
The winter route takes the left-slanting chimney-gully on the corrie face of the Dru. Start right of the the foot of the pinnacle at a left-facing tapering corner, directly below the chimney-gully. Climb the corner to a ledge at 30m (crux). Gain the chimney-gully and follow it for 30m to a belay on the left. Continue in the same line to the bealach where a detached needle on the left abuts the summit ridge. Take the easiest line up the ridge to the top. It may be possible to traverse in above the crux to provide a sensational easier climb.

Am Fasarinen
West of the Pinnacles rises the bigger dome-shaped buttress of Am Fasarinen, forming the back wall of a small hanging corrie, which in turn is bounded on the right by P.C. Buttress. The left face of Am Fasarinen has 3 icy gullies, the leftmost being the deepest (Jerbil) while the rightmost is only a gully in its top half (Echo Couloir). Right of the gullies is a left-slanting chimney (**Toll Dubh Chimney** (V,5), mostly mixed), then a big icefall (**The Shining Path**, IV,6).

Jerbil   120m   V,5 **
M. Fowler, B. Craig   10th March 1985
The deepest and often iciest of the gullies looks steep, hence the grade. Start in a high snow bay shared by a left-slanting gully. Climb a steep ice pitch leading to a small snow amphitheatre in the deep gully (45m). Continue in the same line, avoiding difficult obstacles on the left or right as necessary, to an easy bay leading to the main ridge.

The Andes Couloir   180m   V,5 **
A. Cunningham, A. Nisbet   22nd February,1986
A steep start up an ice curtain in a gully, quite slow to form, leads to a snow ledge under a steep iced corner. Pull into the corner over a strenuous bulge (where the ice may be thin) and take the superb right-facing and easier ice corner above to an easing below the main ridge.

Echo Couloir   250m   III**
Direct Start   V,6
S. Birch, C. Collin, M. Moran   1st March 1993
Variation Left-Hand Start
A. Nisbet, G. Nisbet   19th March 1994
In good conditions the rightmost gully, whose upper part is better defined than The Andes Couloir, is best identified by a wide ice smear which flows out of the gully. This can be gained from the left by starting up a short groove (also the start to Andes Couloir) and slanting up right on snow, then mixed ice and turf. Alternatively, the Direct Start climbs two steep icefalls to the same belay right of the base of the smear. Climb the smear and the superb upper gully.

Twisting Gully   180m   II **
R. Urquhart, D. Stevens   31st March 1955
The deep snow gully on the right of Am Fasarinen, which finishes at a notch on the main ridge, is easy except for an ice pitch at two-thirds height. This may sometimes be avoided by a through route.

Gully 7   180m   I
This is the wide open couloir left of P.C. Buttress.

P.C. Buttress   210m   III
The big buttress in the centre of the corrie looks rather scrappy.

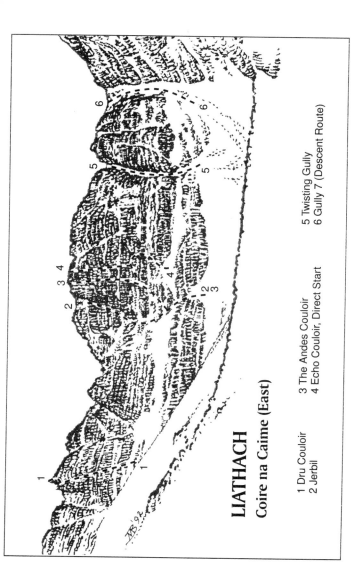

LIATHACH
Coire na Caime (East)

1 Dru Couloir
2 Jerbil

3 The Andes Couloir
4 Echo Couloir, Direct Start

5 Twisting Gully
6 Gully 7 (Descent Route)

West of P.C. Buttress is a high broad broken face cut by numerous shallow chimney lines. Although escapable onto many terraces, this is not obvious during the routes and would only lead to another chimney of similar standard. The face ends in a buttress of more compact rock, Bell's Buttress, situated above the entrance to upper Coire na Caime and forming a high point on the main ridge.

Titanium Gully   200m   III
D. Rubens, G. Macnair, G. Cohen   21st February 1984
At the left end of the face and starting at a snow bay just above the lowest rocks is an obvious narrow ice line running virtually the full height of the face. A good line in lean icy conditions, perhaps Grade IV at the start, but it can fill up with snow and all but disappear.

The centre of this face is more broken and there is a squat buttress low down and right of centre. The right side of this buttress forms a deep gully, the start of Fat Man's Folly, and there are several parallel chimneys to the right. These generally have steep starts, followed by easier upper gullies which are better quality than they look.
Fat Man's Folly (200m IV,5) breaks right out of the deep gully and follows a line of weakness *via* a short slot and slanting corner. The start is steep, then easier climbing follows. **The Faultfinders** (250m IV,5) starts below the chimney of Valentine Buttress, slants up left on mixed ground and climbs a bulging ice wall to reach a good but easier fault line parallel to Valentine Buttress.

Valentine Buttress   250m   IV,4 *
D. Broadhead, W. Tring   14th February 1987
Start 30 metres left of Vanadium Couloir at the top of a snow bay and take the right-hand of two chimneys close together. Climb the chimney line for about 100m, with unusual subterranean moves, until easier climbing leads out right onto the buttress. Follow a series of grooves up the rocks above leading to the ridge.

Vanadium Couloir   300m   IV,4
A. Paul, D. Sanderson   24th February 1979
The obvious open gully line immediately left of Bell's Buttress, starting from the highest point of the snow bay. After a steep start (45m), it is then much easier with icy steps, or largely banked out. The route can

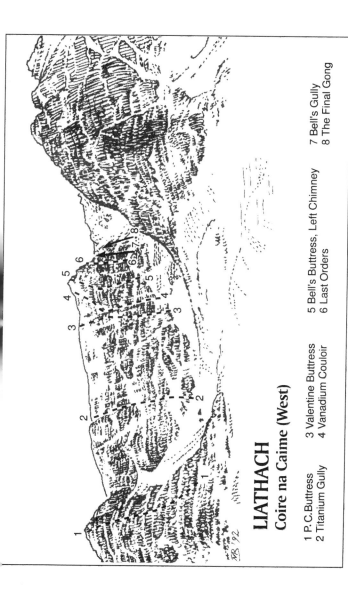

LIATHACH
Coire na Caime (West)

1 P.C.Buttress
2 Titanium Gully

3 Valentine Buttress
4 Vanadium Couloir

5 Bell's Buttress, Left Chimney
6 Last Orders

7 Bell's Gully
8 The Final Gong

AB '92

be reduced to Grade III, or even Grade II in good conditions, by trending right from the base, then going back left into the upper runnel (or by traversing under Bell's Buttress into the upper runnel). There are no cornice problems, as the finish is near the top of Bell's Buttress.

Bell's Buttress is a high area of steep compact rock forming a small top on the main ridge. It is streaked with two shallow chimney-gully lines on the left side and two deeper gullies on the more continuous right side. All the routes merge into an easy finish up the upper crest. A snow terrace at the base of the routes can be gained from either end.

Bell's Buttress, Left Chimney   230m   IV,5 *
G. Cohen, D Broadhead   11th January 1987
This route takes the furthest left chimney line on Bell's Buttress. Start up the left of a pair of chimneys and step into the right-hand one at 10m. Where it overhangs, climb out right and go up the gully above to a huge block belay on the left (30m). Continue up the chimney line to snow ledges, turning two blocking overhangs on the right (30m). Follow the gully on the right through several narrowings past a right-slanting ramp at 45m, and continue in the same line to finish.

Cube's Chimney (280m IV,5) takes the next chimney which fails to reach the base despite the attempts of an icicle to bridge the 10m gap. Start by traversing in from the left.

Last Orders   230m   IV,5 *
S. Pearson, G. Cohen   23rd January 1993
The left-hand of the two gully lines on the right side of Bell's Buttress is blocked by a huge roof, making the grade hard to believe! This can be passed by climbing the right wall to reach a crack above the overhang. Move back left into the gully line which gradually eases and becomes straightforward.

Bell's Gully   230m   IV,5 **
R. Anderson, M. Hamilton   22nd February 1986
The right-hand and most obvious of the two gully lines on the right side of Bell's Buttress. Follow the increasingly difficult gully over two steepenings to a *cul-de-sac* at 125m. A dribble of ice may flow down from the upper gully, but it looks reasonable without. Move left, climb the ice and follow the shallow upper gully above to easy ground.

The Final Gong   200m   III
J. Lyall, A. Nisbet   10th January 1995
The right-bounding buttress right of Bell's Gully. Start up an easy chimney in the lowest tier, then trend slightly right to avoid slabby ground on the left. Return left to the crest between two steep tiers, climb the second, then climb a right-facing corner and continue in the same line to the easier upper section.

The upper corrie of Coire na Caime, Coireag Cham, feels almost Alpine. It is guarded on the left by Bell's Buttress and on the right by the spectacular Northern Pinnacles of Mullach an Rathain which top the back of the corrie. Since this corrie is high and sheltered, it seems to come into condition sooner and holds snow longer than elsewhere on the mountain. The wide snow slope leading up to the bealach between Bell's Buttress and Mullach an Rathain may be used as an easy descent or ascent to the main ridge.

The Northern Pinnacles
These are numbered ascending from right to left, One to Five. The gullies between the top pinnacles provide the following routes:

Left-Hand Trinity Gully   90m   I
G. Sang, W.N. Ling, G.T. Glover   1928
This wide gully, normally snow-filled, lies between the fifth pinnacle and Mullach an Rathain.

Central Trinity Gully   100m   I
D. Stevens, R. Urquhart   29th March 1955
The gully between the fourth and fifth pinnacle can give two ice pitches, but these are often banked out.

Right-Hand Trinity Gully   120m   III *
D. Stevens, R. Urquhart   29th March 1955.
This lies between the third and fourth pinnacles. It is usually the best and most difficult of the Trinity gullies.

The Northern Pinnacles   130m   II **
W.W. Naismith, A.M. Mackay, H. Raeburn   16th April 1900
Short and sharp, the Northern Pinnacles guard the north ridge of Mullach an Rathain. Combined with a west to east traverse of the main

ridge of Liathach, this gives one of Scotland's finest winter mountain days. It is possible to approach *via* the Coire Dubh path from the National Trust carpark to the base of Meall Dearg (2-3 hours), with grand views into the northern corries. An alternative is to approach from the Beinn Alligin carpark (Coire Mhic Nobuil). The start of the route, at the col between Meall Dearg and the Pinnacles, is reached from either side at Grade I. From the west approach, a hidden wide couloir on the north west flank of Meall Dearg leads into an easy narrow gully and so to the base of the first pinnacle. For the east approach, the col is easily gained from Coireag Cham. There are five pinnacles in all; the first two are small, the third has the longest ascent and the fourth is the crux. The general line is on the right of the crest.

THE SOUTH SIDE OF LIATHACH

In comparison to the northern corries, the south side of Liathach offers only a few climbs. The Glen Torridon glacier has scraped and plucked the south side relatively smooth, leaving only one small hanging corrie, Coire Liath Mhor to the east of Spidean a' Choire Leith, and very little in the form of continuous gullies.

PYRAMID BUTTRESS OF SPIDEAN A' CHOIRE LEITH

This is the shapely buttress easily seen from the road that terminates the short south-east ridge of Spidean. To reach it, follow the path on the right of the Allt an Doire Ghairbh and make a rising leftward traverse over awkward ground. There are basically two obvious icefalls split by a tapering rocky rib. These are well seen from the road, the left icefall being wide while the right one is narrow. Although the ice forms readily, the buttress faces due south and is seriously affected by the sun. Even early in the season it may not be a good choice on a sunny day and is rarely in condition in March. The steepest sections of the icefalls can be avoided by climbing the central rib for a pitch, as on the first ascents.

Pyramid Left Icefall   180m   V,5 **
K. Hopper, C. Rowland   *23rd February 1986*
The wide left-hand icefall has a steep second pitch. There can be a choice of vertical icicles here; the choice and difficulty will depend on

The Northern Pinnacles of Liathach   *Climber: Ronald Turnbull*
Photo: Donald Bennet

the precise formation, which will always be spectacular. Easier ice leads to an interesting mixed final section.

Pyramid Right Icefall   180m   V,4 *
D. Jenkins, C. Rowland, M. Webster   February 1977
The right-hand icefall is sustained and serious with little protection, but it is not too steep. For an easier route (IV,4), or if the direct line is not complete, avoid the steep initial section by starting up the central rib.

Pyramid Right Edge   180m   III
B. Ledingham, C. Rowland   Early 1980s
Climb the right crest of the buttress, starting up a groove with a steep finish. Further turfy grooves lead logically up the crest to a final barrier which forces a traverse left into an easy finishing gully. An icefall leads directly into this gully from below (**Busman's Holiday, V5**)

BEINN EIGHE
1010m   (Map Ref 952 612)

COIRE MHIC FHEARCHAIR   *(Map Ref 945 605)*

Coire Mhic Fhearchair, on the north side of Beinn Eighe, is one of the classic corries in Scotland and is justly famous for its magnificent Triple Buttresses. Secluded from the road by a relatively long approach, they dominate the lonely corrie and offer routes of great length and character. Some of the climbs here compare with the best available anywhere in Scotland.

Weather and Conditions
In winter, the corrie is a paradise for modern-style mixed climbing. The steep blocky quartzite provides good axe placements, reliable protection and sensational lines. There is less reliance on frozen turf than, for example, in the Cairngorms so the corrie is a possibility in marginal conditions, especially early season. Also, the corrie usually holds more snow than one might imagine from the view of the south-facing slopes from the carpark. Good ice conditions are rarer, but the easier gullies of Sail Mhor fill readily. When in condition, two of the most spectacular ice routes in Scotland are to be found in the corrie.

The Triple Buttresses of Coire Mhic Fhearchair, Beinn Eighe
Photo: Anne Murray

The corrie is sheltered from southerly or south-westerly winds and deep snow does not alter the climbing, but it is too serious to be considered as an option for poor conditions. A problem for traditionally-minded climbers is being discouraged by lack of snow on the crag. The harder routes are too steep to hold much of the white stuff, but they are often verglassed and feel more wintry than their appearance may suggest.

Access

The initial approach to Coire Mhic Fhearchair is to follow the well made Coire Dubh path between Liathach and Beinn Eighe, starting from the National Trust carpark in Glen Torridon (Map Ref 959 569). When the path levels off, there is an important choice: either continue along the path into the bottom of the corrie or climb the steep slope on the right and approach from the top. The approach over the top is normally much quicker for most routes, except Central Buttress, unless there is deep soft snow above 500m and little below. But first-time visitors may well choose the longer route, as the panorama of the cliff from the loch is not to be missed.

1. If continuing along the path, fork right at a cairn about 1½km beyond some stepping stones and follow another path contouring below Sail Mhor and rising gradually to the lip of the corrie. This takes about 3 hours and a further 30 minutes to the foot of the Triple Buttresses.

2. There are two possible lines recommended up the slope on the right of the path, depending on snow conditions. There is a shallow trough running up the scree and leading to a left-slanting ramp, which in turn leads to the col between Spidean Coire nan Clach and Coinneach Mhor. The trough fills with snow and it is a good option if this reaches its base. Slightly further on, at the boundary between scree and rocky tiers further left, is a deeper stream bed (not the gully further left). Follow its left side, then slant left near the top to reach the base of grassy slopes leading up to Coinneach Mhor. In deep snow, pick the most windswept line.

From the east cairn of Coinneach Mhor (reached in about 2½ hours and a possible place to leave a rucksack), descend to the col leading to Ruadh-stac Mor. From there, descend the gully into the corrie (Grade I). For access to West Central Gully or West Buttress, descend into the corrie west of West Buttress, *via* the col leading to Sail Mhor.

Descent

Reverse one of high level options, chosen on the walk-in when snow conditions are visible. With limited snow, go to the south-east end of the grassy slopes below Coinneach Mhor. Below and left from there is the stream bed described above; its right side is grassy. With good snow, particularly if the snow allows glissading, continue along the ridge until just before the first rise towards Spidean Coire nan Clach, then descend south to the ramp and trough. With care, the descent is effortless compared to the approach.

Layout
Seen from Loch Coire Mhic Fhearchair, the wall in the top left of the corrie is the Far East Wall. To its right is Far East Gully, then the steep left flank of the East Buttress, known as the Eastern Ramparts. Because the crests of the triple buttresses incline to the west, each buttress has an extensive left wall of steep quartzite facing north-east and a much narrower right wall tucked into the flanking gully. The left wall of Central Buttress is known as Central Wall, and the gullies have the obvious nomenclature East Central Gully, West Central Gully and Far West Gully. (Alternatively called Fuselage Gully).

The buttresses are composed of three tiers, the upper tiers of quartzite standing on a plinth of sandstone. There is a big terrace above the sandstone tier, Broad Terrace, and two further fault lines crossing the buttresses higher up. The middle fault starts on the left at the base of the Eastern Ramparts proper, continues across the top of the lower quartzite tier of East Buttress and marks the level where more continuous climbing on the left walls of Central and West Buttresses begins. The highest fault is the line of the Upper Girdle, a sensational 700m climb across all three buttresses. It crosses the Eastern Ramparts about one-third of the way up and on the crests of the Central and West Buttresses it marks the level where the steep climbing on the final towers begins.

EAST BUTTRESS
The sandstone tier of this buttress has few weaknesses, but it can (and usually is) bypassed by a traverse along Broad Terrace. The left edge of the quartzite tier forms a fine ridge which is not too steep and gives the most amenable climbing on the Triple Buttresses.

East Buttress   250m   IV,4 ***
First ascent unknown.
This fine natural line has an imposing appearance, but it is the easiest of the buttresses. It is climbable in any conditions and can often be used to salvage a day for those originally intent on harder things. The

normal start, and consistent in standard with the rest of the buttress, is to traverse all the way along Broad Terrace from the left. This has one very exposed icy section, about Grade II. Start the buttress proper just left of the crest and climb the steep face on good ledges and some turf to an easier section (30m). Continue up an interesting and varied series of pitches to the top.

The Icefall Start   V,5
R. Arnott, E. Clark, A. Nisbet, S. Thirgood   12th February 1983
Climb the steep icefall towards the left of the lower tier, ending on Broad Terrace.

The Chimney Start   VI,7
R. Anderson, G. Nicoll   30th March 1986
This mixed start takes the conspicuous chimney near the right end of the lower tier. Climb the chimney, then a continuation corner, finishing on the left.

East Central Gully   250m   III *
The normal start is to traverse all the way along Broad Terrace from the left and enter the gully easily from the base of the East Buttress quartzite. The gully provides several ice pitches, none too long or steep.

Direct Start   V,4
The sandstone section of the gully is the logical direct start but it is deceptively hard and serious. The ice is often hollow, covering a deep crack, and there is minimal protection.

CENTRAL WALL

Central Wall is the name given to the north-east facing left flank of the upper part of Central Buttress. It is bounded on the left by East Central Gully and on the right by the crest of Central Buttress. The lower part of the wall is formed by what appears from below to be a tower about 45m high rising from East Central Gully at the level of Broad Terrace.

In winter the easiest access is to traverse above the sandstone tier of East Buttress into East Central Gully and follow this until one can break out right onto the Tower (Grade II). A more satisfying approach is to climb the first pitch of East Central Gully, then take the right fork between the Tower and Central Buttress, finally breaking out left onto the Tower (Grade V,4). The right fork can also be reached by the traverse across East Buttress (Grade II) if the initial chimney of East Central Gully is insufficiently iced.

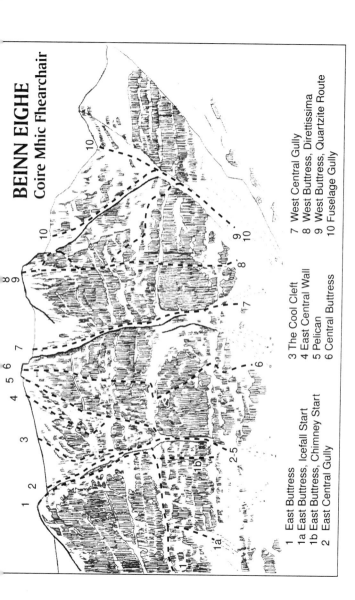

BEINN EIGHE
Coire Mhic Fhearchair

1 East Buttress
1a East Buttress, Icefall Start
1b East Buttress, Chimney Start
2 East Central Gully
3 The Cool Cleft
4 East Central Wall
5 Pelican
6 Central Buttress

7 West Central Gully
8 West Buttress, Direttissima
9 West Buttress, Quartzite Route
10 Fuselage Gully

The Cool Cleft   120m   V,5 *
R. Arnott, E. Clark, A. Nisbet, S. Thirgood   12th February 1983
P. Thornhill, C. Watts, T. Saunders, M. Fowler (direct, as described)
9th April 1983
This takes the shallow curving fault immediately right of the upper part of East Central Gully. It is often a continuous line of ice, particularly late in the season, and is best started by the icefall below East Buttress or by East Central Gully direct start (both of a similar grade), then climbing the gully until an easy traverse right leads to the foot of the fault. The second pitch in the fault is the crux.

East Central Wall   300m   V,4 *
P. Barrass, A. Nisbet   22nd December 1981
This is a good first excursion away from the buttresses with a fine mountaineering atmosphere. Climb East Central Gully direct start through the sandstone (probably the crux), then take a steeper right fork (Pelican), which is also hard if there is no ice. From the top of this gully, go up left on broken ground until about 10m below and right of a very prominent wide crack. Traverse 5 metres right along an overhung ledge to the base of a chimney. Climb this and a further right-slanting chimney to reach a triangular bay with ice in the overhanging corner at its top. The ice is very steep and may be avoided by climbing a shallow chimney to the right of the bay which leads to easy ground. The route can be started *via* the normal start to East Central Gully, along the Broad Terrace; this reduces the grade to IV,4.

Pelican   250m   VI,6 **
A. Cunningham, A. Nisbet   9th January 1987
A steep and sustained direct route formed by a chimney and groove line which starts from East Central Gully, just above its Direct Start (the logical start to this route), and leads up right to slopes at the top of Central Buttress.

CENTRAL BUTTRESS

In appearance at least, this is the finest of the Triple Buttresses, tapering skywards to a splendid quartzite tower. There is excellent climbing on both the sandstone and quartzite tiers; no easy ways but plenty of scope for variation. Good route-finding is very important.

Central Buttress (Piggott's Route)   250m   VI,7 ***
K. Spence, J. Rowayne, K. Urquhart   February 1971 (2 days)
A. McIntyre, A. Rouse   February 1978 (as described)
One of the finest winter expeditions in Scotland, this is a climb of Alpine stature worthy of its illustrious originators. Climb the sandstone tier by a left-slanting diagonal line which starts about one-third of the way from the right-hand end. It has a difficult section past a cave at half-height (90m). Climb the first quartzite tier by starting up a central corner line and moving left, then moving easily to the foot of the final tower (110m). This top tier is the crux, taking a line just left of the crest, and strong parties have used a little aid, particularly when the chimney is heavily verglassed. This section is described in detail:
1. 20m   Above is a left-facing corner and above this an obvious short bottleneck chimney with a crack just to its right. Gain the corner by first moving left into a groove, then go up and right to the base of the corner. This leads to a belay below the narrow chimney.
2. 35m   Climb the bottleneck chimney with difficulty and continue up flakes on the right of an obvious cracked groove. Step up left onto the wall and move up to a flake overlooking the groove. Pull round into a continuation groove and follow this to ledges and a belay on the right.
3. 40m   Above is a corner and on its right more broken stepped ground on the edge. Move up and right to gain a ledge, then pull up onto easier ground which leads to the top.
Right-Hand Finish   IV,6
S. Allan, A. Nisbet   3rd January 1990
An easier but indirect option for those who have run out of energy, time or weather. Traverse right for 15 metres from the crest of the buttress to a right-slanting line, initially turfy, then climb a tricky short wall to easier ground. Gain the final crest by an awkward short corner. If a little aid is used, this line is perhaps only Grade III.

West Central Gully   350m   VIII,7
M. Fowler, M. Morrison   5th April 1987
A very hard, serious and spectacular climb. The story goes that, pushed to the limit, Mick Fowler was forced to take a rest by hanging from his ice-axe cords that he had tied to the top of his rucksack. Fortunately, this precarious arrangement held while he rested, grimly trying to avoid slipping from the shoulder straps! The gully is easy except for an impasse near the top, a very steep 60m step sporting an ice-smeared overhanging chimney leading to steep, pure ice climbing.

The grade is a guess; on the first ascent conditions were good, with some ice under the big overhang, but this may have made it poorly protected. Late season, after freeze-thaw from above, seems to provide the best chance for enough ice. From the base of the step, ascend the chimney forming the back of the gully and belay beneath a prominent overhang (25m). Climb into the groove-chimney below the overhang, move up to another overhang and follow an ice-choked crack to small ledges (20m). Take the mixed groove to the final overhang; step right onto icy smears (rest point) and follow these to good thick ice and easy ground 50m from the top (25m).

WEST BUTTRESS

The lowest tier of the West Buttress is easily the most formidable of the sandstone tiers on the Triple Buttresses, and is bypassed by the ordinary winter route. The direct route, **West Buttress Direttissima** (VII, 8**), climbs this and the quartzite more directly.

West Buttress, Quartzite Route   300m   IV,4 *
R. MacGregor, A. Nisbet   13th January 1979
Start up Fuselage Gully (Far West) and traverse left along Broad Terrace. Climb on the right of the buttress crest, with some awkward short walls depending on route finding, to the base of the final tower. This is characterised by a steep wall on the frontal face, sometimes referred to as a 'domino-shaped block'. Traverse right on ledges until near the edge where the buttress turns round to the right towards Far West Gully. Climb a line of weakness and traverse back left along ledges. Climb a deep chimney to the top of the 'domino-shaped block', then continue more easily to the top.

Fuselage Gully (Far West Gully)   400m   I **
This is the gully to the right of West Buttress. At half-height, take the left fork which includes the crux, climbing into the wreckage of a Lancaster bomber which crashed in 1952. Grade II in lean conditions.

SAIL MHOR
981m   (Map Ref 938 606)

When entering Coire Mhic Fhearchair from the north-west, the beetling crags and terraces of Sail Mhor on the right cannot fail to impress, and the gullies give sporting winter climbs. The routes are described from right to left as this is the way one would normally approach them.

Morrison's Gully (No.1 Gully)   300m   I
The big gully on the north face of Sail Mhor is obvious before reaching the corrie and presents no difficulties.

Lawson, Ling and Glover's Route (No.2 Gully)   300m   II *
First ascensionists as above   2nd April 1899.
The next obvious gully, starting above the north-west end of the lochan. Climb the gully until it turns sharply left, then break out up easy slopes on the right to gain the crest. Follow this to the top over rocky steps and pinnacles. A scenic route.

White's Gully (No.3 Gully)   120m   II *
S. White and party   26th April 1910
The broad gully running up from the head of the lochan is joined a third of the way up by a narrow gully whose foot is a quarter of the way down the lochan. The route follows this narrow gully and is easy up to the final 30m, which is a chimney with three chockstones. This final section is often banked out and provides steep snow.

BEINN ALLIGIN
985m   (Map Ref 860 602)

Beinn Alligin is the most westerly of the three great mountains of the Torridon Forest. It is a noble mountain, well worth a visit for its winter climbs, or for the traverse of its tops, which is a convenient circuit somewhat easier than Liathach and shorter than Beinn Eighe.

Conditions and Weather
Beinn Alligin has fewer ice climbs than its neighbours and, being nearer the sea, is less often in good winter condition. The Eag Dubh always seems to be windy, but the other climbs can be sheltered. Deep South and Deep North Gullies can be good options in stormy weather as the descent is quick.

Access and Layout
Leave the road from Torridon to Diabaig at a large carpark by the bridge over the Abhainn Coire Mhic Nobuil and follow the good path on the east side of the burn through beautiful Caledonian forest. The first

corrie to be seen high on the left is Coir' nan Laogh. The next corrie, Toll a' Mhadaidh Mor, between Tom na Gruagaich and Sgurr Mhor, is much more impressive and offers several good ice routes on the north-east face of Tom na Gruagaich. On the opposite side of this corrie is a long vertical wall angling up to form a deep-cleft gully, the Eag Dubh, which reaches the ridge just south-west of the highest top, Sgurr Mhor. There are further winter climbs on the north side of the Horns of Alligin and in the remote Toll nam Biast. The descents are generally by following the traverse in the most convenient direction.

Beinn Alligin, Ridge Traverse   I **

The ridge can be traversed in either direction but anti-clockwise is easier; this goes over The Horns of Alligin first. There is a considerable path leading up towards the Horns, which involves some short and awkward, but unexposed walls. The Horns can be traversed on the crest (Grade II in icy conditions) or passed on the left (south) by a long exposed traverse. The ascent to Sgurr Mhor is steep but only walking. On its descent, the initial bearing will appear to lead diagonally rightwards off the ridge, but thereby misses the Eag Dubh. Continue easily towards Tom na Gruagaich; on its ascent there is some easy scrambling, exposed at one point. Normally the summit of Tom na Gruagaich would be included but it can be passed on the right by traversing into a snow gully which leads up and over directly to the descent down Coir' nan Laogh (a good glissade if there is sufficient snow). This leads fairly directly to the carpark.

TOM NA GRUAGAICH, NORTH-EAST FACE

West Coast Boomer   300m   IV,4 **
D. Gardner, N. Crawford, C. Ferguson   February 1973
The obvious gully on the left of the face can be recommended as a sustained and scenic route. Pass the lower crag on the right and angle up left to reach the main gully. There are numerous short pitches in the lower part and a continuous steep section in the upper part.

Eag Dubh   400m   I or II
The diagonal vertical wall facing the road from Sgurr Mhor and on the opposite side of the corrie from the previous route is thought to be the side wall of a huge rock avalanche whose debris can be seen on the corrie floor below. The wall leads up to and forms the right wall of the Eag Dubh, a deep narrow snow gully (Grade I). The gully can either be

gained by a long scramble up the ramp immediately below the impressive wall or more directly up a shallow gully further left. The latter requires some consolidated snow at that level but it can have several low-angled ice pitches and is a more satisfying approach (Grade II). The gully area is a windy place, susceptible to a fierce up-draught.

THE HORNS OF ALLIGIN

On the north-east face of the Horns of Alligin are the following climbs, reached by continuing along the vague path after the more obvious path to the ridge has been left.

Deep South Gully   250m   I ***
This is the first gully seen on the approach towards the col between Beinn Dearg and Beinn Alligin. It curves from left to right and finishes between the first (lowest) and second Horn. In lean conditions there is a big chockstone with an easy through route followed by an easy ice pitch.

Deep North Gully   250m   II **
This gully, which finishes between the second and third Horns, requires a good build-up; otherwise an introductory pitch can be very hard.

Diamond Fire   225m   IV,4 **
S. Chadwick, G. Livingston, G.S. Strange   10th February 1985
This climbs a huge deep cleft on the north-west face above Toll nam Biast. It is rarely climbed, but it is recommended for an adventure into the unknown. First climbed in very lean conditions, it held good ice even when the surrounding buttresses had little snow. The steepest ice pitch was avoided on the left, but with a good build-up it might not be too difficult.

FUAR THOLL
907m   (Map Ref 975 489)

This fine mountain has two major cliffs, a large number of smaller crags and good scope for winter climbing. The most important winter cliff is the South-East Cliff, which overlooks a small corrie just south-east of the summit, and is therefore visible from the road at Achnashellach. The other major cliff is Mainreachan Buttress, which rises from a north-facing corrie and abuts the north-west ridge, but it is remote and formidably steep. The South-East Cliff should not be confused with a lower band of crags which line the north-east face of the mountain and show up from the Achnashellach approach as a clean nose falling from the east ridge. This band continues round to the north side, facing the grand Coire Lair and producing broken crags with good easy gullies of Grade I and II.

SOUTH-EAST CLIFF   *(Map Ref 978 488)*

This is a very extensive north-east facing cliff, base 750m. In winter it provides several long and exacting climbs, among the hardest in the area.

Conditions and Weather

This is a typical Torridonian sandstone cliff, steep and hostile, but providing tremendous icefalls. There is also hard mixed climbing which is icy in good conditions. Although best known for its steep icefalls, there are two easier climbs. The cliff is lower than the Liathach corries, so the season is shorter and more susceptible to thaw. It faces the road so conditions can be assessed (weather permitting) from the car, but January and February are most likely to provide good climbing. The corrie is very sheltered from winds south-westerly through to northerly and can provide a venue when other cliffs are too stormy. The disadvantage of this is that the corrie collects huge amounts of snow and is prone both to big unstable cornices and windslab avalanches. It is a good choice on windy showery days, but assess snow conditions carefully.

Access

Follow the railway for 400 metres west of Achnashellach station, thus crossing the River Lair, then strike off right and go up steep rough slopes to a plateau at 420m. Reach the burn issuing from the corrie, and climb past a small lochan to gain the corrie (about 2 hours).

Descent

1. The direct descents are steep and rough, so in bad weather or complete snow cover (when the cornices cannot be seen), head away

from the cliff southwards to the flat area near Carn Eididh, descend a gully eastwards and traverse back to the plateau at 420m (or continue from Carn Eididh to Balnacra).

2. From the harder routes on the main face or the easier routes in good weather, descend south-eastwards along the top of the cliff (cornices). When the ground begins to steepen after about 200 metres, turn right (west) and soon reach a snowy trough which leads south-east again. This slope is convex and briefly 50 degrees. Follow snow as long as possible, because the ground here is very rough, and trend left to the plateau at 420m.

3. To return to the corrie, Access Gully is rarely used, as the cornice has to be abseiled. The usual choice is to descend the ridge on the north side of the corrie until it is possible to go down a short Grade I gully to the floor of the corrie.

Layout
The left side of the corrie is the main face. The big corner of Fuhrer is to the left while the icefall of Tholl Gate in the centre is the most obvious feature. At the top of the corrie there are two snow gullies, the cul-de-sac of Cold Hole is the left one and Access Gully the right one, with Right End Buttress between them.

Fuhrer   190m   VII,6
M. Fowler, C. Watts   15th February 1986
This route follows the big left-facing corner up the left-hand side of the cliff. It was climbed in very icy conditions (perhaps at a lower grade) and may be unrepeated.

Il Duce   200m   VII,7 *
S.M. Richardson, D. Hesleden   20th February 1994
The left-hand of three icefalls in the centre of the cliff was in excellent condition in 1994, but normally the route has thinner ice and is more mixed. Start left of Tholl Gate and gain a crescent-shaped snowfield via an icy ramp (crux). It would be possible to avoid this by starting up Tholl Gate, thereby dropping a grade. Mixed climbing with good cracks leads to a tongue of ice and then the main icefall. Climb this through the icicle fringe and continue to the top, keeping left of Tholl Gate

Tholl Gate   170m   VI,6 ***
P. Butler, M. Fowler   31st March 1984
This takes the magnificent icy line in the centre of the cliff, 50 metres right of Fuhrer. Sometimes it is the central of 3 icefalls, but it is often the only one formed. A thick icefall on pitch 2 is always present but the difficulty will depend on how far it extends down an overhanging wall to the ledge below. This section is the most susceptible to thaw but it can be mixed climbed. Start slightly right of the line in a shallow bay.
1. 40m   Climb a shallow icy groove (or mixed climbing trending left then right) to a ledge line. Traverse 10 metres left to belay below the ice streak.
2. 35m   Gain the icefall (moving out right is often easiest) and follow it to a good ledge.
3. 50m   The steep and fine icy corners on the right lead to a good ledge.
4. 45m   Move left and continue straight up by corners and a final gully.

The Ayatollah   190m   VII,7 *
I. Dring, M.E. Moran   23rd February 1989
This route takes an uncompromising line right of Tholl Gate, following an obvious steep slab corner in the second tier, then a series of icy grooves directly above. The key to the route is reaching the ice on the slab (pitch 2). Start as for Tholl Gate at a shallow bay beneath the highest part of the cliff.
1. 50m   Climb tricky icy grooves to a snow terrace, then traverse right to a spike belay beneath the slab corner.
2. 30m   Make some radical moves up the smooth corner until usable ice can be gained on the slab to the left. The second ascent climbed an ice smear which can form between the corner and Tholl Gate's icefall. Follow the ice smears to a narrow terrace, traverse right under an icicle, then go up a rocky groove for 4m to belay at a cracked block.
3. 35m   Bridge across left to the icicle, then climb up directly. If no icicle is present, it can be mixed climbed. A short groove, an easier snow bay and a further iced groove lead to belays at a wedged block below a steeper icefall.
4. 45m   Climb the icefall, then go left and back right in easier-angled mixed grooves to a terrace below the final rock wall.
5. 30m   Traverse 5m left, then go up steep snow and a runnel to the cornice.

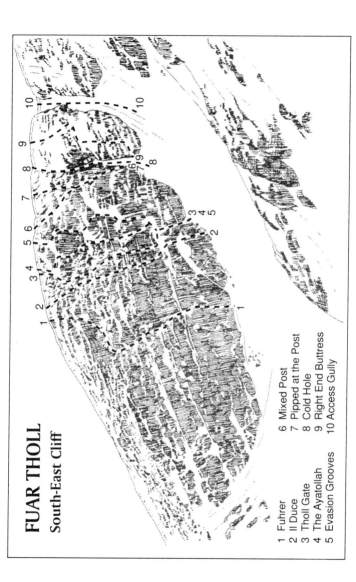

FUAR THOLL
South-East Cliff

1 Fuhrer
2 Il Duce
3 Tholl Gate
4 The Ayatollah
5 Evasion Grooves
6 Mixed Post
7 Pipped at the Post
8 Cold Hole
9 Right End Buttress
10 Access Gully

Evasion Grooves   220m   VI,6
S. Jenkins, M.E. Moran   4th March 1988
This mixed line up the buttress to the right is usually in condition. Start as for Tholl Gate and The Ayatollah.
1. 50m   Climb the icy grooves to the snowy terrace. Go right along this to belay below a prominent steep corner.
2. 45m   Traverse 4 metres right to a very steep groove. Climb this to a hard exit, then continue to giant spike belays.
3. 45m   Go down right to a big easy snow ramp. Follow this for 25m to a left-sloping break in the tier above. Struggle up this to reach another terrace directly beneath a fine ramp.
4. 40m   Climb the ramp to belay in an overhung corner.
5. 40m   Traverse left for 15 metres, then trend left up snowfields and rocky grooves to an occasionally monstrous cornice.

A prominent gully ending in a *cul-de-sac* separates the right side of the cliff from an easier buttress. About 30m lower down the gully from the back of the *cul-de-sac* (Cold Hole) is a continuous ice streak on the left wall. This ice is hidden on the approach, even from the lip of the corrie. The following two routes take diverging lines from there.

Mixed Post   100m   IV,5
D. Jarvis, A. Nisbet   December 1993
Although a mixed route early in the season (V,6), this later becomes a less sustained option to Pipped at the Post and can be iced when the thinly covered wall of Pipped has thawed away. Start at the left side of the ice streak and go leftwards into a short steep groove. Continue in the same line leftwards and climb more easily to the top.

Pipped at the Post   100m   V,5 **
M. Fowler, C. Watts   10th January 1987
A fine short ice route with a big first pitch, a good belay at its top, and easier climbing thereafter. Start in the centre of the ice streak.
1. 40m   Climb the ice direct to a thinly covered wall at 15m (crux) and continue to a big spike belay on the right.

Opposite: On the ridge of Beinn Alligin at the top of the Eag Dubh
Photo: Robin Chalmers

Next page: Il Duce, South-East Cliff of Fuar Tholl
Climber: Dave Hesleden   Photo: Simon Richardson

2. 30m   Continue in the same line to belay below an overhanging wall.
3. 30m   If there is sufficient ice, climb the wall; otherwise traverse delicately right to easier ice or mixed ground leading to the cornice.

Cold Hole   50m   VI,5 **
M. Fowler, C. Watts   10th January 1987
The gully is easy up to the *cul-de-sac* which forms a very steep 45m step. This climb takes the ice sheet forming the left corner of the step. Although short, it is highly recommended and often in condition, even when the other ice routes are too thin. This is a big and tiring pitch, but never vertical, and the crux is at the top. Finish either on steepening snow or traverse left and climb a long pitch on lower angled ice (III).

Tubular Bells   40m   VII,7 *
D. Wills, M. Fowler   16th February 1991
The obvious icicle-ridden corner just right of Cold Hole; its ridiculous appearance has scared off any repeats!
1. 25m   Battle up through overhanging Damoclean icicles to a belay in a cave beneath the final overhangs.
2. 15m   Break out left through the icicle fringe, go round the overhang and gain easy slopes leading to the cornice.

Right End Buttress   180m   III *
W.S. McKerrow, D.M. Nichols   22nd February 1976
The separate buttress at the top right of the cliff, between the Cold Hole *cul-de-sac* and Access Gully, can provide a fine icy climb or an easier option in bad conditions (if safe from avalanches). The belays are good but hard to find. Start at the bottom left corner and gain the centre. Climb a steep pitch, usually mixed, then a slabby pitch, quite thin, to the left side of a big snow terrace. Regain the centre and climb rightwards, often on ice, then move back left to the upper snow field.

Access Gully   130m   II *
The obvious gully to the right of Right End Buttress has a steep exit, often dangerously corniced. A steeper right fork gives an alternative finish of 50m.

Previous page: In the dark recesses of Gully of the Gods, Coire nan Fhamhair, Beinn Bhan   Climber: Robin Clothier
Photo: Bruce Goodlad

Opposite: Coire na Feola, Beinn Bhan   Photo: John Lyall

SGORR RUADH
960m   (Map Ref 959 505)

Sgorr Ruadh, the highest peak of the Coulin Forest, presents an impressive north-east and north face to the walker ascending Coire Lair from Achnashellach. The rock is sandstone throughout and rather broken. In winter several of the gullies and faces provide good middle grade climbs in a fine situation.

Conditions and Weather
The climbs are mostly mixed, so the turf must be frozen. With the cliff base around 700m, the best conditions will be found from January to March on average. Deep snow on the longish but easy approach can be a problem.

Access
The best approach is on the good path from Achnashellach station to upper Coire Lair (2-3 hours). The path starts over a stile on the north side of the railway line just west of the station.

Descent
The best descents are either by the Central Couloir or on a bearing south to the Bealach Mhor.

Layout
Seen from Loch Coire Lair on the Achnashellach approach, the furthest skyline ridge marks Raeburn's Buttress. Coming left from this is a broken south-east face, then the broad Central Couloir then, in front of the Couloir and partially hiding it, the long line of Academy Ridge with an easy section in the middle and a steep upper part. Left of this is another large broken area with a number of rakes which run up from left to right and terminate in gullies. Robertson's Gully defines the left boundary of Academy Ridge and the next buttress left is Robertson's Buttress. The large north face is hidden beyond Raeburn's Buttress.

Robertson's Gully   180m   IV,4
A. Nisbet, N. Spinks   31st January 1976
A long snow approach climbing diagonally right leads to this steep gully on the left of Academy Ridge. There is a deep cave just over halfway

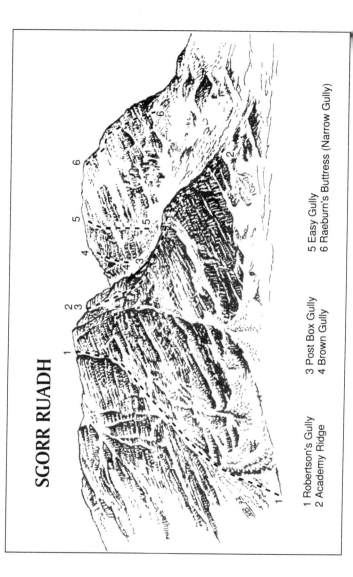

SGORR RUADH

1 Robertson's Gully
2 Academy Ridge

3 Post Box Gully
4 Brown Gully

5 Easy Gully
6 Raeburn's Buttress (Narrow Gully)

up. Climb the gully by a series of chockstone-filled chimneys to the cave (this section can bank out). Traverse right and re-enter the gully by the higher of two traverse lines above the cave.

Academy Ridge   350m   II
A long mountaineering route, mostly easy. Move left at mid-height to regain the crest after a discontinuity. Avoid the steep upper section on the right by traversing into the top of Post Box Gully. Alternatively, a fine direct finish through the upper section is IV,5. Gain the grooves on the right of the top arete and follow them to a spike. From there gain and follow the arete.

Post Box Gully   180m   II *
A. Fyffe   March 1969.
This is a narrow well defined gully on the left wall of Central Couloir, recognisable by a huge chockstone near its foot. Climb up to the chockstone and continue beneath it to emerge from a slot. Continue direct over small pitches to the top of Academy Ridge. Ice is not required so this route is climbable in most conditions.

Croydon Chimney   160m   IV,5
H. MacInnes and party   1969
Just left of High Gully is a left-slanting chimney line. Climb this direct with a hard slot (crux, mixed) at mid-height and a sustained upper groove. Escape left to easy ground below the final capstone. Again, ice is not required.

High Gully   120m   III *
M. Hillman, A. Nisbet   1st February 1976
High on the left wall of Central Couloir, just below and opposite Brown Gully, a large two-tiered icefall can form below a deep narrow gully. Climb the icefalls trending right and enter the gully from the right.

Brown Gully   100m   III
A. Fyffe   March 1969
This is the narrow gully on the right of and starting high up Central Couloir. Climb up right past a bend in the gully and go up an ice pitch. Climb straight up the gully to where it narrows and steepens. Either take a through route or follow a groove on the right and return to the gully as soon as possible. Continue easily to the top.

Easy Gully   180m   II *
J. Cleare, P. Gillman   March 1969
Halfway along the right wall of Central Couloir is an obvious long gully starting just right of an isolated pinnacle. It may have several short ice pitches.

Raeburn's Buttress (Narrow Gully)   300m   III *
H. Raeburn, E.B. Robertson   4th April 1904
G. Cohen, D. Rubens (Narrow Gully)   February 1978
On the approach from Coire Lair, Raeburn's Buttress appears to have a well defined crest, but in fact the buttress gradually curves round to form the north face. Only above a steep lower section does the buttress become a ridge up which all the routes finish. The steep section is bounded on the left by the well defined Narrow Gully, the first obvious feature. Either climb the gully or the vague ridge on its right (the original route) or start up the gully and move onto the ridge. The difficulty on the ridge soon eases into a long mountaineering adventure.

BEINN BHAN
896m   (Map Ref 804 451)

This superb mountain offers some of the finest winter climbing in the Northern Highlands. There are six corries lining its north-east face. The first corrie, Coir' Each, is somewhat open and less impressive than its neighbours. The second and third corries, Coire na Feola and Coire na Poite, each rise from an outer corrie to a high inner corrie with a magnificent back wall. Coire na Poite is enclosed by two narrow ridges with precipitous sides whose outer ends form the great castellated buttresses of A'Chioch on the left and A'Phoit on the right. Beyond A'Phoit the fourth corrie, Coire nan Fhamhair, contains on its south side one of the steepest cliffs on the Scottish mainland. There is a fifth corrie, Coire Toll a' Bhein, which is unnamed on the O.S. map and a smaller sixth, Coire Gorm Beag, near the north end of Beinn Bhan.

Access
1. Coir' Each, Coire na Feola and Coire na Poite are all approached from the road bridge at the head of Loch Kishorn *via* a good track. The ground is heathery and the approach takes longer than expected, especially with fresh snow.

2. For Coire nan Fhamhair, either approach as above or, if the Bealach na Ba road is open (nowadays it is often ploughed) and high level walking conditions are good, follow the stalkers' path across Coire nan Cuileag to the col between Sgurr a' Chaorachain and Beinn Bhan, climb to the Beinn Bhan plateau and descend into the corrie from the north. Note that the start of the path and the shieling at Map Ref 763 437 are hidden from the road. This approach is not recommended in poor visibility or for first time visitors.

Descent
A straightforward descent to the road at Tornapress may be made by following the summit ridge and the south-east flank of the mountain. In white-out conditions, admittedly rare on the windswept plateau, there may be a danger with cornices, particularly where the plateau projects out towards A' Chioch, so keep well away from the edge.

Conditions and Weather
While there are a number of excellent gully climbs, the climbs on the buttresses tend to be open to traversing variations owing to the horizontal bedding of the sandstone. So, typical of sandstone, many of the best climbs here are gullies or icefalls.

The mountain is quite often in good winter condition, basically the colder the better, although the length of the cold spell coupled with the amount of drainage water makes conditions not completely predictable. January and February are the most likely since the low altitude of the cliff base allows damaging thaws later on. Applecross sometimes escapes a heavy snowfall, and it may be worth visiting when inland mountains are swamped with unconsolidated powder. On the other hand, being low and near the sea, there are inevitably times when the climbs have little snow and ice while the higher inland mountains are in good condition. However, the magnificent mountain scenery of these corries, with their open views east to the Coulin Forest, make them well worth a visit.

The corries can be very sheltered during strong westerly winds. However, the presence of a 60m band of 50 degree snow around their rims makes them very prone to windslab avalanches. It is easy to underestimate the deposition of windslab because the cliffs are so big and the puffs of spindrift seem far away. The traverse of A' Chioch is safe from avalanche and can be a bad weather option.

COIRE NA FEOLA

There are some interesting features on the walls of the enclosing arms of this corrie, but the best routes are on or near the back wall. This curves round to the left into the prominent Suspense Gully, which is split into parallel runnels by a narrow ridge with an apparent tower, and may be used as a descent route. To the left of this is Suspense Buttress, which has a very steep icefall in a recess on its left side (**Acid Queen**, V,5).The amount of ice in the corrie is very variable and the same routes have been described from tedious turf to brilliant ice. The routes have not had many ascents compared to the other corries.

Suspense Buttress   150m   III *
Avoid the big lower wall by traversing in above it from Suspense Gully. Continue the traverse to gain the upper section, consisting of short walls broken by terraces.

Suspense Gully (Easy Gully)   150m   I **
A straightforward snow climb between Suspense Buttress and the main back wall. There are two branches; the right one is steeper and more scenic but may be corniced or threatened by avalanche. The left one is a possible descent.

Crab Nebula   275m   IV
D. Dinwoodie, A. Williams   1980
This takes the line of the hanging snowfield at about half-height in the huge buttress right of Suspense Gully. Start by traversing right on a snow terrace from the base of the gully. The crux is at the top (2 PA).

Flesheater   220m   IV,5
I. Dring, M.E. Moran   21st February 1989
A prominent diagonal fault line in the steep cliff to the right of Suspense Gully slants steeply leftwards between Sheet Whitening and the hanging snowfields of Crab Nebula. The fine line is not quite matched by the quality of the climbing.

Sheet Whitening   250m   V,5
M. Fowler, S. Fenwick, M. Lynden   30th December 1981
This is the leftmost of the obvious runnels on the back wall of the corrie. The crux is a hard ice pitch up a steep barrier rock band at 90m. The rest of the climb is straightforward.

Sniper's Gully   280m   IV,4
J. Mothersele, A. Nisbet   17th February 1986
The shallow gully just right of Sheet Whitening.

In X.S.   250m   V,5
C. Downer, D. Scott   1st March 1986
This continuously left-slanting ice smear starts in a small basin about 45 metres left of Y-Gully. It is very good but rarely forms.

Y Gully   250m   V,5 *
There is one big pitch, but the rest is easy. At the right side of the back wall is a very prominent Y-shaped feature. The lowest band may be climbed slightly right of the steepest ice. After crossing some easier ground, climb a long steep ice pitch in the 'stem' of the Y. Higher up, either the left or the right branches of the Y may be taken, both giving pleasant climbing to the top.

Man's Best Friend   220m   IV,5 *
G. Ettle, J. Lyall   5th January 1994.
Climb the big corner line to the right of Y Gully, including a through route. The final wall is easier than it looks.

COIRE NA POITE

Surely one of the most dramatic of Highland corries.

The Traverse of A'Chioch   II ***
J. Brown, T.W. Patey   1968
This is the best mountaineering route on Beinn Bhan, and also a good choice for those who wish to venture out on a wild westerly day. Climb easily up and along A'Chioch, then with more difficulty down to the col. The crux is the ridge from this col beyond A'Chioch to the summit plateau, which has some tricky little walls (150m). For a more sustained climb, start by the following route.

North Gully   120m   II *
A. Fyffe, C. MacInnes, M. Alburger   2nd March 1969
This is the prominent chockstone gully on the left side of the Coire na Poite face of A'Chioch. It finishes halfway up the A'Chioch spur. Start easily, then climb a couple of steeper pitches near the top. It is still good in lean conditions.

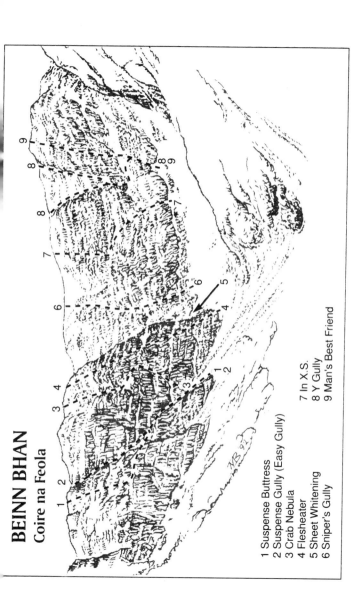

BEINN BHAN
Coire na Feola

1 Suspense Buttress
2 Suspense Gully (Easy Gully)
3 Crab Nebula
4 Flesheater
5 Sheet Whitening
6 Sniper's Gully

7 In X.S.
8 Y Gully
9 Man's Best Friend

March Hare's Gully   300m   IV,4 **
C.J.S. Bonington, T.W. Patey   1st March 1969
This fine route was the first of the major winter climbs to be done on Beinn Bhan. The hard sections are short, and it takes the obvious line on the left side of the upper corrie finishing at the point where the upper connecting ridge of A'Chioch meets the summit plateau. There can be several ice pitches of which the first is often the hardest, particularly if unfrozen. In unusually heavy snow conditions much of this climb may bank out, but the grade will still be IV,3 because rock protection is limited. A bad choice if there is spindrift (potential windslab).

Mad Hatter's Gully   300m   V,5 *
M. Freeman, G. Stephen   1st February 1976
This is the large gully in the back left corner of the corrie. A huge feature, but it can be disappointing because there is only one good pitch, impressively steep ice though it is.

To the right of Mad Hatter's Gully is the huge back wall of Coire na Poite, the base of which often holds the biggest ice sheet in Scotland. The climbs here are long and impressive. In the upper part of the face the obvious snow terraces allow numerous variations, though the routes will always be serious. Several routes have been recorded, but it is not possible to be sure how much they have in common.

Silver Tear   350m   V,5 ***
N. Muir, A. Paul   12th February 1977
In good conditions this gives a superb ice climb. Climb the great icefall somewhat left of the centre of the wall directly for 120m to a terrace. Above this the icefall may continue, or, more likely, it may be necessary to take a more circuitous line up the bands of the upper half of the face. The easiest finish is up a right-slanting natural fault line.

Wall of the Early Morning Light   370m   V,5 **
K. Spence, J. Horsfield, B. Jones, P. Thomas   February 1971.
The snow can turn soft in early morning sun! Somewhat less continuous icefalls usually form in the centre of the back wall, to the right of Silver Tear and starting slightly lower. There are several possible options; choose a line from below. The route usually climbs fairly directly up, then finishes by a natural fault line of chimneys and grooves leading up and slightly right through the upper bands of the face.

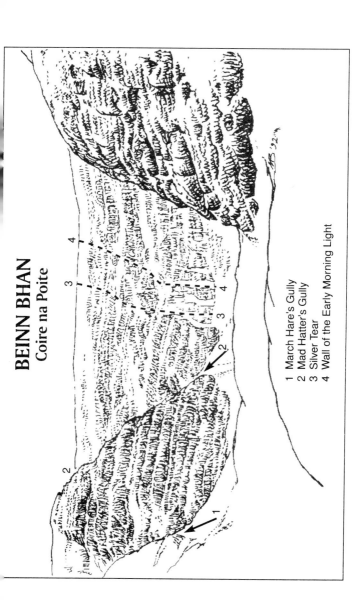

BEINN BHAN
Coire na Poite

1 March Hare's Gully
2 Mad Hatter's Gully
3 Silver Tear
4 Wall of the Early Morning Light

COIRE NAN FHAMHAIR

A huge and very steep face on the left of the corrie provides some of the best routes in Scotland, but they are not for the faint-hearted!

Die Riesenwand   400m   VII,6 ***
A. Nisbet, B. Sprunt   26th-27th January 1980
This outstanding and exciting route takes the line of least resistance up the large face left of Gully of the Gods. A prominent zigzag of snow ledges marks the line in the upper part. It can be climbed with little ice, but recent ascents have found a lot and it has added to enjoyment and speed. Start towards the left of the face below a secondary corner. Climb steep ice for two or three pitches to a niche below a huge roof, 80m (at half-height is a short barrier wall which may be passed on the left if there is insufficient ice). Traverse right from the niche across steep rocky ground to gain a large snow ledge, 30m. Continue traversing right for about 80m until another ledge leads back up left across the wall. Follow this for 60m passing some narrow sections and finishing with a memorable swing round a bulge in a very exposed position. The ground is now easier and a short traverse left leads to a shallow gully which gives a pleasant route to the plateau, 150m.

Gully of the Gods   180m   VI,6 ***
M. Fowler, S. Fenwick   3rd April 1983
The uniquely overhanging central gully splitting the cliff gives a tremendous climb. It is intimidating but surprisingly accommodating, providing unexpected runners and rests.
1. 25m   Largely bridging on ice leads to an excellent ledge on the right.
2. 45m   Back and foot with ice in front and a good crack behind (with less ice, back and foot outwards to reach it). Follow this into a very steep and difficult icy groove above the main overhangs. Pass the final capstone on the right.
3. and 4. 110m   Climb more easily to the top.

Great Overhanging Gully   180m   VI,7 **
M. Fowler, P. Butler   17th March 1984
C. Cartwright, D. Hesleden (FFA)   1994
This is the exceptionally steep chimney line about 45 metres right of Gully of the Gods. It was originally climbed with many short pitches, and the crux was an overhanging section in the middle, climbed on the left with two pegs for aid.

SGURR A' CHAORACHAIN
792m   (Map Ref 797 417)

The very accessible east-facing Summit Buttress is about 200 metres south-east of the radio mast at the summit of the hill. Two very steep gullies split this cliff into three roughly equal sections.

Access
Walk up the Landrover track from the Bealach na Ba road summit to the radio mast at the top of Sgurr a' Chaorachain. From there go east for about 100 metres to the top of the gully in the north-west corner of the east corrie. Descend this gully and traverse below the cliff on the right.

Blade Runner   100m   IV,4
P. Long, B. Owen   2nd February 1986
The right-hand gully forms an icefall which starts with steepish ice (30m), then a right-slanting chimney leads to easy ground.

Excitable Boy   75m   V,5
P. Long, B. Owen   2nd February 1986
The left-hand gully has steep ice which leads to a bay. Finish by a short chimney on the left, then easier ground trending right, or more directly by an ice streak on the right wall.

MEALL GORM
710m   (Map Ref 779 409)

Scotland's most accessible cliff. It may not be as impressive as others in the area, but 15 minutes from the road makes it an attractive option. The Bealach na Ba road is now often ploughed and even when not open over the pass, one can often get as far as the climbs. Meall Gorm is near the sea and the most important factor for good conditions is that the turf be frozen (which happens more quickly on the steeper pitches than on terraces which may be insulated by snow). The climbs described are near the top end of the cliff, making this more likely.

Access
Park opposite and slightly below the climbs in a layby just beyond the South Face of Sgurr a' Chaorachain, then walk across and up to the routes.

Descent
Descend to the first hairpin (often *via* the summit trig point), having walked beyond the top end of the cliffs. From Gorm Gully, the right-slanting gully above the three-tiered buttress gives a quicker descent.

Layout
Close on the left of the lower hairpin, the highest buttress is terraced and split by a gully (**The Six-Track Mono Blues**, Grade II). Next left is an easy gully, bounded on its upper left by Wedge Buttress, then the massive and conspicuous Cobalt Buttress which has a big steep left-hand face. Close to its left is the steep and narrow subsidiary buttress of Blue Pillar, the two being separated by Lobster Gully. Left of Blue Pillar is an easier gully, then a right-slanting Grade I gully.

Cobalt Buttress   170m   IV,4 *
I. Clough, G. Drayton, C. Young   10th February 1970
There are several short hard sections on the front of the buttress, generally well protected. Start about 30m up right from the toe of the buttress, just above the toe of Wedge Buttress (to the right) and below a pitch in the gully bed. Follow a ledge to the left to belay below a short corner.
1. 35m   Climb the corner, step left and go up to a big terrace.
2. 30m   Go up to a higher terrace.
3. 30m   Climb up leftwards, pull right to stand on a block and pull over a bulge to gain the terrace above.
4. 40m   Move up to the next ledge.
5. 35m   The last wall is perhaps the crux.

Rattlesnake   200m   V,6 **
G. Ettle, J. Lyall   13th December 1993
Sustained and varied climbing up the obvious line of corners running up the centre of the buttress, high in the grade. Climb the first unavoidable tier by a groove line just right of a black patch. Climb the first and most impressive corner to half-height, then take the edge on the left. Follow the corner system to the top.

Lobster Gully   180m   IV,5
M. Fowler, A.V. Saunders   15th March 1987
The prominent well protected chimney has a number of steps to start, then two big steep chimney pitches. Some ice forms in the back, along with frozen vegetation; this requires cold conditions.

Blue Pillar   180m   V,6 *
J. Brown, T.W. Patey   February 1958
This is the conspicuous narrow pillar on the left of the massive Cobalt Buttress. Follow the crest, trying hard to find the easiest line, and finish by a deep chimney on the right of the final tower.

Gorm Gully   150m   II *
A. Fyffe and party   1970
This good wee route holds snow better than the other routes on the face. Climb the deep narrow gully left of a three-tiered buttress (**Blaeberry Corner**, old IV, probably new V,5) on increasingly steep snow to a final ice pitch which can be either 30m with fine ice formations or just steep snow.

THE SADDLE
1010m   (Map Ref 935 131)

The shapely mass of The Saddle is west of the main South Glen Shiel Ridge directly across the A87 road from the Five Sisters of Kintail. The best ascent of the mountain is undoubtedly by the east ridge of Sgurr nan Forcan; the Forcan Ridge. The commonest approach is *via* an obvious stalker's path leaving the road at Map Ref 968 143. In reasonable snow conditions, and certainly in descent, it is quicker to take a direct line south of Meallan Odhar to the ridge, avoiding the path's deviation to the north.

Forcan Ridge   I or II ***
A classic Alpine-style ridge. Climb close to the crest (Grade II) or take minor variations just below it if wished (Grade I). The crux is a short steep descent from Sgurr nan Forcan, either abseiled down the crest or climbed down on either side. One should expect to use a rope. The route is usually climbed with one axe, as there are excellent handholds on the steep sections.

From the summit of The Saddle, descend to the south-east (beware of avalanches), cross the Bealach Coire Mhalagain and traverse east under the Forcan Ridge following a drystone dyke north-east back to the start of the ridge, and so down the approach path.

The Cairngorms

Being a high plateau area and far away from the prevailing Atlantic westerlies, the Cairngorms offer a different style of climbing to all the other areas. The reward is to climb in a remote mountain setting, the colder climate provides reliable conditions and the turfy granite offers a unique style of climbing. The challenge is sometimes to cope with wind and spindrift, producing the navigational difficulties of white-out on the plateau. There are reliable ice climbing venues, like Hell's Lum Crag, but it is for mixed turf and rock climbing that the Cairngorms have become famous. Many of the easier routes follow gullies whereas the harder ones often climb the turfier rock climbs under rime (hoar frost) and verglas. The challenge is the technical move with axes on rock, in cracks or embedded securely (you hope) in the turf of the next ledge. Despite their colourful history, their popularity does not match Ben Nevis and Glen Coe, with the exception of the accessible Coire an t-Sneachda and Hell's Lum on a good day.

The most remote cliffs have not been included, because a day visit is only possible for the very fittest, and as a result they are rarely visited. The exceptions are the icy Creagan a' Choire Etchachan with its grand central setting, and a small selection of climbs in Garbh Choire of Beinn a' Bhuird, because their quality defied omission. The selection fits into three groups: those approached from Aviemore in the north; from Ballater or Braemar (the Dee valley); and from the Dundee direction in the south. The northern Cairngorms are very popular, probably because of the excellent road links to Aviemore and the convenience of the ski road to the Cairn Gorm carpark at 620m. They even offer a retreat from mild conditions in the Northern Highlands, perhaps in the direction of home. The southern Cairngorms — Lochnagar, Creag an Dubh-loch and Eagles Rock — are less convenient, except from Aberdeen, and will probably be approached *via* the A93 over Glen Shee to Braemar and Ballater, then to the Glen Muick carpark. The high cliff of Lochnagar has the most continental climate and provides the most reliable conditions, except that powder may lie deep for weeks and ice forms only reluctantly. The third area, Glen Clova, is the most southerly and in Dundee climbers' backyard. The glen is not extensive, but it offers many lower grade routes in a charming setting and is popular.

Sgoran Dubh Mor and, in the far distance, Creag Meagaidh seen beyond the cliffs of Cairn Lochan   Photo: Rab Anderson

A word of warning. While the Cairngorms are a good option when the weather is too warm further west, the same does not apply to escape wind. The high plateau has even stronger winds, and coupled with the colder temperatures, produces excruciating spindrift leading often to huge windslab avalanches in sheltered locations (Lochnagar being a common example). If the snow is deep and soft in the west, conditions may be better in the Cairngorms because there was less snowfall, or they may be worse because the last thaw was longer ago.

Maps
The maps required for the Cairngorm area are: Lochnagar, Creag an Dubh-loch, Eagles Rock, Glen Clova – Sheet 44; Braemar and the Dee approach, Sheet 43; the Aviemore approach and the northern cliffs, Sheet 36. The 1:25,000 Outdoor Leisure Map *Aviemore and the Cairngorms* is also useful.

THE NORTHERN CORRIES OF CAIRN GORM

COIRE AN T-SNEACHDA   (Map Ref 994 033)

Coire an t-Sneachda is the central of the three north-facing corries of Cairn Gorm. It is separated from Coire Cas, the main ski area, by the Fiacaill a' Choire Chais and from Coire an Lochain on its west by the Fiacaill Coire an t-Sneachda (unnamed on the 1:50,000 map). The latter is a hump-backed ridge which steepens after a shallow col to form a narrow rocky ridge called the Fiacaill Ridge leading to the plateau near Cairn Lochan, the westerly top of Cairn Gorm.

The corrie itself is deceptive in size as it has a recess which extends westwards. This cannot be seen from the Glenmore area and it contains a large mass of rock buttressing the Fiacaill Ridge. Due to the wealth of good easy and middle grade routes, combined with the ease of access, this is a very popular corrie.

Weather and Conditions
The corrie is high (cliff base at 970m) and north-facing and therefore it has a very long season. It is a good choice in poor weather and conditions (within reason) as a route safe from avalanche should be

The Fiacaill Ridge   Photo: David Ritchie

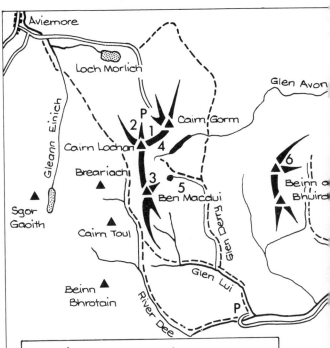

1 Coire an t-Sneachda
2 Coire an Lochain
3 Carn Etchachan & Shelter Stone Crag
4 Hell's Lum Crag & Stag Rocks
5 Creagan a'Choire Etchachan
6 Beinn a' Bhuird, Garbh Choire
7 Lochnagar
8 Creag an Dubh-loch & Eagles Rock
9 Driesh, Winter Corrie
10 Mayar, Corrie Fee

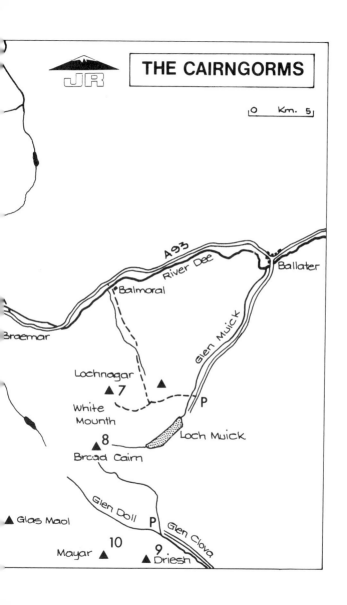

THE CAIRNGORMS

JR

0 Km. 5

A93
River Dee
Ballater

Balmoral

Braemar

Glen Muick

Lochnagar
▲ 7   ▲

White
Mounth   P

8
▲
Broad Cairn   Loch Muick

Glen Doll   P
▲ Glas Maol   Glen Clova

10
Mayar ▲   9
              ▲ Driesh

available, the Fiacaill Ridge being the ultimate resort (although not approached direct from the corrie). However, the corrie is a very windy place, never sheltered. South-westerly winds, from which one might expect to find shelter, funnel down the Goat Track to a vortex in the corrie. In general, hard snow and ice are more likely in the second half of the season.

Layout
There are four main rock masses in the corrie. High on the left is a rectangular buttress, The Mess of Pottage, which is bounded on its right by Jacob's Ladder, an obvious straight gully. Aladdin's Buttress lies in the centre of the corrie and has the lowest cliff base; its lower section is characterised by some obvious corner lines. Above and to the right the rock is more broken but shows three prominent ribs jutting up to the skyline. This buttress is bounded on the left by the large dog-leg of Aladdin's Couloir. It is separated from The Mess of Pottage by a wide area of broken ground. Right of Aladdin's Buttress is the more complex Fluted Buttress. This is cut by many gullies, particularly on its left where Central Gully, the leftmost of the Trident Gullies, forms the boundary between these two buttresses. On the right, Fluted Buttress fades out near the lowest point of the skyline where the Goat Track, usually a snow slope around 40 degrees, leads onto the plateau at the head of Coire Domhain. The fourth buttress, the Fiacaill Buttress, lies at the head of the westerly recess below the Fiacaill Ridge.

Access
Follow the ski road to the Coire Cas carpark and go to the White Lady Shieling. Then go diagonally up the corrie on good tracks to cross the Fiacaill a' Choire Chais above the Fiacaill ski tow in the vicinity of the snow fences crossing the ridge. An easy descending traverse then leads into the corrie floor.

Descent
The normal descent is to follow the corrie rim round northwards to the big cairn at point 1141m and descend Fiacaill a' Choire Chais. This is usually easiest on the right, down a strip of snow overlooking Coire Cas (beware of cornices).

To return to the floor of Coire an t-Sneachda, descend the Goat Track. This is the snow slope down from the col between the top of the corrie rim and Cairn Lochan, i.e. the back right of the corrie as seen from the approach. From Fiacaill Buttress it may be quicker to descend the Fiacaill Ridge and drop down into the corrie.

THE MESS OF POTTAGE

This small, fairly slabby buttress lies high on the left of the corrie. Its left side consists of a dome-shaped mass of rock which has some defined corner and crack lines running up it. The right side is more broken and cut by a couple of diagonal faults and some large areas of easier ground. The right edge of the buttress is defined by the straight regular gully of Jacob's Ladder. The cliff base has an obvious bay right of centre from which a diagonal fault system leads up and left to peter out below roofs near the top of the dome. The Message starts here and No Blue Skies is a parallel slabby fault further left. The climbing has a none too serious atmosphere and comes into condition very quickly, only needing a decent covering of snow. On many of the routes it is possible to interchange pitches and to escape fairly easily. It is best early in the season before the build-up is too extensive and first pitches shortened. The slopes round the base of the crag are prone to avalanche. The slopes left of the crag are easy (35 degrees) and can be used for approach or descent.

Honeypot   90m   IV,6 *
J. Lyall, M. Sclater   25th March 1989
This route climbs near the left side, finishing by the obvious square-cut chimney near the left boundary of the upper slabs. Start at a triangular recess at the bottom left corner of the face. Go diagonally right up the obvious slanting line, hard to start but it soon banks up, then go straight up a gully. Climb the wide but shallow chimney, passing the capping roof on the right wall (crux). It is easier when icy, but this only occurs in prime conditions.

No Blue Skies   110m   VI,7 *
A. Fyffe, L. Healey   20th December 1990
An interesting route with a deceptive first pitch. Start left of the bay where an obvious diagonal line leads left to a shallow horizontal cave. The first pitch is very thin, but ice will ease it considerably. Climb the diagonal corner to near the apex, traverse left, then go up the left side of the apex to exit onto a ledge by a horizontal cave. Continue up the

crack and corner (or a left-facing one further right) to easier ground and belay by a squat pillar. Climb broken ground, then gain a fine flake crack below and left of the big roof and follow it to its end. Traverse left to a crack which goes through a short bulging wall and finish up this.

The Message   90m   IV,6 **
A. Cunningham, W. Todd   23rd January 1986
A natural system of grooves gives three fairly consistent and well protected pitches. It starts up the diagonal fault, but then takes the deepest groove running straight up the cliff on the right. Start at the top of the main bay right of the lowest rocks. Climb a blocky chimney and two short corners trending left to the foot of the main deep groove. Climb this, break out left, then go up the fault to the foot of a square right-facing corner. Climb the corner to a bulge at the top, swing left onto the edge and climb cracked slabs to finish.

Pot of Gold   90m   V,6
J. Lyall, S. Spalding   26th November 1988
The crack line in the buttress just right of The Message is very well protected and therefore low in the grade. Start as for The Message and climb the blocky chimney. A move right leads to the crack-groove line. Follow this and a short squeeze chimney, then go over blocks until near The Message. Climb up right to a large ledge, then climb the centre of the wall above by cracks and shallow corners. Follow a chimney to finish.

Jacob's Ladder   110m   I *
A. Henderson, F. Mitchell   Easter 1939
The gully bounding the right side of the buttress is the hardest at its grade in the corrie. The finish is the crux; in lean conditions a small cave blocks the way, and a large build-up can produce a big cornice. The answer to either problem is usually to finish on the right, sometimes Grade II.

ALADDIN'S BUTTRESS
This is the obvious buttress in the centre of the corrie right of Aladdin's Couloir. Its lower section is a steep dome-shaped mass of rock at the top left of which is a 10m pinnacle, Aladdin's Seat. Above and right of the lower buttress and separated from it by a diagonal break of easier ground are several triangular rock buttresses. The right-hand and best

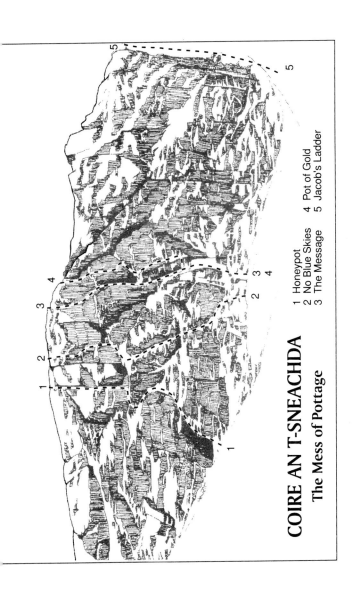

COIRE AN T-SNEACHDA
The Mess of Pottage

1 Honeypot
2 No Blue Skies
3 The Message
4 Pot of Gold
5 Jacob's Ladder

defined is Pygmy Ridge; the ground below this is easy-angled and much of it banks out in winter. The lower rocks of Aladdin's Buttress give some of the most interesting climbing in the corrie. The two main features to aid route location are the big left-facing corner of Doctor's Choice in the centre of the buttress and the wide chimney of Patey's Route near the right side. Routes on this part of the cliff finish on easy ground just below the level of Aladdin's Seat where the plateau can be gained *via* the top of Aladdin's Couloir or Aladdin's Mirror, or these routes can be used to return to the corrie floor.

Aladdin's Couloir   180m   I **
A. Henderson, E.M. Davidson   24th March 1935

The obvious large dog-leg gully bounding the left of the main buttress. In lean conditions an easy ice pitch may form at the narrows before the bend. This is the steepest section even when banked out; this happens readily and the gully becomes the easiest Grade I in the corrie. Above, the gully widens and leads to a col above the pinnacle of Aladdin's Seat. A long pitch then leads to the top, any cornice normally petering out on the right. It is frequently skied when in prime condition.

Original Route   100m   IV,6 *
W. March, B. Manson   13th February 1972

This line on the left of the buttress overlooking the couloir is a good choice under powder and is sometimes a little sheltered from the wind. One abseil to the left gains Aladdin's Couloir from the route and sometimes there is an *in situ* sling at the top. Start about 5m up and right from the foot of the narrow rib on the left of the buttress.

Climb a shallow corner to gain a flake and continue to the obvious break. Alternatively take the line just on the left of the toe (harder). Go diagonally up the easy ramp above and continue the same line in an exposed position until a route leads up to the crest of the buttress.

The Lamp   100m   IV,5
A. Liddell and party   January 1988

An interesting line up the linked diagonal breaks just right of Original Route. Start at the top of the bay right of the narrow rib. Climb an open groove, then follow an inclined ledge right to its end in the central bay. Go diagonally right to below an obvious break leading back left (or continue right to the final corner of Doctor's Choice, which may be temptingly icy). Follow this break, then climb the buttress crest.

COIRE AN T-SNEACHDA

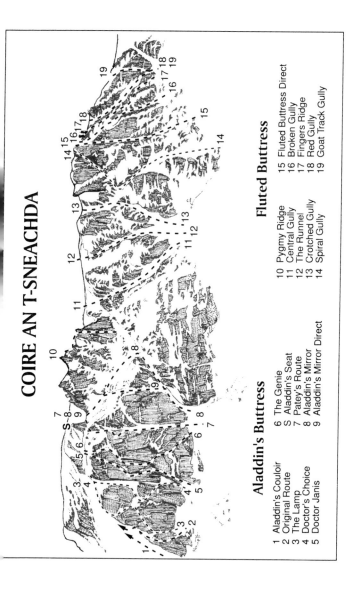

Aladdin's Buttress

1 Aladdin's Couloir
2 Original Route
3 The Lamp
4 Doctor's Choice
5 Doctor Janis
6 The Genie
S Aladdin's Seat
7 Patey's Route
8 Aladdin's Mirror
9 Aladdin's Mirror Direct

Fluted Buttress

10 Pygmy Ridge
11 Central Gully
12 The Runnel
13 Crotched Gully
14 Spiral Gully
15 Fluted Buttress Direct
16 Broken Gully
17 Fingers Ridge
18 Red Gully
19 Goat Track Gully

Doctor's Choice   105m   IV,4 *
W. March, N. Dilley   12th February 1972
An interesting climb taking the prominent large left-facing corner in the centre of the buttress. It is only recommended when the top corner is iced; this is visible from below. Start below the corner and climb to a cave below an overhang. From the foot of the cave go diagonally left to a snow bay, exit from this on the right and return on easy ground to below the main corner. Climb this to the top. A more direct start can be taken when it is very icy (5).

Doctor Janis   130m   V,7 *
J. Grosset, J. Lyall, A. Nolan   4th April 1987
The slightly hidden slanting corner right of the main corner of Doctor's Choice requires a good build-up for pitch 2. The top corner fills readily with ice, but it would be desperate under powder. Start on the right side of the bay below Doctor's Choice.
1. 45m   Climb the right-slanting groove until it is blocked by an overhang.
2. 15m   Cross the overhang direct and move delicately left to a snow bay.
3. 25m   Step up right to a ledge and climb the wall leftwards by an awkward ramp-groove (crux).
4. 45m   Climb the upper corner.

The Genie   110m   V,6 **
D. Sanderson, J-C. Tomasi   14th March 1982
A fine climb taking the central of the three main corners. It is graded for powder but if icy it may be a little easier. Start at the foot of Patey's Route and gain a ramp line and the following open corners which curve up to the foot of the main corner. Climb this to the top.

White Magic   120m   VII,7
A. Cunningham, A. Nisbet   7th December 1985
The highlight is the unique torquing crack right of the main corner of The Genie; it is strenuous to climb and even more strenuous to place the excellent protection. Follow The Genie to its stance below the main corner. Make a thin move right to gain the right-slanting crack, then follow it to an overlap. Traverse right (inventive torquing but overhead protection) to a ledge at the top of a corner (**Damnation**). Finish above *via* a narrow chimney.

Patey's Route   120m   IV,5 **
T.W. Patey   February 1959
This follows the obvious wide chimney line on the left side of the buttress. The more ice, the easier the climb; it is graded for average conditions. There are two main pitches, both of which have a difficult bulge where they narrow. The top one is usually climbed by going up left at the top, then making a long move back right above the bulge. It can also be climbed by continuing leftwards.

Aladdin's Mirror   180m   I
E.U.M.C. Party   Easter 1946
An exposed snow route taking the easy ground right of the lower part of the buttress. Climb the diagonal snow shelf on the right-hand side to reach open slopes. Trend back left under the upper rocks to reach Aladdin's Seat and finish up Aladdin's Couloir.

Aladdin's Mirror Direct   25m   IV,4
A popular ice problem, sometimes underestimated, which varies in length and steepness according to build-up. Climb the steep ice pitch on the right of the buttress up from the start of Aladdin's Mirror. An easy chimney leads to the main route.

Pygmy Ridge   90m   IV,5 *
The right-hand ridge in the upper tier above Aladdin's Mirror gives an excellent little climb starting from the lowest rocks and following the well defined rib, at one point crossing a horizontal arete. The start, to the right of the toe of the ridge, is the crux. It is a good combination with Aladdin's Mirror Direct, offering contrasting styles. Traditionally Grade III, but it has been graded for those not used to snowed up rock.

FLUTED BUTTRESS

This is the cliff between Aladdin's Buttress and the lowest point of the corrie rim. A recessed section on the left is split by the Trident Gullies which spring from the same prominent snow bay which extends high up into the cliffs. Central Gully, which slants left and is the left-hand of the three, forms the boundary between Aladdin's and Fluted Buttresses. The Runnel is the prominent direct line while the rightmost of the Trident Gullies is Crotched Gully; this uses the wide fault in the upper cliffs. Right of this the rocks are less broken and are cut high up by the right-slanting upper section of Spiral Gully . This lies above a fairly unbroken section of cliff which from below appears as a tapering wedge of rock bounded by Broken Gully on the right. After Broken Gully is Fingers Ridge, with its distinctive pinnacles high up near the plateau. Right again are Red Gully and Goat Track Gully, before the buttress fades out into the easier ground of the Goat Track.

The area of the Trident Gullies is quite low-angled and the ribs between the gullies give routes only slightly harder than the gullies themselves. Further right at the highest part of the cliff the buttress has a slabby lower section which can bank out. If this is not the case, Spiral Gully and routes in the area of Fluted Buttress Direct may have an extra easy pitch to start.

Central Gully   135m   I
T.E. Goodeve, A.W. Russell   1st April 1904
The leftmost of the Trident Gullies separates Aladdin's and Fluted Buttresses. It is straightforward with no pitches and an easily out-flanked cornice. It can contain much ice in very lean conditions.

The Runnel   135m   II **
E.U.M.C. Party   Easter 1946
The central and best defined of the three gullies rises from the top of the snow bay. It is arguably better (but no harder) in lean conditions. Straightforward climbing leads to a fine icy chimney (well protected) near the top.

Crotched Gully   135m   II
E.U.M.C. Party   Easter 1946
The right-hand of the Trident gullies leads out from the snow bay, steepens and finishes by an easier gully on the right. It reduces to Grade I in peak conditions, when there is often a big cornice.

Spiral Gully   160m   II *
T.W. Patey   February 1959
The longest of the gullies is quite easy under heavy snow, but rock belays are not obvious and the line is not simple. Start right of the Trident Gully bay and climb steep broken ground which readily banks out. Aim for twin gullies which usually offer an easy ice pitch. Above these, climb snow and bend right into a well defined right-slanting fault which leads to a small col just below the plateau. It is rarely corniced. A direct finish from the base of the diagonal fault is Grade III.

Fluted Buttress Direct   135m   IV,4 **
A. Fyffe, S. Crymble   18th March 1978
A good climb which follows the narrow but defined chimney-groove system on the left of the most continuous section of slabby rocks. It is best when iced, but still good and a grade harder when lean. Climb the main groove to where it forks and increases in size. The left fork (**Wavelength**) is easier and suitable for icy conditions. The right fork is technically more interesting and leads to the crest of the buttress, thence to the col between Spiral and Broken Gullies and the top.

Broken Gully   130m   III
T.W. Patey, J. McArtney, J. Cleare   February 1967
The fault between the highest part of the buttress and Fingers Ridge has a good start but is disappointingly discontinuous thereafter. The upper section of the gully is large and funnel-shaped. Start in the first bay right of the lowest rocks. Climb the gully up and right until a left traverse (crux) can be made onto the top of a slabby pillar and thus into the main gully (this is not very obvious but is at the top of a fairly long pitch). Follow the upper gully to finish up the right or the left of the upper funnel.
Variation:
The Left-Hand Start takes a smaller gully left of the ordinary start and leads directly into the upper fault. This can be harder but it may also contain ice in quantity.

Fingers Ridge   140m   IV,4 ***
J.R. Dempster, J.I. Wallace   19th January 1969
The slabby rib which culminates in two obvious pinnacles which are visible on the skyline from the corrie floor gives a fine climb with sustained mixed climbing, but never too hard. Start at the foot of Red Gully.
    Go up and left over slabs and ledges to a bay near the left edge of the buttress (close to Broken Gully). Climb a broad rib overlooking Broken Gully, then a short wall on the right *via* a flake to gain a large right-facing open groove left of some slabs. Climb this groove to a narrow ridge (there is an easy escape left from here into Broken Gully) and follow this past the 'fingers' to a col. A short wall leads to the top.

    Broken Fingers (IV,4) is a good combination, more sustained than Broken Gully and offering both ice and mixed climbing. Start up Broken Gully when icy but continue up, past the traverse, to join and follow Fingers Ridge.

Red Gully   120m   II *
The fault right of Fingers Ridge gives a fine climb, graded for good conditions when it has a lot of ice in the chimney and excellent rock runners. Unfortunately its popularity thins the ice and it is easy after the first pitch which leads into the easier funnel-shaped upper gully.

Goat Track Gully   120m   II
Starting at the same point as Red Gully, the gully on the extreme right of the buttress has short but sharp difficulties. It cuts up deeply rightwards to a short pitch which is usually taken on the right, sometimes on ice, or by struggling past a small chokestone. Above, the line is more open and less defined and it is possible to traverse right.

FIACAILL BUTTRESS
This is the fine mass of rock high up in the western sector of the corrie buttressing the Fiacaill Coire an t-Sneachda. It is split in two by the large diagonal gully of Fiacaill Couloir, but this is hidden from most angles. Left of the gully the face is wedge-shaped and the upper section above a ledge which cuts the face from the left is scored by several right-slanting ramps. The face above and right of the gully has more large scale vertical features. The winter climbing here can sometimes be better than elsewhere in the corrie because it is sheltered from west winds.

The Stirling Bomber   55m   V,7 *
A. Cunningham, A. Fyffe   4th January 1990
This great little climb takes the obvious right-facing chimney right of centre on the lower part of the buttress. Gain the chimney by flakes and cracks leading leftwards into it, and climb it by an inch-by-inch struggle to a diagonal fault. The chimney is rather too wide for comfort, more back and neck than back and foot, but it is well protected. Finish up the fault to the halfway ledge which leads easily off left, back to the corrie.

Fiacaill Couloir   150m   II/III **
T.W. Patey   17th January 1958
The diagonal gully which cuts deeply through the buttress gives a sustained climb with limited protection and sometimes continuous snow-ice. Start in the snow bay in the centre of the buttress and follow the gully up and left. Near the top a chokestone may be difficult if there is a poor build-up. Above the col go left to a smaller col, then continue up to finish.

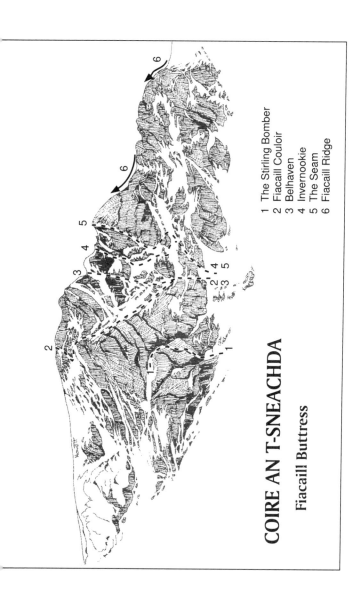

COIRE AN T-SNEACHDA

Fiacaill Buttress

1 The Stirling Bomber
2 Fiacaill Couloir
3 Belhaven
4 Invernookie
5 The Seam
6 Fiacaill Ridge

The next route climbs the wall overlooking Fiacaill Couloir and starts some way up that fault.

Belhaven   75m   V,6 *
A. Fyffe, K. Geddes   *19th February 1979*
A good climb up the prominent corner immediately above the start of Fiacaill Couloir. It sometimes ices up and it will be easier but less well protected. Climb Fiacaill Couloir for a pitch to below the corner. Either climb directly into the corner (good build-up or good torquing technique required), or continue up the gully to use the big ledges going right. Climb the main corner in one long pitch; protection is strenuous to place at the start and the climbing is sustained throughout.

Invernookie   120m   III,4 *
K. Spence, J. Porteous   *4th January 1969*
An interesting climb which takes a line of ramps on the wall above and right of Fiacaill Couloir. It is very popular since the quality and grade vary little with conditions, but the grade may in due course increase as the amount of turf is reduced by traffic. Start just right of Fiacaill Couloir. Slant right, then go back left to a short wall which leads to the ramps. Follow these to below an overhanging wall. The right-hand corner leads into a chimney-cave from which a right traverse leads to a groove and the ridge.

The Seam   100m   IV,5 *
J. Grosset, J. Lyall   *2nd January 1986*
A good route, low in the grade, which follows the obvious chimney immediately left of the steep triangular wall on the buttress edge. Start as for Invernookie, but continue the initial right slant until underneath the triangular wall. Pull up left round the edge of this wall and continue up to the base of the chimney. Climb the chimney-fault directly to the top; tricky and sustained but well protected. An easier start is to follow Invernookie further and gain the base of the chimney from the ramps.

Fiacaill Ridge   130m   II
This is a good option under powder, when other routes are deeply covered and possibly avalanche-prone. Stick to the crest as closely as is sensible. It offers some short technical sections but an escape right to much easier ground is slightly too convenient.

Opposite: Traversing round the pinnacles of Fingers Ridge, Coire an t-Sneachda   Climber: Tracy Bryden   Photo: Jonathan Preston

Next Page: Reaching the top of The Migrant near the crest of Ewen Buttress, Cairn Lochan   Climber: Rob Milne   Photo: Rab Anderson

COIRE AN LOCHAIN   (Map Ref 984 026)

The corrie lying below Cairn Lochan, the most westerly top of Cairn Gorm, is compact and well defined. Its crags are short but steep, the home of technical mixed climbing. Some easier mixed routes and a limited selection of easier gullies are also available, but they have a more serious feel than the neighbouring Coire an t-Sneachda, largely because of the steeper approach (effectively Grade I) and consequent exposure caused by The Great Slab.

Layout

There are four main buttresses separated by obvious gullies. These form an arc overlooking the corrie's most outstanding feature, The Great Slab. This is a huge, easy-angled slab of pink granite which is also a notoriously avalanche-prone slope, both for windslab and for the huge full-depth avalanche which often occurs in spring. It is usually advisable to approach winter routes up the flanks of The Great Slab, but beware of windslab. The four buttresses are numbered from left to right. The Vent separates No.1 and No.2 Buttresses while the obvious diagonal fault of The Couloir in the centre of the corrie lies between No.2 and No.3. Between No.3 and No.4 is a large recess tucked in the corner of the corrie, which houses the two branches of Y-Gully.

Weather and Conditions

The corrie is very high, with a base at 1100m, and it is amongst the first places in Scotland to come into good winter condition, with a potential season from October to May. This is also because the majority of routes are mixed. Ice does not usually form until later in the season. Rime (often incorrectly called hoar frost) builds up to great depth and the steeper routes are best avoided in these conditions, although it is difficult to know the thickness from a distance. There is slightly better shelter from the wind than in Coire an t-Sneachda, but this is counter-balanced by the longer approach and greater avalanche risk. This shelter allows windslab to accumulate, particularly in The Vent, along the top of the Great Slab and around No.4 Buttress. Great care should be taken to assess avalanche risk when approaching routes.

Previous page: In the icy recesses of Deep Cut Chimney, Hell's Lum Crag
Climber: Mick Hardwick   *Photo: Allen Fyffe*

Opposite: Climbers at the foot of Hell's Lum Crag starting the first pitch of
Auld Nick   *Photo: Andy Nisbet*

Access
1. From the head of the carpark in Coire Cas, contour round the base of the Fiacaill a' Choire Chais and follow the well marked path to the Allt Coire an t-Sneachda. Cross the burn and follow any one of a number of paths which lead roughly south into the corrie. Despite the short distance, the target is quite small and navigation is not easy in mist and snow; it is quite easy to land up in Lurcher's Gully.
2. From the top station of the chairlift, traverse Cairn Gorm on its north side, go over the top of Coire an t-Sneachda and continue to Cairn Lochan. It is probably best to descend The Couloir (if you can see where it is), but various abseil descents have been made by those with local knowledge and confidence. This approach is not recommneded in poor visibility.

Descent
The easiest descent is to the west, but care is necessary as the slope is steep and there are small cliffs and ice slopes. At first, keep away from the cornices, but note that lower down the convex slope can divert you too far left (west). In white-out, a dogleg away from the cornice is best. The east side of the corrie is steeper (close to Grade I). The top of the Goat Track and a descent into Coire an t-Sneachda is also nearby.

No.1 BUTTRESS
The buttress on the left side of the corrie has a steep right wall rising out of The Vent and a front face which merges into more broken ground on the left. The front and side walls are cut by some large corners which offer hard and distinctive routes. **Auricle** (V,7) climbs the prominent overhanging groove at 40m on the front face while **Ventricle** (VII,9) and **Big Daddy** (VIII,8) take the corners in the vertical wall left of The Vent.

The Vent   110m   II/IV *
E.M. Davidson, R.F. Stobart, Miss Macbain, J. Geddes
13th April 1935
A pleasant but short-lived route up the obvious gully between No.1 and No.2 Buttresses. It is narrow and defined at the bottom, but it opens out into an easy-angled funnel above. The difficulties depend on the build-up and the amount of ice on the lower chokestone section. It is a bad choice in early season when the chokestone will be Grade IV. It requires a large build-up to be Grade II.

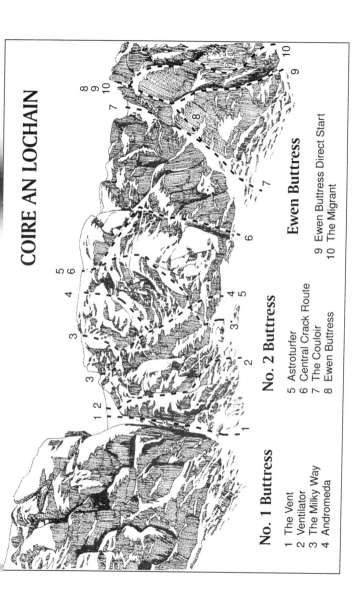

COIRE AN LOCHAIN

No. 1 Buttress

1 The Vent
2 Ventilator
3 The Milky Way
4 Andromeda

No. 2 Buttress

5 Astroturfer
6 Central Crack Route
7 The Couloir
8 Ewen Buttress

Ewen Buttress

9 Ewen Buttress Direct Start
10 The Migrant

No.2 BUTTRESS

This is the widest buttress in the corrie, extending between The Vent and The Couloir. Its left-hand side consists of several vertical ribs which do not continue all the way to the plateau. The central and right-hand sections are characterised by steep walls and horizontal breaks and there is a conspicuous square-cut wall at the top. There are several worthwhile middle grade mixed routes here.

Ventilator   100m   II
D.S.B. Wright and party   1969
Start in the big snow bay about 30 metres right of The Vent. From the foot of the bay, climb a ramp slanting out left to a corner on the right of The Vent's rib. Climb the corner, then the rib, to finish up The Vent.

The Milky Way   100m   III
T.W. Patey, V.N. Stevenson, I.W. Armitage   February 1959
This is a pleasant route, low in its grade, which takes the obvious diagonal line on the left of the more massive section of the buttress. In early season, start in the big snow bay about 30 metres right of The Vent. Go up the bay towards a steep groove but soon pull out right onto the spur. Climb the spur (or the fault on its right – Andromeda), then trend left to the top of the rib right of Vent. Finish up a shallow groove leading rightwards (possible big cornice), or finish up The Vent.

In late season, the wall blocking the base of the Andromeda fault is banked out and there is a small bay 10 metres right of the big bay and just left of the main buttress. Climb the big open shallow gully and take the easiest line out left to the spur. Continue up the spur and trend left as above. In good conditions this is easier, perhaps Grade II.

Chute Route (V,4) climbs the icy groove at the head of the snow bay to join The Milky Way after a pitch. It is usually in condition only late in the season.

Andromeda   120m   IV,4 *
R.D. Barton, J.C. Higham   30th December 1971
This route takes a big open fault left of the central part of the buttress, about 10 metres right of the early season version of The Milky Way, then it follows a big groove line which slants up right. Start up the open fault, then trend right and follow the deep groove which abuts a steep wall. This is excellent when icy and leads to the buttress crest; finish as for Central Crack Route on the left of the conspicuous upper wall. The cornice may be large.

Astroturfer   120m   III *
J. MacKeever, I. Dawson   31st December 1985
A good middle of the grade mixed line. Start as for Andromeda, but take the lowest chimney line leading right onto a ledge on the crest. Climb the subsequent wall on its right, then climb the front of the buttress to finish as for Central Crack Route.

Central Crack Route   120m   IV,5 *
T.W. Patey   2nd February 1958
A fine climb taking the fault right of the centre of the buttress. Start just right of the lowest rocks. The start is very technical but a lot easier with a big build-up; thereafter it is Grade III. Climb the slanting right-facing corner crack and continuation fault for about 75m, then zigzag up to below the great square wall and exit on its left. The cornice can be huge and necessitate a long traverse.

The Couloir   150m   I *
E.M. Davidson, A. Henderson   24th March 1935
The slanting gully in the centre of the cliff, above the top of the Great Slab, is serious for the grade because the approach is as hard as the route itself. In early season it is a good Grade II climb. Approach from the right (under No.3 Buttress) by icy steps and usually an easy pitch in the gully itself. The gully leads to a small col (Y-Gully Left Branch is on the other side) and this always allows a way through any cornice.

EWEN BUTTRESS (No.3 BUTTRESS)

This well defined buttress lies between the diagonal of The Couloir and the Left Branch of Y-Gully. Its left flank forms an easier-angled rib, Ewen Buttress, overlooking The Couloir. To its right is a huge overhanging groove-recess, right of which is a steep and more massive frontal face. Where this turns into the Left Branch of Y-Gully there is a set of well defined vertical features, mostly corners.

Ewen Buttress   90m   III *
T.W. Patey, V.N. Stevenson   February 1959
This route follows the left edge of the buttress overlooking The Couloir. Start just inside the narrow part of The Couloir. Climb steep broken ground to a saddle. The face above and right is cut by an open gully; reaching this provides a short but sharp crux, but above it the climbing becomes straightforward and leads to the top at the same point as The Couloir.

Direct Start   45m   IV,5
The obvious fault right of the toe of No.3 Buttress leads steeply up and left to join the normal route above the first pitch, near the saddle.

The Migrant   100m   VI,7 **
A. Cunningham, A. Nisbet   13th March 1986
A devious but spectacular line to the left of the huge groove on No.3 Buttress. Start just right of Ewen Buttress Direct Start. A more direct start is easier with a good build-up, but this misses the good first pitch.
1. 20m   Climb the deceptively steep right-hand groove and make a delicate step right to a belay. **The New Age Traveller** (VI,7) continues up the groove and climbs the wall on the right.
2. 20m   Work up right under the overhanging wall and go through it at the first possible place to the base of the huge groove.
3. 40m   Return a short way and break out onto a ledge on the arete (exciting). Follow the ledge left, then go up over a chokestone to the top of a pinnacle. Move left to gain the rib above and follow it to easier ground.
4. 20m   Go easily right to the finish of Ewen Buttress.

The Overseer Direct   70m   V,6 *
A. Nisbet, E. Clark   10th December 1983
N. Main, A. Nisbet (as described)   28th November 1992
A steep, interesting line towards the right edge of the buttress. Start at the foot of the Left Branch of Y-Gully. Pull onto a ledge and climb two consecutive steep corners to reach slabs. Climb direct to the base of a capped chimney. Pull out left and climb a vertical corner to emerge on easier ground.

The Hoarmaster   60m   V,6 **
R. Anderson, G. Nicoll, R. Milne   19th November 1988
This varied and exciting route takes a line of chimneys on the right edge of the main face of the buttress. It is strenuous but well protected, and high in the grade. Pull onto the same ledge as the start of The Overseer, but climb the square-cut chimney on the right for the first pitch and continue in the same line up a chimney with bulges for the second. Instead of climbing the last bulge, it is slightly easier to exit left onto a pinnacle and go up the corner-crack above (the original line of Overseer).

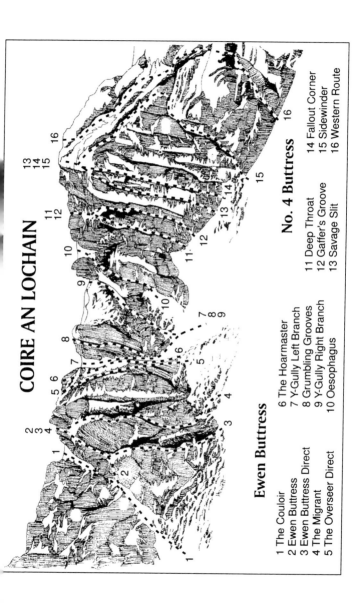

COIRE AN LOCHAIN

Ewen Buttress

1 The Couloir
2 Ewen Buttress
3 Ewen Buttress Direct
4 The Migrant
5 The Overseer Direct
6 The Hoarmaster
7 Y-Gully Left Branch
8 Grumbling Grooves
9 Y-Gully Right Branch
10 Oesophagus

No. 4 Buttress

11 Deep Throat
12 Gaffer's Groove
13 Savage Slit
14 Fallout Corner
15 Sidewinder
16 Western Route

Y-Gully Left Branch   100m   III
T.W. Patey, A.G. Nicol, A. Wedderburn   16th November 1952
This is the wide gully between No.3 Buttress and the steep pillar at the head of the bay between No.3 and No.4 Buttresses. Start at the top left of the bay and climb up to a belay right of the icicle. Surmount this (crux), then follow easier ground to the top. It may be very hard unless the icicle is fairly well formed, and this is surprisingly rare (although it was climbed on 1st June 1994).

A steep narrow pillar is the main feature of the recess which bites back into the plateau between No.3 and No.4 Buttresses. This rises between the two branches of Y-Gully.

Grumbling Grooves   60m   VI,6 *
S. Allan, A. Nisbet   17th December 1983
Climb the big groove on the left side of the pillar direct. There is a potential cornice problem.

Y-Gully Right Branch   100m   II **
R.F. Stobart, T. Stobart, Miss Harbinson   14th April 1934
This branch starts from the top right-hand end of the bay. In mid to late season it is a wide high-angled gully generally without pitches, although the cornice can be large and difficult to pass. It is also a good climb in freezing but lean conditions when it can contain continuous ice. After a big early season thaw and refreeze, it may be the only climb in condition in the Northern Corries.

No.4 BUTTRESS
The largest and most important buttress. On its left side, starting from the Right Branch of Y-Gully, it presents a fine steep wall cut by a series of compelling vertical lines of which the large central corner of Savage Slit is unmistakable. On the right side the wall swings round to form a longer but less steep face looking north. This degenerates into easier ground on its right flank.

Oesophagus   70m   III *
W. March and party   9th April 1971
About 10 metres right of the Y-Gully Right Branch is a groove which often holds ice in quantity. Climb the groove into the upper snow amphitheatre, then follow this to the top.

Deep Throat   70m   V,6 *
R. Anderson, T. Prentice, R. Milne   2nd December 1989
This unusual route takes an unlikely line up the wide crack through the stepped overhangs up the left side of the pillar left of Gaffer's Groove. Climb a wide groove, move up to gain the crack, then follow it over a tricky roof (crux). Continue up until a delicate traverse left below a huge roof leads to a stance and belay. Step right into a continuation crack and follow it to the top of the pillar and an easy finish.

Gaffer's Groove   80m   VI,7
R. Anderson, P. Long   1988
This is the big line of disconnected grooves starting a few metres left of Savage Slit (not to be confused with the wide corner-crack in Savage Slit's left arete; **Bulgy**, VII,7). Traverse left above a low rectangular roof to reach the three consecutive grooves.

Ice Variation   80m   V,5
J. Cunningham, A. Fyffe   February 1975
Occasionally, and almost always late in the season, a fine icefall flows out of a wide chimney and down the main groove of the summer route. It may be necessary to gain the icefall by starting up the summer route.

Savage Slit   90m   V,6 ***
G. Adams, J. White, F. Henderson (1PA)   21st April 1957
A very fine climb up an impeccable line, technical but well protected. It takes the wide chimney-crack in the big right-angled corner in the centre of the buttress. There is no turf so it comes into condition with the first snows. Climb an introductory tricky little pitch to belay at the foot of the slit. The main chimney can be climbed inside or out depending on girth, conditions or fear factor. Occasionally the lower section of the crack (crux) fills with ice and the route becomes a little easier. It is normal to belay on large chokestones at half-height. Because of the inconvenience of rucksacks in the narrow chimney, it is possible to leave them at the foot of the climb and abseil down from the top of the chimney to retrieve them. The more aesthetic finish is up a left-slanting gully and awkward short wall.

Fallout Corner   80m   VI,7 ***
A. Cunningham, A. Nisbet   9th December 1985
An excellent climb, sustained, technical and very well protected, which goes up the impressive corner right of Savage Slit. Start below the

corner and go up to just under the roof blocking it (10m). Cross the roof and climb the corner to a ledge on the right (30m). There is an optional belay at half-height on the left. Continue in the same line (15m). Finish as for Savage Slit either by abseiling or by climbing its last pitch.

Sidewinder   100m   III *
A. Nisbet, E. Clark   11th December 1983
This route finds a way up the buttress by a big zigzag around Savage Slit; an easier route threading the hard classics. Start below Savage Slit and three corners (of which the top-most is Fallout Corner), where a ramp leads round onto the frontal face. Climb the ramp line leading up and right onto the north face, then go up a short wall onto easier ground. Climb a chimney on the left, the opposite side of Savage Slit, and squeeze through a gap to gain and finish up the top of that route.

Western Route   120m   IV,6 ***
T.W. Patey   February 1959
Starting from the left corner of the buttress, this route slants out right to finish up the front face. A very technical wall on the second pitch becomes much easier when banked up with snow; the grade assumes some snow, but not as much as found by Patey, who soloed the first ascent and graded it III. Start near the left corner of the buttress. Climb the diagonal crack slanting right to a platform, then move up to a snowy recess. Next is the crux; climb the crack on its right wall. An awkward chimney on the right follows, then easier climbing up the prominent final gully leads to a finish up flakes on the right wall (not direct!).

THE LOCH AVON BASIN

Loch Avon lies at 730m in the heart of the Northern Cairngorms enclosed between Cairn Gorm, Ben Macdui and Beinn Mheadhoin. At its head, a superb arc of cliffs cluster round its main feeder streams, the Garbh Uisge, Feith Buidhe and Allt a' Choire Domhain. Dominating this scene is the spectacular square-topped Shelter Stone Crag and on its left is the triangular Carn Etchachan. High at the west end of the cirque are the glaciated and often ice-covered slabs of Hell's Lum while overlooking the head of the loch on the north side are the Stag Rocks.

Although still fairly accessible from the Cairn Gorm ski road, dropping out of sight from ski development and Aviemore produces a better mountain atmosphere coupled with the knowledge that return to civilisation is more than just a plod downhill. Each of the cliffs offers a different aspect and consequently differing rock formations, each with its characteristic style of winter climbing.

CARN ETCHACHAN   *(Map Ref 003 012)*

This is a crag for the connoisseur of mixed climbing, and it has some of the best chimneys in the Cairngorms. It is composed of the Main Face, split into Upper and Lower Tiers at its left end, and the Gully Face, which rises above Castlegates Gully.

Conditions and Weather
The crag is north-facing with a base at 850m. The Main Face offers fine mixed climbing with much turf and often good cracks for protection and torquing moves. As such, no special conditions are required; indeed the Main Face is climbable in almost all conditions and at any time of the winter season when the turf is frozen. Route Major has been climbed in October and in May! The cliff is sheltered from a southerly wind. The Gully Face has gullies and ramps which are best with ice. This forms slowly, so the second half of the season is generally better.

Access
By far the most convenient approach starts from the Cairn Gorm carpark. Climb Fiacaill a' Choire Cas to point 1141m, then descend Coire Raibert. Depending on conditions, either follow the burn as it steepens towards Loch Avon or take the rib on the right. Beware of avalanches, particularly into the burn. Either way, cut right before the loch and descend diagonally to the head of Loch Avon. Traverse this, hoping the Feith Buidhe burn is frozen or low, and go up to the base of the cliff. For the Upper Tier only, gain The Great Terrace from the left.

Descent
There are several choices, depending on snow conditions and weather. Castlegates Gully is possible in good conditions, otherwise it may be best to head west over the top of The Shelter Stone crag and descend the line of the Garbh Uisge Mor back to the floor of the corrie.

Layout
The left side of the Main Face is split into two tiers at half-height by The Great Terrace. The climbs have been described by pairing a route on the lower tier which leads directly into one on the upper tier, but these can easily be climbed separately. The lower tier routes are easier and less interesting than those on the upper tier, but a continuous ascent is more satisfying to some. Others will climb the more technical upper routes alone, either approaching from the right by the obvious left-slanting Diagonal Shelf or from the left along The Great Terrace. At the right end of the Terrace is a vague buttress with many turfy ledges and ramps (Route Major and Red Guard weave up here) before the gully of Scorpion. This starts just inside Castlegates Gully, but its upper half is more obvious.

Eastern Approach Route   100m   IV,5
A. Fyffe, A. Liddell   4th February 1979
This is the right-slanting fault line near the left end of the crag which leads to The Great Terrace.
Crevasse Route   100m   V,6 *
S. Kennedy, A. Nisbet   13th January 1981
The best continuation has four short, technical but very different pitches. Go up to the leftmost main buttress in the Upper Tier which lies between a large diagonal ramp (**Inside Edge**, V) and the obvious gully-fault of Equinox. Start right of centre and take the turfiest line leading to a corner on the right (40m). Climb a large leaning block, then the overhanging curving crack above (technical crux). Step left and climb huge flakes to a crevasse. A queer contorted chimney exits through a hole to a fine eyrie. Climb the first crack above for 25m, veering right at the top, and go up a nose to the true finish of the buttress.

Western Approach Route   110m   III
A. Nisbet, D. McCutcheon   19th December 1989
The climbs of this combination are both fine natural lines, and both can be icy in good conditions. Start left of the lowest point of the buttress, which is next to Castlegates Gully, just left of a mound of huge blocks. Climb a series of three narrow left-slanting ramps (parallel to Diagonal Shelf) and a short chimney to The Great Terrace below Equinox.
Equinox   110m   VI,6 **
S. Kennedy, A. Nisbet, N. Morrison   14th February 1981
The gully line of Equinox is best distinguished by an overhanging square-cut tower high on its right. Climb the left side of the fault for two

pitches, then move steeply right to an obvious chimney with a constricted top which is tucked under the square-cut tower on the right. Finish straight up or out left if the cornice is large.

The Silent Approach   110m   IV,5
J. Lyall, A. Nisbet   28th December 1989

The highlight of this combination is a cavernous chimney on Guillotine. Start at the left side of the cliff base, gain a low ledge below a steep wall, follow this right and take a right-slanting line to cross Western Approach Route and finish in the trough below Guillotine.

Guillotine   110m   V,6 *
A. Fyffe, A. Liddell   4th February 1979

Guillotine takes the deepest part of the next recessed section right of Equinox and left of a pink spur. Zigzag to the foot of a wide chimney on the immediate left of the pink spur. Climb this, then take the second chimney on the right which cuts deeply into the spur and passes below a huge blade of rock. Exit by a tunnel roofed with blocks to a platform on the spur. Climb the chimney above with an overhang at the top (crux).

Route Major   280m   IV,5 ***
T.W. Patey, M. Smith   10th February 1957

A classic winter route, but more notable for finding a relatively easy route up the centre of the huge face than for the quality of the climbing itself. It is possible in any conditions although it is better when the Battlements Groove is iced. The most obvious feature in the centre of the lower tier is the large left-slanting ramp of the Diagonal Shelf, usually snow-covered. Start on the right wall of the Shelf, about 5m above the lowest rocks.

Move steeply out right to a groove which runs back left and parallel to the Diagonal Shelf. A well defined continuation groove leads to a snow basin. An easier start (the original) follows the Shelf to about half-height, then takes a ramp leading right to the basin. Exit from the basin by the obvious tapered chimney (technical crux, very well protected). Another ramp then leads to more broken ground. Go diagonally right for two long pitches to the foot of a huge V-groove (the Battlements Groove, difficult to see from below). In icy conditions, climb the groove and continue in the same line to the top. Under powder, take turfy ledges on the right to a similar finish.

Red Guard   250m   VI,7 *
N.D. Keir, M. Freeman (4PA)   24th March 1978
G.S. Smith, R.D. Barton (FFA, as described)   1979
A fine lower tier, particularly the unusual chimney, with an easier but less interesting finish. Start below the huge block-filled groove between the Diagonal Shelf and the base of Castlegates Gully. A pitch up the groove, hard if the ice is thin, gains a slightly left-slanting continuation chimney. The chimney is very deep, sometimes heavily verglassed and entertaining for troglodytes. Above a snowy bay is a continuation groove; reach this with difficulty (technical crux) and follow it to easier ground. Go up rightwards and take either of two left-slanting ramps to a finish just right of Route Major. The higher ramp is better and more sustained but common with The Sword (not described). It is possible to escape easily from below the crux by going up then down and left into the basin of Route Major (and down *via* the Diagonal Shelf).

Scorpion   240m   V,5 **
T.W. Patey, J.M. Taylor, A.G. Nicol, K.A. Grassick
6th December 1952
A route full of character and a notorious 'sting in the tail' which is either a hard ice pitch in lean conditions, but more commonly it is a problematical cornice. A subterranean chimney in the lower section is worthwhile but difficult to find, and many parties have accidentally started by The Sword.

The Sentinel is an apparent tower at the left base of Castlegates Gully. Immediately below The Sentinel is a long open groove, **The Sword**, which leads logically but with less interest into the upper fault of Scorpion then out left by a big ramp. Start 15m below The Sentinel, midway towards the initial gully of Red Guard. Climb a steep corner left of a V-groove and, at about 20m, continue left for about 10m to below a steep wall (the right end of the steep smooth wall above Red Guard's initial block-filled groove). Enter a subterranean slanting crack and above the exit, which may be a problem under hard snow, climb an overhung wall on the immediate right on good holds. Go round a corner to the right and go up in a left-trending line to cross left over a slab by a crack in its lower margin. The next pitch is obvious to below the upper fault. A long chimney below a leaning wall leads back right into the main fault which may hold one or several ice pitches. A near impossible cornice can be passed by a finish out left, ending up a short vertical wall which can be trickily freed or pegged, but a more direct finish is satisfying and can be easy in early season.

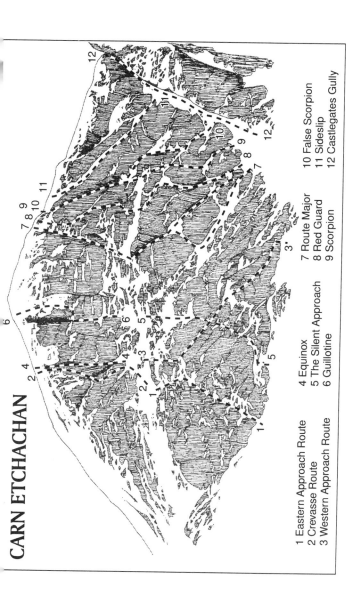

CARN ETCHACHAN

1 Eastern Approach Route
2 Crevasse Route
3 Western Approach Route

4 Equinox
5 The Silent Approach
6 Guillotine

7 Route Major
8 Red Guard
9 Scorpion

10 False Scorpion
11 Sideslip
12 Castlegates Gully

False Scorpion   240m   V,5
W. March, O. Ludlow   March 1970
A logical option following the main fault throughout, with more ice but less variety. It is worthwhile when icy, being scrappy and serious under powder. Start just above The Sentinel inside Castlegates Gully. A steep and narrow section leads left to join the upper fault and Scorpion.

Sideslip   150m   III
A. Fyffe, R. O'Donovan   14th March 1975
A committing outing into a land of snow-sculptured aretes and gullies in heavy conditions, this route takes the line of a big slab leading left out of Castlegates Gully (a pink rockfall feature in summer). Follow the slab to its top (conslidated snow required), go round the corner and traverse left into a hanging gully. Follow this to the top.

Castlegates Gully   250m   I **
J. McCoss, W.B. Meff, R. Clarke   Easter 1914
A straightforward gully, rarely with any nasty surprises.

SHELTER STONE CRAG   (Map Ref 001 013)

This big and impressive cliff is perhaps better known for its hard rock climbs, but it offers a few chinks in its armour which provide magnificent winter routes. Although Carn Etchachan dominates on the approach, the true stature of the crag is well seen from the loch.

Access and Descent
In addition to the way described for Carn Etchachan, above, the route by Coire Domhain past Hell's Lum Crag may also be used

Weather and Conditions
This is a big north-east facing cliff with a base at 800m. Its remote location and the potential hazards of a return across the Cairngorm plateau mean that it is a bad choice in poor weather. It is somewhat fickle in the amount of snow it holds, particularly on the steeper routes. A westerly wind and spindrift will plaster the cliff with powder, but this is stripped quickly in a thaw. Sticil Face requires ice, which is usually present in good conditions. Raeburn's Buttress and Clach Dhian Chimney are climbable in any conditions.

Scorpion, Carn Etchachan   Climber: Steve Blagbrough   Photo: Ian Dillon

Layout
A slabby lower half rears up to a steep prow right of centre. In the centre of the left face are the Central Slabs, with Sticil Face taking an ice line at their left edge and defining the right side of a tapering buttress. On the left side of this buttress is **Breach Gully**, and left again is the left-bounding buttress of **Castle Wall**. Right of the steep prow are the lines of Postern and Clach Dhian Chimney. The cliff is bounded by the snow gullies of Castlegates Gully on the left and Pinnacle Gully on the right.

Raeburn's Buttress   240m   IV,5
W. March, J. Hart   February 1971
A good line, but with little technical interest and perhaps best treated as an option for poor conditions. The big feature of Breach Gully towards the left edge of the cliff marks the start. Start at the bottom right side of the bay below the gully. Follow a line of right-trending grooves to a stance on the right. Traverse left up a series of ledges, then move left to a line of weakness splitting the buttress. Climb this to a steep chimney and exit right at its top onto an arete. Above, the angle eases and the line leads up left.

Sticil Face   240m   V,6 ***
K.A. Grassick, A.G. Nicol   27th December 1957
An excellent long route with varied climbing, following the angle between Raeburn's Buttress and the Central Slabs. It requires good but not exceptional conditions for the ice to form. Basically, the more ice there is, the easier and better the route becomes. The grade is for good conditions (sometimes it is VI,6); a steep ice corner at about 100m is the guide to conditions. Although the route is technically hard, it is not sustained and therefore can be climbed quite quickly by a competent party.
  Start below and left of the ice corner. Climb diagonally out right onto the face, then gain the depression leading up to the ice corner. In good conditions this is mostly on snow and ice and quite easy. Climb the steep ice corner and continue to below a narrow chimney. Climb this awkward chimney (mixed) to easy ledges. Go diagonally right above the Central Slabs (easy but exposed) to a wide finishing fault. This can be straightforward with ice, but it is hard under powder or verglas.

The Crux Pitch, Sticil Face, Shelter Stone Crag   Climber: Kathy Murphy
Photo: Kathy Murphy Collection

The Citadel   270m   VII,8 ***
M. Hamilton, K. Spence   23rd February 1980
A. Rouse, B. Hall (variation)   1975
A magnificent route; hard, sustained and sensational. The first ascent was long sought after, and it was the scene of many epic failuress, like Cunningham and March's bivouac in the early 1970s. The lower section takes the line of shallow chimneys bounding the right side of the Central Slabs, the upper part is on the slabby left side of the prow. Good conditions are rarely found; it requires ice on the slabs below the lower crux, and enough snow to justify a winter ascent on the lower section, but the top slabs have to be not too deep in powder. It has yet to receive a free ascent, although the upper and lower sections have been freed independently. Many ascents have used 2 or 3 points of aid, especially on the lower crux.

Climb the shallow chimney line in two pitches to a ledge system (Low Ledge). A further two pitches follow the chimney until overhangs force an exit to ledges on the left. Trend rightwards on slabs (hopefully ice) to a corner with a crack in the right wall. The next pitch is the lower crux. Climb the strenuous corner with a hard move right (usually with aid) to a grassy fault and belay. Traverse right into an open corner, climb this and the corner into which it develops to gain a ridge. Follow this, then go left to a spectacular stance by a huge flake. Next is the upper crux. Flake traverse left, then climb the crack and chimney system above to a good stance. Continue up the crack above, then traverse right with a step down to ledges (not easy to find under deep powder, but it can be tensioned). Climb the ensuing right-slanting fault until the left of two short chimneys leads to the plateau.

Variation:
A worthwhile route, particularly if the upper section has been stripped by the sun. After the lower crux, go up and left on straightforward snow to either finish up the last pitch of Sticil Face or, 10m up this, take an obvious thin ramp trending slightly left up the headwall.

Postern   240m   VI,6 **
M. Hamilton, K. Spence, A. Taylor (original line)   5/6th January 1980
This is another impressive route which takes a largely diagonal line right of the prow to reach the prominent Second Step on the skyline. It is a good natural line and it is possible in most conditions with harder direct finishes for those with energy to spare. Two earlier starts, the corners of Steeple and the summer line, are very good but require unusually icy or snowy conditions.

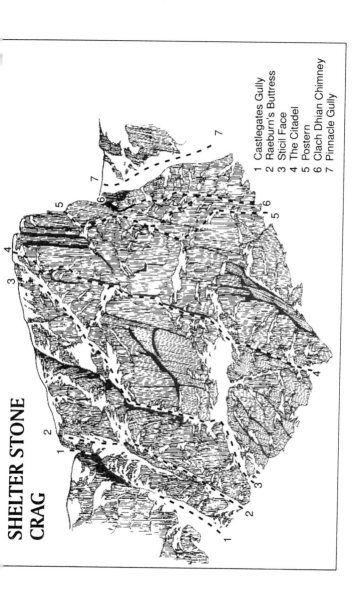

SHELTER STONE CRAG

1 Castlegates Gully
2 Raeburn's Buttress
3 Sticil Face
4 The Citadel
5 Postern
6 Clach Dhian Chimney
7 Pinnacle Gully

Start up a big left-facing corner just left of Clach Dhian Chimney. Climb this past a prominent wedged block, then go up a ramp slanting left to the terrace. Go right to 'the slanting crack' and climb this slanting rightwards to where it develops into a deep chimney. Climb the chimney and traverse left to a long wall and groove which ends at a narrow ledge. Move left on a short catwalk, then climb an obvious right-trending line to the Second Step. Finish out right overlooking Pinnacle Gully.

Variation Finish 1:   7

Climb the obvious groove rising directly above the Second Step (The Direct Finish to Clach Dhian Chimney).

Variation Finish 2:   8

Climb a large rectangular recess above the left end of the Second Step to a perch on the skyline, then ascend blocks and cracks in a dramatic position to the top (the last pitch of Postern Direct).

Clach Dhian Chimney   220m   IV,4
C. Butterworth, A. Frost   *4th January 1972*
Western Grooves Start
A. Fyffe, R.D. Barton   *March 1978*
The normal start of Clach Dhian Chimney, a big chimney left of Pinnacle Gully, is obvious but harder and not so often in condition. Start midway between this and the right edge of the face. Climb wide shallow grooves into a short deep red chimney. Climb this to an awkward exit, and continue in a groove until a ramp goes left into the fault of Clach Dhian Chimney; this leads to the first step on the horizon. Continue up to the final wall and finish up right overlooking Pinnacle Gully.

Pinnacle Gully   200m   I *
First ascent unknown
Another straightforward gully with no nasty surprises. The Forefinger Pinnacle near the top provides scenic interest.

HELL'S LUM CRAG   *(Map Ref 996 017)*

This south-facing slabby cliff, with a base at 930m, is frequently wet in summer but it provides fine icefalls in winter. Although it lies close to Shelter Stone Crag, it is far more accessible and popular since descent to the loch is unnecessary. The Hell's Lum itself is the huge gully on the left-hand side of the cliff, and in a good winter nuch of the right side of the crag is sheathed in ice.

Access
Access is *via* Coire Domhain. From the top of the chairlift, traverse Cairn Gorm on its north side (or go over its top), then traverse south of the summit of Coire an t-Sneachda. Alternatively, from the carpark, ascend the Fiacaill a' Choire Cas to point 1141m and join the former route. Descend Coire Domhain towards Loch Avon and traverse right under the cliff. This may be avalanche-prone.

Descent
Reverse the approach *via* point 1141m.

Weather and Conditions
Because of its south-easterly aspect, conditions are susceptible to sun. Sunny days in December or January are generally alright, but not thereafter. Partially cloudy days in mid-season are also acceptable, but the ice has usually been stripped by mid-March. The ice forms reliably, the longer the cold spell the better. It is a bad choice with north-westerly winds and spindrift, as it will be avalanche prone. Beware of avalanches both on the approach and at the top of the routes.

Layout
Hell's Lum, the huge chimney towards the left, splits the crag into a smaller left-hand section and a large right-hand section. The buttress just right of the Lum contains the prominent narrow chimney of Deep Cut Chimney. Further right are the main slabs and icefalls.

The Gullet   130m   III *
J. Bower, B.S. Findlay   28th December 1969
The central and best of three ice-filled faults on the slabby face left of The Lum. Start about 20 metres left of The Lum and climb the fault, slabby and shallow at first, to reach the deeper central section. Continue up this with occasional diversions to the left. The cornice can be large and difficult, perhaps impossible.

The Chancer   90m   V,6 **
J. Cunningham, W. March   January 1970
First climbed using Cunningham's daggering technique, a transitional step in the development of front-pointing, this route remained as Scotland's hardest icefall for only two years until Labyrinth Direct was front-pointed. The historical significance adds to the atmosphere provided by the scenery. The icefall is slow to form and the difficulty varies

with the amount of ice. In prime conditions there are three icefalls, about Grades IV, V and VI (left to right), but the central icefall is the traditional route. The crux is the middle pitch, which may be a free standing icicle or a short vertical ice wall. There is a good belay below it and behind the ice.

Hell's Lum   150m   II/IV ***
G. McLeod and party   March 1956
This classic route up the major fault which splits the crag gives interesting climbing through superb scenery but with a noticeable lack of good protection. It can vary from high angle snow to having up to four ice pitches. In lean early season conditions it just as good a route, but may be IV,4. The cornice, which may be huge, can normally be turned on the right. It is a dangerous route on a warm day, both from cornice collapse and icicle fall.

Deep Cut Chimney   150m   IV,4 **
T.W. Patey, D. Holroyd   19th January 1958
This intriguingly deep fault is not too variable in condition, and it is possible to climb it in avalanche conditions after approaching by abseil down the route. The normal approach is *via* a left-slanting diagonal fault, but this lower part can be banked out. The chimney becomes increasingly deep and is normally finished by back and foot up to a pile of wedged boulders in the outer jaws. Great fun!

Nobody's Fault   150m   IV,5 *
G. Smith and party   1979
The shallower fault parallel to and right of Deep Cut Chimney gives a good climb, but the difficulties are disappointingly short. The hanging chimney at mid-height is tricky (eased by ice) but well protected.

Brimstone Groove   170m   IV,3 **
S. Docherty, K. Spence   27th December 1970
A fine sheet of ice regularly forms right of Grey Buttress (the buttress with Deep Cut Chimney and Nobody's Fault). It is technically straight-forward but serious, and is graded for good conditions. Follow the left edge of this ice to break through a steeper section, which may be thin in poor conditions, into the largest and widest fault on the left. This is the route perhaps most affected by the sun, deteriorating as the season progresses, but runners appear as the ice thins and it becomes IV,4 or even IV,5.

HELL'S LUM CRAG

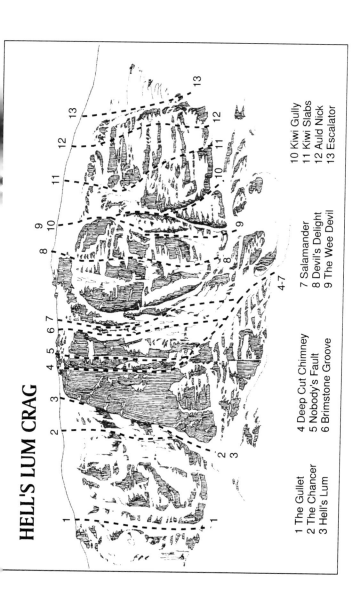

1 The Gullet
2 The Chancer
3 Hell's Lum

4 Deep Cut Chimney
5 Nobody's Fault
6 Brimstone Groove

7 Salamander
8 Devil's Delight
9 The Wee Devil

10 Kiwi Gully
11 Kiwi Slabs
12 Auld Nick
13 Escalator

Salamander   160m   V,4 *
J. Cunningham, W. March, R. O'Donovan   February 1973
Another good ice route with a significantly more technical section than Brimstone Groove. Climb the right side of the ice sheet to belay below a chimney slot in the overlap above, then pull through this to an easier finish. The difficulty will vary unpredictably with the amount and shape of the ice (IV,5 may apply).

Devil's Delight   160m   V,5 ***
J. Cunningham, W. March, R. O'Donovan   February 1973
A superb ice route but slow to come into condition. The icefall forms on the right side of a steeper section, left of the big left-facing corner of Wee Devil and characterised by a large triangular niche. A cascade of ice leads into the triangular niche, then continues to the Haven. Above, narrow ice runnels hopefully exist in grooves and corners; these constitute the crux.

The Wee Devil   150m   IV,4 *
D. Dinwoodie, J. Mothersele   17th November 1971
This route follows the prominent left-facing corner system halfway up the face, hopefully thick with ice and leading up to an overhang, usually bare. Climb the discontinuous gully into the corner, continue up this then exit left below the overhang (or just trend left on thick ice). Above, ignore the overhang and go right by a large flake onto a slab, perhaps thinly iced, until a right-facing corner line above the overhang and right of a steep tower can be followed to easier ground and the top.

Kiwi Gully   150m   III,4 **
W. March, I. Nicholson   2nd January 1972
A line of ice following a shallow left-slanting gully forms regularly, deepest at about two-thirds height. Exiting from this is the steepest section, but it often has good ice. The gully then fades out so trend left to finish up the top right-facing corner of The Wee Devil. The line is slightly sheltered from the sun so it may last longer into the season.

Kiwi Slabs   150m   IV,3
T.W. Patey, V.N. Stevenson   February 1959
Open climbing on ice smears, serious but quite easy in ideal conditions. Either start up Kiwi Gully to its deep section, then break out and climb rightwards on easy-angled ice smears to a slanting left-facing

corner (Grade III) or gain this corner more directly if conditions allow (for which the route is graded). The corner normally has thicker ice and leads to the snow apron at the top.

Auld Nick   150m   III
M. Freeman, G.S. Strange   20th November 1971
Another very variable route, but graded for good ice which forms on the right side of the main slabs. It can bank out substantially.

Escalator   150m   II **
J.Y.L. Hay, A. Thom   January 1960
This route can be anything from continuous ice to a snow slope, but often there is much low-angled and reliable ice. The route is Grade III in early season. Climb the obvious line of ice which forms in a shallow fault at the right edge of the cliff.

STAG ROCKS   (Map Ref 003 022)

These cliffs are on the south side of Cairn Gorm, overlooking the head of Loch Avon between Coire Raibert and Coire Domhain.

Approach
Descend either Coire Domhain or Coire Raibert and traverse round under the cliffs. With a little local knowledge, descend either Diagonal Gully to the right section or a prominent Y-shaped gully at the west end to the left section.

Weather And Conditions
As a dry crag in summer, it forms ice reluctantly. Facing just east of south it is quickly stripped by sun despite a base of 870m, but it is a quiet option to the busy Hell's Lum.

Layout
The cliff consists of two main sections separated by Diagonal Gully. The left section is smaller with several ribs and shallow gullies and is bounded on the left by a Y-shaped gully beyond which is the icefall of Cascade. The right section is more massive and divided in two by Amphitheatre Gully. On its left is the inverted triangle-shaped Pine Tree Buttress with Apex Gully leading out right from Diagonal Gully. To the right of Amphitheatre Gully is the larger slabby Longbow Crag, which is split by Central Route.

Cascade   45m   VI,6 *
W. March, D. Alcock   February 1977
The obvious steep icefall which develops on the largest outcrop midway between Coire Domhain and the left section of Stag Rocks proper. Normally two icefalls form, the left-hand one being considerably steeper while the right-hand fall is always less than vertical (Grade V,5). Ice screws provide the only protection.

Afterthought Arete   150m   III
W. March   November 1969
This route follows the left-hand and most regularly shaped arete bounding the right side of the Y-shaped gully. Gain the arete from the right and follow it as directly as you dare, hopefully finding it a fun route.

Diagonal Gully   200m   I
An easy and friendly Grade I, apart from avalanche risk.

Apex Gully   150m   III
W. March, J. Hart   18th February 1971
The obvious icefall and fault about halfway up Diagonal Gully on the right. Climb iced up slabs into the snow gully and follow this to its fork. The right branch leads to the top at about Grade II. The left fork contains a good ice pitch, then snow leads to the top.

Amphitheatre Gully   225m   V,5 **
W. March, J. Hart (1PA)   17th February 1971
The obvious gully which splits the right-hand section gives an excellent winter route, but it is not often in good condition. Follow the gully into the upper amphitheatre *via* at least one long ice pitch. The final two pitches lie up the left corner of the large wedge-shaped wall which backs the amphitheatre. The lower of these is usually the crux and the final pitch may exit through a rock window.

Central Route   150m   VI,6 *
G. Smith, G. Ball   1979
Right of the smooth clean slabs is a large vegetated depression forming a mossy drape at mid-height (not the grassy gully further right). Climb the depression, passing a diagonal fault below the mossy drape, then bend left above it. Any ice is stripped quickly by the sun, but the steep top section is mixed. If the lower depression is bare, the route is best started by a mixed line on the right (**Wigwag**).

THE STAG ROCKS

1 Cascade
2 Afterthought Arete

3 Diagonal Gully
4 Apex Gully

5 Amphitheatre Gully
6 Central Route

CREAGAN A' CHOIRE ETCHACHAN
(Map Ref 016 998)

This fine icy cliff lies in the remote heart of the central Cairngorm mountains, so it tends to be much less crowded than the Northern Corries. Facing east and at a relatively low altitude, the cliff has more variable conditions than the higher ones. The routes are quite short but they are of high quality and, despite the long approach, a visit here can be highly recommended. The Hutchison Hut, the bothy in the corrie below the cliff, is an ideal base for a weekend visit.

Layout
The left end of the cliff is a large broad buttress, The Bastion, bounded on the right by the deepest gully, The Corridor. The central section of cliff is more broken with several shallow gullies leading up to a snow slope, often corniced. Next right are some big overhangs above half-height bounded on the right by the narrow Red Chimney. The right-hand end of the cliff features the Crimson Slabs, icy in good conditions, with two prominent left-facing corners, Djibangi and The Dagger.

Weather and Conditions
The cliff is of a middle altitude (base at 850m), faces south-east to east, receives the sun particularly in the morning and therefore is generally in better condition in early or mid-season. Red Chimney, The Corridor and the easier gullies, however, are often still good in March. January may be the best month for the other routes, and a cold spell of weather after a wet autumn is ideal. The other consideration is the long approach, not recommended in poor weather, although the cliff has no unusual hazards.

Access
This is either from the south (from the Linn of Dee) or the north (from Cairn Gorm carpark).

The southerly approach is long and may be helped by cycling. From Braemar, drive to the Linn of Dee and park shortly beyond it on the north side of the Dee. A signposted path goes through the forest to reach the private road to Derry Lodge. About 200 metres beyond Derry Lodge, turn right at the public telephone, cross a bridge and follow a path through the forest up into Glen Derry. Under powder it is better to follow the bulldozed road on the east side of Glen Derry. Some 6km from Derry Lodge, a path branches left from Glen Derry towards the Hutchison Hut (another 1½km). In thick weather (and in the dark), both the hut and the correct point to branch left are difficult to find. The crag is at the head of the corrie above the hut. The total distance is 14km total, but it may be possible to cycle a fair distance before snow or ice makes walking more prudent.

The quickest way from the north is to ascend Coire Cas to the plateau and descend Coire Raibert. Alternatively, take the chairlift and traverse the south side of Cairn Gorm into Coire Raibert. Traverse round the head of Loch Avon and take a path leading up towards Loch Etchachan. Continue down to the outflow of the loch, then either cut right to the crag or descend to the hut. Although this is only about 9km, remember that there is a lot of wild and inhospitable country between you and your car should the weather turn nasty at the end of the day.

Descent
Descent is possible at either end of the cliff. At the left (Bastion) end, descend 45 degree snow in or near the left bounding gully (Forked Gully). At the right (Crimson Slabs) end, a line of small crags beyond the slabs must be passed before descending a short gully (Grade I).

Quartzvein Edge   120m   III
J.Y.L. Hay, G. Adams, A Thom   29th December 1956
The left edge of The Bastion is a good choice when snow or weather conditions are doubtful, as it should be possible in most conditions. Start well up left from the base of the buttress and just round the corner, where the wall of Forked Gully becomes defined. Climb a short wall onto the face. Follow the edge at first, then find a way up slabs which develop into a shelf leading round a false tower on the left. A better but harder variation is to climb the false tower on its right side.

Original Route Direct   140m   V,6 *
J. Bower, G. Boyd   23rd December 1969 (Original Route)
J. Ashbridge, S.M. Richardson   29th November 1992 (Direct)
The route follows a line of grooves just right of centre of the Bastion. It is a direct and natural winter line although the Original Route, further left at the start and right in the middle, is easier (IV,5). Start to the right of the lowest rocks on the right of the buttress and go left up an easy

depression which ends at a deep V-groove. This groove is the best means of locating the route, although it is better seen from below the centre of the buttress than from the route's start. Climb the groove (crux) to a snow patch in a depression. Exit from its right side and return left to follow a large V-groove. Alternatively, go further right to a ramp which joins the V-groove higher up (Original Route).

The Corridor   120m   IV,5 **
F.R. Malcolm, A. Thom   20th March 1954
An impressive route, both for the scenery and as an early step-cutting achievement. There are usually two major ice pitches, one leading over jammed blocks into a cave and one above the cave, usually the crux and often very steep. There is often a large cornice, best taken on the left.

Architrave   120m   IV,4 *
A. Fyffe, J. McArtney   29th December 1969
This is the prominent groove in the slabs close to the right wall of the Corridor recess. It can form an impressive ribbon of ice, more sustained than The Corridor but less steep.

Central Chimney   120m   III *
T.W. Patey, A.O'F. Will, G. Adams, M. Smith   27th February 1955
The route takes a shallow chimney between two ribs on the left of the central section of cliff (not far right of The Corridor recess). It is the best of the easier routes, and it can be reduced to Grade II in good conditions by starting up a fault leading leftwards from the base of Square-Cut Gully into the chimney proper.
   Climb an obvious V-cleft which splits the lowest rocks and leads into the chimney. The chimney itself gives 60m of climbing over small ice pitches to the foot of a right-slanting snow ramp, which provides a beautiful finish. Beware of windslab on the final slopes.

Square-Cut Gully   150m   V,6
M. Forbes, M. Low   March 1966
The shallow slabby gully is dominated by a magnificent ice pillar. The start is easy but the finish may include a tricky slabby pitch if there is unconsolidated snow.

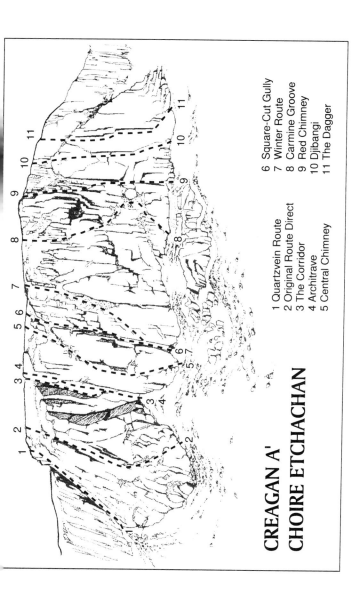

CREAGAN A'
CHOIRE ETCHACHAN

1 Quartzvein Route
2 Original Route Direct
3 The Corridor
4 Architrave
5 Central Chimney

6 Square-Cut Gully
7 Winter Route
8 Carmine Groove
9 Red Chimney
10 Djibangi
11 The Dagger

Winter Route   150m   III
W.D. Brooker, J.W. Morgan, D.A. Sutherland   2nd January 1949
This is the easiest line on this section of cliff, only Grade II in good conditions. Start up Square-Cut Gully and take an obvious line of weakness leading up onto the buttress on the right (Pioneer Buttress). Mixed climbing leads to an ice pitch on the left near the top.

Carmine Groove   140m   IV,5 *
R.A. Smith, G. Stephen   November 1974
A barrier of overhangs rises diagonally rightwards from the foot of Pioneer Buttress to the upper reaches of Red Chimney. Two prominent snow scoops, The Meadows, are situated below the largest section of overhangs, just left of Red Chimney. Carmine Groove takes a steep ice-filled groove which starts at the left edge of the upper Meadow and runs left of the big overhangs. It is not to be mistaken for an ice line even closer to the overhangs which is **The Red Snake** (V,4).

Red Chimney   150m   V,5 **
J.Y.L. Hay, R. Ibbotson   February 1959 (Flanking Ribs finish)
I.A. Paterson, S.P. Hepburn   January 1967 (Direct Finish)
This very fine ice climb may be relied on to give good conditions in all but the leanest winters. The lower section is usually filled with a cascade of clear ice overflowing the Crimson Slabs on the right. This is not steep but often thin. The upper chimney becomes choked by a series of very steep ice bosses, threaded up leftwards (ice screw runners) into the final corner. The cop out is to pull out onto the rib on the right and follow it to the top (**Flanking Ribs**; IV,4).

Djibangi   140m   V,4 ***
J. McArtney, W.J. Barclay   31st January 1965
The left-hand of two corners on the Crimson Slabs is well worth a gamble on conditions, and not to be missed if it is iced. It is quite easy in perfect snow-ice conditions. Either start directly below the corner and climb ice directly, or more commonly climb a series of corners to the left. The main corner has an overlap which may be the crux. Above the corner, a snow ramp leads rightwards to join The Dagger, but it is better and easier to finish up icy grooves trending left. Continuing directly up the slabs from the left start is **Djibooty** (V,4 or easier), a superb route on the rare occasions when the ice is thick enough.

Opposite: The Left Cascade, Stag Rocks   Climber: John Lowther
Photo: George Reid
Next page: Creagan a' Choire Etchachan from the Hutchison Hut
Photo: Neil Bielby

The Dagger   130m   V,5 *
A. Nisbet, A.T. Robertson   29th January 1977
The right-hand corner provides an excellent climb, but it is rarely iced.
Take a left-trending turfy line to the base of the corner. A thin ribbon of
ice is sufficient in the corner. Pass the next bulge on the left (mixed)
and continue to a large platform below the last slab. This may well be
the crux. Climb the slab by a crack slanting right, then continue straight
up to the top.

BEINN A' BHUIRD
1196m   (Map Ref 092 006)

This is a rather remote mountain towards the east end of the main
Cairngorm massif. There are many good climbs in three different
corries, but with the long approach limiting its popularity, only a small
number of routes on the best known cliff, Garbh Choire, have been
selected. Coire na Ciche has good shorter routes, a possibility for a
second day, but it is not described here.

Weather and Conditions
Being high and east, good conditions occur at similar times to Lochnagar. The buttresses are possible at any time of a long season,
November to April, but they are better without deep powder or rime so
March or early April are recommended. The gullies are definitely better
in late season. Good conditions for the long approach are also important, i.e. hard or little snow, so a freeze after a good thaw is best. Good
weather is also important as it is a long way to retreat or escape, and
a mishap would be very serious. The climbs face north-east and the
cliff base is at 920m.

Access
The best winter approach starts from the A93 Braemar-Aberdeen
road, 100 metres east of the gates to Invercauld House. Follow the
upper road past the house and go through a locked gate just beyond
the house. Continue past Alltdourie cottage and enter Glen Slugain
through a conifer plantation. A good stalkers' path goes through Glen
Slugain, passes the ruined Slugain Lodge and enters upper Glen
Quoich. Turn to the north and continue up the path to a huge boulder

Previous page: The approach to Lochnagar   *Photo: Andy Nisbet*

Opposite: Easy snow slopes at the top of Giant's Head Chimney, Lochnagar
Climber: Bill Church   *Photo: Brian Findlay*

called Clach a' Chleirich. Follow the stream past the stone to the Sneck between Beinn Avon and Cnap a' Chleirich, then enter the corrie by contouring left, avoiding rock ribs by descending. Although this is some 15km in total, the routes are sometimes climbed in a day from the road; otherwise some accommodation must be arranged. There are good camp sites in the Fairy Glen below Slugain Lodge.

Descent
The quickest route off the plateau in wild weather is to follow the corrie edge back to the Sneck. Keep well up the slope from the cliff edge and take care to avoid a small slab outcrop on the east-facing slope of Cnap a' Chleirich about 400 metres south of the Sneck. In better weather, and especially when there is powder in the valleys, it is easier to go to the summit of Cnap a' Chleirich and follow the blunt ridge back to Clach a' Chleirich (the edge of Coire nan Clach on the right is often corniced).

Layout
First reached and on the left of the corrie is the North Face with a large basin high up, The Crucible. Occasionally twin icefalls flow out of this; the left-hand one is **Gold Coast** (VI,5) and the right-hand one is **Crucible Route** (V,4), although neither climbs the icefall direct. High on the right of this face is the west-facing Squareface. The central part of the cliff is more broken with several easy gullies, the exception being the waterfall at the head of the Allt an t-Sluichd which freezes to form The Flume. Right of The Flume is Mandarin Buttress, beyond which is the mighty Mitre Ridge, the most impressive feature of the corrie. Between Mandarin and Mitre is the shallow South-East Gully.

The Flume   200m   II **
The Flume Direct   200m   IV,4 **
J.M. Taylor, G.B. Leslie   31st March 1954
D.F. Lang, N.W. Quinn   15th December 1974 (Direct)
The stream drops from the plateau in a big waterfall which provides the Direct Route when frozen (two pitches). The easier version, also very icy, threads its way between the Direct icefall and another big ice pitch which forms to the left (**Flume Left-Hand**; IV,4).

South-East Gully   200m   V,4 *
R.H. Sellers, G. Annand   February 1959
The gully bounding the Mitre Ridge on the left gives a fine climb in good conditions but, with minimal rock protection, it becomes very serious when there is unconsolidated snow. Beware of avalanches when there

BEINN A' BHUIRD
Garbh Choire

1 The Flume
2 South-East Gully
3 The Grail
4 Mitre Ridge
5 Cumming-Crofton Route

is a south-westerly or westerly wind and spindrift. The crux is a steep narrows just above half-height. The cornice is seldom troublesome.

East Wall Direct (IV,5) takes the left side of Mitre Ridge East Face, roughly parallel to South-East Gully. A long shallow chimney system leads to an ice couloir in the centre of the face. Finish at the top of Mitre Ridge.

The Grail (V,5) is in the centre of the East Face. Follow a direct line up a vegetated fault, then climb by a ramp overlooking the couloir of East Wall direct.

Mitre Ridge   220m   V,6 ***
W.D. Brooker, T.W. Patey   2nd April 1953
J. Anderson, A. Nisbet (Direct)   April 1979
A great classic with short hard sections. With good snow it is much easier and a fine finish over the towers is possible. With consolidated snow or ice, start up a big groove (the rightmost) at the base of the ridge near the right corner of the East Face. Climb the groove past a steep section to a rising shelf which leads into a deep chimney on the West Face. In less icy conditions, start up a line of weakness further up and right which leads to the shelf and chimney. Climb the chimney and shallow gully to a shoulder on the ridge. The short wall above is the crux; climb it by tricky torquing, moving up and right. Above and to the left is a platform, usually gained by moving left across a slab and climbing a splintered chimney. Now climb the wall above and ascend rightwards to the col between the First and Second Towers. The latter is normally turned on the left to an impressive finish along the final arete. Bell's Variation (see below) is another possible finish.

Cumming-Crofton Route   160m   VI,6 **
R. Renshaw, G.S. Strange   26th February 1977
R. Anderson, G. Nicoll (Bell's Variation)
This is a steep, sustained and exciting winter route in the modern style of snowy rock. One of the 'last great problems' of the seventies, there were at least two previous attempts, one very nearly successful in a storm, by Norman Keir. The route follows a right-slanting corner parallel to and on the right of the crest of Mitre Ridge, ending at the col behind the First Tower.

Start directly below the corner and go straight up to climb a prominent chimney blocked by a flake. Pulling out right at the flake is hard

(30m). Traverse right and continue rightwards up a smooth groove. When stopped by a vertical wall, return left into the main corner (optional belay). Climb the corner to a platform (40m). Continue in the same line to the col. Either finish by Mitre Ridge on the left or more directly by Bell's Variation (technical 7). For the latter, follow a shelf rightwards and climb a very exposed crack on the west face. Step back left from the crack and finish straight up.

Commando Route (IV,5) follows a mirror image corner to the Cumming-Crofton Route, finishing at the same col. It is a fine line, but has had only two known ascents, both using tension from the right to get established in the main corner.

North-West Gully (III) is the corner-gully tucked hard against the West Wall of Mitre Ridge. It is graded for its fine 30m ice pitch and is harder under powder.

LOCHNAGAR
1155m   (Map Ref 244 862)

Lochnagar is undoubtedly one of Scotland's most famous mountains. Its distinctive outline rises gracefully above Royal Deeside and provides a fine mountain landscape for residents, tourists and climbers.

The climbing is situated in the magnificent North-East Corrie with its cliff front extending for 1½km, reaching a height of 230m and encircling the loch which has given its name to the mountain. It is split by great gullies into several well defined buttresses which give long natural winter routes.

Weather and Conditions

Conditions are particularly reliable, but only for those who are willing to climb any style, ice or mixed. Good ice often appears only as late as March, after the powder has lain unchanged throughout January and February. The classic buttress climbs are traditionally climbed and graded for powder, progress being reliant on frozen vegetation. The deep enclosure of the corrie protects the snow from the effects of a thaw and protects the climber from strong south-east through to west winds, so it is often possible to climb in reasonable comfort after battling up to the corrie in wind. The consequence of this shelter, combined with the colder eastern climate, is that windslab avalanches are common on days with spindrift (which are frequent). The buttresses are generally well defined with ridges up to the plateau and some provide safe options in dubious conditions, as long as they can be reached safely. Even gullies on the opposite side of the corrie to the recent or current wind may be safe. After a long cold spell, the buttresses may be heavily rimed, but they should still be possible, although determination and about twice the normal time may be required. As a general rule, don't have fixed ideas about choice of route, but go for the best conditions on the day. If powdery, climb a buttress; if icy, climb a gully. The season is long, often lasting from November to April.

Layout
The corrie has two different sectors. The southern sector, reached as soon as the Meikle Pap col is crossed, is a wide bay with a frieze of rock under the plateau. Further on there is a first aid box on a small terrace above the loch, from where routes can be identified and conditions assessed. For ready identification, a division of the buttresses into four natural groups has been made, the groups being divided by the three largest gullies. From left to right these are:
1. Central Buttress and the Shadow Buttress Group. Central Buttress is the left edge with Shadow Buttresses A and B up and right, bounded by the obvious Douglas-Gibson Gully, a straight-cut gash between high walls.
2. Eagle Ridge is immediately right of Douglas-Gibson Gully, then to its right are the Parallel Gullies (the narrow slit of Parallel Gully B is particularly distinctive) and finally the large and smooth Tough-Brown Face. Raeburn's Gully bounds this group but it is hidden from the first aid box by its slanting course, although its snow fan is obvious.
3. Black Spout Pinnacle ('The Pinnacle') is the slabby triangular face left of The Black Spout, unmistakable as a wide Grade I snow gully.
4. West Buttress forms the right-hand limit of the cliffs. The lower icefall of West Gully is often prominent near its right end.
   The following are grid bearings from the first aid box to major routes. It should be noted that all the direct approaches cross regular avalanche paths: Central Buttress (initial gully) 185 degrees; Shadow Buttress A, Original Route, 209 degrees; Parallel Gully A, 253 degrees; Raeburn's Gully, 273 degrees; The Black Spout, 281 degrees.

Access
The most common approach is from Glen Muick, which is reached from Ballater by 15km of motor road (sometimes blocked by snow in

winter) which ends at a large carpark at the Spittal of Glenmuick. From the carpark, walk through the wood past the visitor centre, turn immediately right and follow a private unsurfaced road across the valley to a T-junction beside an outbuilding of Allt-na-giubhsaich Lodge. A path follows a fence westwards into the wood from the southern end of this building. Take this path which leads through pine trees to join a bulldozed landrover track. This is followed all too obviously out of the pines and up the open hillside to the Muick-Gelder col. Here a well marked path branches off the track to the left and leads towards the mountain. At some point the path will disappear under snow and the easiest line through bouldery terrain will have to be chosen. Go over the col between Meikle Pap and the main mountain (Cuidhe Crom) to descend into the corrie. Descend leftwards until not far above the south-east corner of the loch, then climb slightly to the first aid box. Being very popular, there are often tracks in the snow and other parties to follow.

Descent

The normal winter descent from the summit plateau is to follow the cliff edge back to near the Meikle Pap col (beware of cornices). Returning from there to the Landrover track is surprisingly difficult in poor visibility without using a map and compass. In stormy weather, a foolproof but longer descent can be made *via* the Glas Allt and Loch Muick. From any point near the cliff top, head south (if at the top of West Buttress, beware of The Black Spout which cuts into the plateau). Gentle slopes soon lead into the upper basin of the Glas Allt, which leads to Loch Muick. To return to the corrie floor, descend The Black Spout. Either branch can be descended with care, but the main branch is recommended as the cornice is almost always easily passed on the left (looking down). It is also slightly less steep.

Central Buttress   300m   II *
S.R. Tewnion, J. Tewnion   January 1948

This is the easiest of the major buttresses and the first on the left; it gives a good introduction to Lochnagar-style mixed climbing. The slopes above the arete can avalanche and will funnel down Shallow Gully. Start up an introductory gully on the right which faces the first aid box. At its top traverse right as soon as possible and climb the crest to two gendarmes set on a level arete. From there take the easiest line to the plateau, usually *via* snow on the left. The route has ever-present easier ground on the left which can be used as an escape.

Shallow Gully   300m   IV,4
D.L. Macrae, F.G. Henderson   8th February 1959
The shallow depression between Central Buttress and Shadow Buttress A gives a good climb when in condition, but not being recessed, it fills up less readily than the major gullies. It rarely holds continuous ice, but would be easier in such conditions (although poorly protected). Difficulties are confined in the lowest 60m, after which snow leads to the upper slopes of Central Buttress (but since these avalanche, it is not a safe choice in doubtful snow conditions).

Shadow Buttress A, Original Route   300m   III,4 ***
W.D. Brooker, J.W. Morgan   27th December 1949
This first class mountaineering route is a good choice for strong parties in poor conditions. There is interesting route finding, sustained turf climbing and a short sharp crux. The buttress is recognised by its prominent curving band of snow (the Spiral Terrace) starting low down below large overhangs. Start in the bay below the large overhangs, climb towards them, then follow the Spiral Terrace round right underneath them. From its end continue trending right to a vague rib alongside Shadow Chimney. Climb the rib, including a steep section which is a notorious short crux which has recently been made more difficult by a rockfall (possibly Grade IV). It is worth noting that a single abseil from below the crux down Shadow Chimney gains the corrie floor. Go left and climb a shallow gully to regain the crest. Follow the crest to a small tower and pass it by a short descent on the right (climbed direct it is technical 5).

Giant's Head Chimney Direct   200m   V,5
D. Dinwoodie, N.D. Keir   12th February 1972
This fine route has an exposed technical mixed crux, but the rest is much easier. It is hidden from the first aid box behind Shadow Buttress A and starts at the same place as Polyphemus Gully. Start in the bay between Shadow Buttresses A and B. Shadow Chimney cuts into Shadow Buttress A; Giant's Head is the much more obvious chimney on its right. Climb the narrow lower chimney with one ice pitch, usually short, to a large overhang. Move out right to belay. Traverse left across the overhang (crux) to belay. Once in a blue moon this section can be climbed direct on ice. Enter the shallow upper chimney and follow it to a snow bowl. Now gain Giant's Head Arete on the right which leads to the crest of Shadow Buttress A and the top.

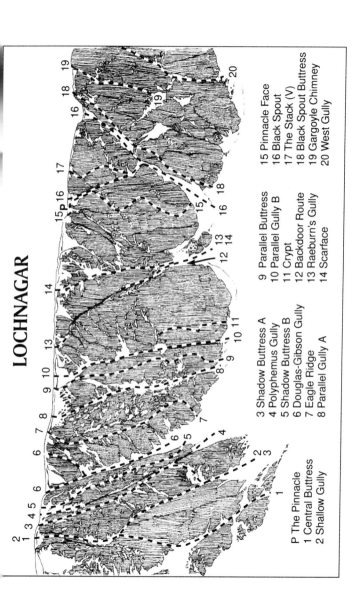

LOCHNAGAR

P The Pinnacle
1 Central Buttress
2 Shallow Gully

3 Shadow Buttress A
4 Polyphemus Gully
5 Shadow Buttress B
6 Douglas-Gibson Gully
7 Eagle Ridge
8 Parallel Gully A

9 Parallel Buttress
10 Parallel Gully B
11 Crypt
12 Backdoor Route
13 Raeburn's Gully
14 Scarface

15 Pinnacle Face
16 Black Spout
17 The Stack (V)
18 Black Spout Buttress
19 Gargoyle Chimney
20 West Gully

Giant's Head Chimney   220m   IV,4 *
W.D. Brooker, J.W. Morgan   29th January 1950
Another fine climb but graded for ideal conditions of thick ice on the
crux (this is not common; when lean, the grade is V,5). Climb the initial
chimney to the overhang and move right to belay as for the Direct.
Follow the terrace round the corner to the right into a trough. The initial
30m of the trough may contain much ice and in these conditions gives
a superb pitch. Higher up the trough becomes an easy snow scoop.
Here, more difficult climbing may be found by moving right on to the
'Feathered Arete' and following it to the plateau.

Polyphemus Gully   200m   V,5 ***
K. Grassick, H.S.M. Bates   24th January 1953
This excellent gully has good rock belays below the two hard pitches
and is a soft touch for the grade in good conditions. The lower pitch is
ice, then 60m of snow leads to a cave. Climb this direct on ice or, in
normal conditions, either by a little corner on the right or an obvious
V-groove on the left. The cornice is often huge, but it can usually be
outflanked by a traverse right onto Shadow Buttress B.

Shadow Buttress B   200m   IV or V **
A rewarding climb, typical of the best of the winter buttresses. A
technical lower section is followed by enjoyable climbing up the crest
via snow aretes and short steps leading to a steep finish and occasionally a tricky cornice. The difficulty depends on which of three starts
is chosen:
Bell's Route   V,6
T.W. Patey, A.O'F. Will   23rd January 1955
The traditional route is technically interesting but very hard for its old
Grade IV. Start just inside the foot of Douglas-Gibson Gully where a
grassy break leads left to the centre of the buttress. Go up a crack on
the right until two teeth are encountered below a vertical wall. From a
perch on the left tooth, traverse left (or flit across the blank wall) and
climb a groove to reach the easier upper section.
Original Route   IV,4
A. Bolton, C. Butterworth   5th March 1972
This is more consistent in standard but not so interesting. Start about
10m above Bell's Route and follow shallow turfy grooves for a long pitch
to the crest.

Raeburn's Groove   VI,7
D. Dinwoodie, A. Nisbet   19th January 1986
This is a fine line, but it is distinctly the hardest variation. Climb the obvious groove on the left edge of the buttress to where it ends under a steep wall. Traverse left beneath it and climb its left edge (crux). Go left again and climb a short groove to reach the crest.

Douglas-Gibson Gully   200m   V,4 **
T.W. Patey, G.B. Leslie   28th December 1950
The great gully between Shadow Buttress B and Eagle Ridge was the first attempted route on Lochnagar, in March 1893. It was finally 'conquered' (to use tabloidspeak) by a youthful and inexperienced Tom Patey. "When the ability to climb back down is lost, the only choice is to carry on." Although it has lost much of its original aura of impregnability, the gully still provides a fine and serious climb in impressive surroundings. It is perhaps unique among Lochnagar's major climbs in that it reserves all its defences for the final 60m, the last obstacle of which may be a huge unavoidable cornice. The choice of finish may be the smallest cornice. From the foot of the top wall, move left and climb grooves until it is possible to move left into an easier snow runnel leading to the cornice. In peak season the climbing will be easy, but the cornice may be impossible. In early season it may provide continuous ice but an easier cornice.
Alternative finishes:
Right Fork   V,5
This runs up the Eagle Ridge side of the top wall.
Central Fork   VI,5
Climb the icicle, then a take right-trending line.
Far Left Fork   V,5
A gully on the far left has a huge chokestone.

Eagle Ridge   250m   VI,6 ***
T.W. Patey, J.M. Taylor, W.D. Brooker   25th January 1953
This is the queen of Lochnagar's winter climbs, following the elegant ridge right of Douglas-Gibson Gully. The first ascent time of 4½ hours shows how advanced winter buttress climbing had become at the time. The grade is for free climbing in average conditions; a couple of points of aid, or the presence of good ice will make it considerably easier. The climbing is very sustained but well protected. Start just inside Douglas-

Gibson Gully and climb an obvious V-groove (hard, but it soon banks out). Follow a shallow gully bending right, then return left to the crest by a groove and climb a left-facing corner. Above is the Tower. Pull into a recess on the right (hard), then continue up steep rock and trend slightly left to gain a sentry box with relief! Follow the crest (approximately) until forced right to a short corner. Climb this to an airy knife edge, above which is a short vertical wall. Occasionally this builds up with snow, without which it is very hard (a peg is often used). Climb the crest to a projecting square-cut overhang. Traverse right across the wall and pull up to follow a corner slanting right to finish.

Parallel Gully A   270m   III ***
G.W. Ross, R. Still   28th March 1948
The initially shallow gully left of the obvious steep narrow slit of Parallel Gully B gives an extremely variable climb which may have several long ice pitches, or it may completely bank out into a snow chute. The direct first pitch may give 30m of sustained ice, but even if well banked it usually provides the crux. It can be avoided by a traverse from the left. Avoid a chimney above by going left on ice to a long stretch of snow leading past a minor gully on the right to a bifurcation. A rising traverse left gains entry to the left fork which is straightforward to the cornice, often bypassed on the left.
Right Fork   IV,4
A steeper and more direct finish.

Parallel Buttress   280m   VI,6 **
T.W. Patey, J. Smith, W.D. Brooker (4PA)   4th March 1956
The flat-fronted buttress between the Parallel gullies tapers to a ridge near the plateau. This is another sustained climb, but consolidated snow will considerably ease the difficulties. Start up a wide groove just right of Parallel Gully A. Above is a big groove (the variation start, harder). Move right into a defined chimney. Climb this, then slant right up two recessed corners to a big flake, from where easy ground slants left to an easing in angle. Go diagonally right up easy ground to the edge of Parallel Gully B. Gain a shelf overlooking the gully and climb it to its end. Move left onto the face and ascend a succession of turfy grooves to The Tower. Gain a small ledge up on the left, then climb the shallow groove above for 3m to a large jammed spike (crux, particularly under powder). Move left onto a sloping snow shelf and follow this until it is possible to return to the crest behind The Tower. A graceful snow arete leads to the plateau.

Parallel Gully B   280m   V,5 ***
J.R. Marshall, G. Tiso   22nd February 1958
An outstanding climb up the unmistakable narrow slit. The poaching of this last great problem by Jimmy Marshall persuaded Aberdonians (like Patey) of the advantages of crampons over tricounis. It is usually in condition late in the season after a big thaw and re-freeze has provided melting water from the big snow patches in its upper reaches. Normally start on the left to gain the chimney which is sustained but well protected. The middle section is usually easier but entry to the top pitch is blocked by a bulge, easier on the left side. If there is a huge cornice, possibly extending over Parallel Buttress, slant right from below the top pitch to the top of Tough Brown Ridge. Note that a huge rockfall in the summer of 1995 removed a vast slab from the buttress to the right of the gully. This may have affected the chimney, and dangerous debris may be lodged in the gully.

Crypt   80m   VI,7 **
B. Sprunt, A. Nisbet (1PA)   4th February 1979
R. Anderson, M. Hamilton (free, direct)   March 1980
The Tough-Brown Face is the steep smooth face right of Parallel Gully B. To the right of the huge rockfall scar, the most prominent feature is a pair of corners, slightly offset and one above the other, situated left of centre and trending slightly left towards the scoop above the chimney of Parallel Gully B. This is the line of Crypt, which requires good conditions to ice the corners, when it is at its best. Climb the grassy right-hand corner to exit left on a ledge (mixed; if ice comes this far down, it will form on the slabs to the left). Continue up a steep mossy section to the second corner, follow this to an overhang and pass it on the left. Descend leftwards down a terrace into Parallel Gully B. For convenience or to avoid an ascent to the plateau, either abseil twice down its chimney, or continue a descending traverse left across Parallel Buttress and Parallel Gully A.

Backdoor Route   220m   IV,4 *
T.W. Patey, A.O'F. Will, G. McLeod, A. Thom   20th March 1954
This fine natural line is relatively easy after the first pitch. Just right of the crest of Tough-Brown Ridge, a prominent groove system descends in a direct line to a point immediately below the bend in Raeburn's Gully. Start up a big corner, but after 10m traverse left, then go up and back right to gain its top (or climb it direct, harder). Follow the groove system above to reach the crest about 50m below the plateau.

Raeburn's Gully   200m   II ***
G.R. Symmers, A.W. Clark, W.A. Ewen   27th December 1932
This classic gully is arguably better early in the season when it has
much ice and is Grade III, but it fills quickly to leave only one ice pitch.
There is often a very large cornice which may require a steep traverse
to the top of Tough-Brown Ridge.

   Avalanche warning: There have been many accidents in Raeburn's
Gully caused either by climbers starting an avalanche or being hit by
one. The gully has a very large catchment area, including the corniced
rim of The Amphitheatre, and for this reason it is probably more prone
to avalanches than any other gully in the corrie.

Scarface   170m   V,4 *
D. Stuart, G.S. Strange   12th February 1972
This route starts on the right wall of Raeburn's Gully, just above the
bend, and climbs a shallow depression into a big amphitheatre. At
times, particularly towards the end of the season, or after a long thaw,
the depression becomes very icy. The best winter line (with the most
continuous ice) is usually the leftmost of three faults above The
Amphitheatre.

Pinnacle Face   250m   VI,7 **
K.A. Grassick, J. Light, A.G. Nicol (3PA)   16th January 1966
D. Dinwoodie, A. McIvor (FFA to plateau)   1974
This demanding route covers a fair area of The Pinnacle's lower slabs,
but only to take the easiest line, which is not always obvious. It is best
in icy conditions, when it will still have some short technical sections
although the line will be open to more variation. Occasionally it is very
icy and then much easier; in these conditions a direct line up The
Pinnacle should be possible (**Winter Face**).

   Start at the base of The Black Spout on the left wall where there is
an obvious 10m V-groove.
1. 35m   Climb the groove, then traverse left into a parallel line which
leads past a shallow chimney and cracks (or climb the parallel line
throughout).
2. 25m   Climb a few metres to a corner and pull onto the right-hand
slab. Work left up a slabby fault to a large grass stance.
3. etc. Climb turfy corners to a steep wall, traverse right and pass the
wall's right end into a groove which leads to Route One. Follow this to
the top.

Route One   200m   V,6 **
J. Smith, W.D. Brooker (1PA)   11th March 1956
Notable for a fine technical first pitch, this route finishes with spectacular situations over The Pinnacle (if it is still daylight!). With good conditions and correct route finding it will be Grade IV. Start on the left wall of The Black Spout above Pinnacle Face and a vertical groove in a steep smooth wall. Climb a prominent slabby ramp passing an overlap (easier with ice). About 3m above the overlap traverse left and gain The Springboard (a well named ledge) *via* a short wall. Go up ledges above, then traverse left into the left-most of three faults. Follow the fault out onto the front face. Here one can continue left but a better line goes up right, starting by a big flake to gain the crest at a point overlooking the fork in The Black Spout. A wall and an arete lead to the summit of The Pinnacle. Descend to the col above the Pinnacle gullies (often abseiled) and continue up to the plateau.

The Ice Ox   100m   IV,4 *
G. Livingston, A. Mathieson   24th December 1984
A good early season route up the big corner starting from the fork in The Black Spout and leading to the summit of The Pinnacle. **Twin Chimneys Route** (IV,5) has the same first pitch but moves onto the rib on the right up a steep chimney.

The Pinnacle (via Pinnacle Gully 2)   150m   II *
A.W. Clark, W.A. Ewen   28th December 1932
This entertaining day out has some tricky manoeuvres. Head up The Black Spout and its Left Branch. Pinnacle Gully 2 is the short prominent gully running up behind The Pinnacle. The chokestone can be difficult in lean conditions. From the col, descend slightly on the other side, climb a crack going right, then go round a corner onto slabs which lead to the top of The Pinnacle. Return to the col (possibly by abseil) and continue up to the plateau by a long but easy pitch.

The Black Spout   250m   I ***
J.H. Gibson, W. Douglas (Left Branch)   12th March 1893
A prominent feature with spectacular scenery, but set at an angle of only about 40 degrees it is easy for its grade, and rarely corniced enough to cause trouble. The left branch is 45 degrees, more prone to cornicing and very early in the season it can be steeper low down (over the chokestone). **Crumbling Cranny** is a steeper right branch, often easy but with a huge cornice (Grade II).

Black Spout Buttress   250m   III,5 **
J. Tewnion, C. Hutcheon, D.A. Sutherland, K. Winram   9th January 1949

A good winter route which follows the buttress on the right of The Black Spout. Start at a chimney-fault at the top of a grass slope about 10 metres right of The Black Spout. Climb this and continue to a level arete at half-height. Above the arete, a ridge of piled blocks leads to a deceptively difficult short chimney. Easy climbing leads to a 5m wall (crux), which is started in the centre and finished by an awkward corner on the right. Make a peculiar traverse right into the head of a flanking gully and return left to the crest as soon as possible.

Gargoyle Chimney   120m   IV,4
J.M. Taylor, W.D. Brooker   20th January 1952

The prominent thin chimney in the middle of the upper face right of Black Spout Buttress can give an excellent pitch of up to 30m of ice. Thereafter go up and left on snow to a sometimes difficult cornice.

West Gully   250m   IV,4 *
P. McIntyre, A. Nash   21st March 1948
A.F. Fyffe, M.D.Y. Mowat (Direct)   4th April 1966

The obvious big gully on the right side of the West Buttress leading down to a big icefall. The lower section soon ices up and provides an excellent introduction to steep ice climbing. The upper gully, although impressive, is relatively straightforward. At the top, the left branch is easy but the direct chimney is more sporting.

CREAG AN DUBH-LOCH
(Map Ref 234 824)

The Dubh Loch is set in a high secluded valley between the extensive White Mounth plateau to the north and the cone-topped plateau of Broad Cairn to the south. Creag an Dubh-loch is the huge Broad Cairn precipice guarding the loch. At more than 1km in length and 300m in vertical height, it is the biggest cliff in the Cairngorms.

The Dubh Loch is a lonely and intimidating place in winter, when the cliffs take on an impressive scale. But a visit will be memorable even if the easier option of a route on Eagles Rock is chosen.

Creag an Dubh-loch from the Dubh Loch   Photo: Brian Findlay

Weather and Conditions

In prime conditions this largely north-east facing cliff is one of the best and iciest in the Cairngorms. But with the cliff base at about 700m, Creag an Dubh-loch is less frequently in condition than the higher cliffs such as Lochnagar. Prediction of prime conditions has perplexed even the closest observers, but there are some reliable routes. Normally a long cold spell early in the season suggests good conditions. But a spell of very cold weather can freeze the springs at source while even a day's thaw can strip the cliffs bare. Deep powder in the valley is usually an indicator of poor conditions. An attempt has been made to choose the routes most liable to be icy, particularly the Hanging Garden area because ice also forms here later in the season, after heavy snow followed by thawing and freezing. The cliff is often a windy place, with less shelter than might be expected. The absence of big snow slopes means that avalanches are rarely a problem.

Layout

The cliff is split into two main sections by Central Gully, a very easy Grade I which provides access up and down. At the left-hand end is South-East Gully. Above and right of it, under the plateau, is the very steep Broad Terrace Wall. In the centre of this left section is the Hanging Garden, a 'White Spider' in winter, with several ice lines leading out from it. Between there and Central Gully are the long and smooth Central Slabs. Beyond Central Gully is the big slab face of the Central Gully Wall, facing the top end of the loch. Its top right extension is the steep tilting False Gully Wall which forms the left flank of the broken North-West Buttress which curves round to the right and out of sight. North-West Gully is tucked in there.

Access

Drive to the Spittal of Glenmuick carpark as for Lochnagar. Walk past the visitor centre, ignore the Lochnagar turn-off and continue on towards the south-east side of Loch Muick. Ignore the left fork to Glen Clova *via* the Capel Mounth path. Just before the loch, a small path leaves the road on the right and follows the shore across the valley. Cross the bridge and gain the road which follows the north-west shore of Loch Muick to Glas-allt-Shiel. From the head of the loch, continue up a good path to the Dubh Loch, which has a small path on either side. Occasionally it is possible to ski from the carpark, ideal for Nordic

Labyrinth Direct, Creag an Dubh-loch   *Climber: Greg Strange*
Photo: Brian Findlay

skis as it is long but gentle. Very occasionally, early in the season, one can cycle to Glas-allt-Shiel. There are possible approaches from Glen Clova or Glen Callater, but these are much longer.

Descent
There are easy descents at both ends of the cliff, or more steeply by Central Gully.

South-East Gully   200m   I **
W.A. Russell, M. Smith, W. Stephen.   26th January 1947
The left-slanting gully near the left end of the cliff is overhung by steep walls on the right. It is Grade II in lean conditions, but an ice pitch near the bottom banks out in mid-season, leaving a steeper section.

The Last Oasis   100m   VI,6 **
A. Nisbet, N. Spinks (2PA)   30th March 1980
D. Hawthorn, F.R. Malcolm (free, direct)   January 1993
A tremendous icefall forms left of the steepest section of Broad Terrace Wall (but alas, not very often). Start near the foot of South-East Gully and zigzag up to the left end of Broad Terrace, which is the snowy promenade under the steepest section of wall. Traverse left to the foot of the fault containing the icefall (Grade II, not included in the length). The icefall is slightly right-slanting but ends direct in 10m of vertical ice. An easier option is the original finish, which misses the vertical section on the left (mixed, 2PA, could be freed). Freddie Malcolm also made the first ascent of The Corridor, Etchachan, in 1954!

The Snow Desert (300m V,4) is a line of icy grooves and traverses working out left from The Last Oasis. It provides a good option after having second thoughts about The Last Oasis.

THE HANGING GARDEN
This sector provides reliable ice climbing, some of the best Grade V routes in the Cairngorms and a 'White Spider' atmosphere. Generally there is continuous ice, steep but less than vertical, but ice screws are required as rock cracks are limited. Access to Broad Terrace, the snowy promenade under the steepest section of wall, is as described for The Last Oasis, above. Traverse along The Terrace and enter The Hanging Garden. This is intricate Grade II so retreat would be difficult. A better and more direct approach in good conditions is the lower half of Labyrinth Direct (Grade III), and if its icefall is complete, The Aqueduct gives a lower tier of consistent standard.

CREAG AN DUBH-LOCH

1 South-East Gully
2 The Last Oasis
3 The Aqueduct
4 Bower Buttress

5 Hanging Garden Route (Left Fork)
6 Labyrinth Direct
7 Labyrinth Edge
8 White Elephant
9 Theseus Grooves

10 Central Gully
11 Sabre Cut
12 Vertigo Wall
13 North-West Gully

The Aqueduct   120m   V,4
J. Moreland, R.A. Smith   February 1975
In favourable conditions a steep icefall flows from The Hanging Garden directly over the lower tiered rocks. It is poorly protected.

Bower Buttress   150m   V,5 *
J. Bower, G.R. Simpson   March 1970
The buttress which forms the border between the right edge of the vertical Broad Terrace Wall and the left wall of the Hanging Garden area is good when icy, but it also provides a mixed option if the ice routes further right are out. Starting from The Hanging Garden, climb grooves slanting left to a big ledge, The Gallery. Follow ice-choked cracks trending slightly right to enter a shallow gully which leads to snow slopes under the cornice (avoided on the left). A harder line further left can be taken in good conditions above The Gallery. This is the finish of **The Sting**, a very steep and impressive icefall at the right end of Broad Terrace Wall (VII,6).

Yeti   140m   V,4 **
R.A. Smith, J. Moreland   February 1975
Between Bower Buttress and the prominent gully of Hanging Garden Route is an impressive set of slabby ramps. These can become sheathed in ice providing an exposed and serious route, sustained but not steep for the grade. In the lower section the icefall may split in two; either branch can be climbed. It is hard to predict whether Yeti or Hanging Garden Route will be in better condition; they certainly vary, so choose the better-looking line.

Hanging Garden Route (Left Fork)   150m   V,4 **
A. Nisbet, A. Robertson   6th January 1977
This is usually the first of the steeper ice routes to come into condition. It has a steeper section than Yeti, but it is less sustained. Follow the gully at the top of the Hanging Garden to an imposing triangular buttress which splits the route into its two forks. Continue up the groove until a steep wall forces a left traverse across an exposed iced slab to a difficult cornice. Occasionally, the cornice will force a traverse to Bower Buttress to finish. The right fork is often easier but with cornice problems.

Labyrinth Left-Hand   150m   V,5 *
D. Dinwoodie, A. Williams (1NA)   March 1979
G. Harper, A. Nisbet (FFA, as described)   24th February 1983
On the left side of Labyrinth Direct is a big roofed slab, often sheathed in ice. An icefall forms from this slab towards the right edge of the Garden. The exact line depends on the length of this icefall; its base is reached from the left. The slab can be gained without ice by a short hard overhanging cleft (1NA). Climb the slab for about 20m to a big corner running up left to a potentially big cornice. Continuing up the slab gains the upper reaches of the Direct.

Labyrinth Direct   300m   VII,6 ***
A.J. Bolton, P. Arnold   11th March 1972
An amazingly steep climb for the early days of front pointing, before wrist loops! It is probably in condition most winters, but not for long. The lower couloir (easy snow after an initial ice pitch) leads into the right edge of The Hanging Garden. The continuation is all too obvious, following a steep and poorly protected groove to a good belay on the right side of the *cul-de-sac* (if rock is visible). About 10m of near vertical and perhaps thin ice (crux) leads up the left wall. A steep groove continues for another 30m before the angle eases for the last 40m to the plateau. Perhaps not too hard for the grade, but the route has a serious feel.

Labyrinth Edge   300m   IV,5
W.D. Brooker, D. Duncan   10th February 1959
This route takes the vegetated left edge of The Central Slabs, not far right of Labyrinth Direct. It is a long route with increasing difficulty but it is possible in most conditions, although the chosen line may vary. Start up the grassy right bank of the Labyrinth Couloir (the Direct). Soon trend right, then climb grassy grooves to emerge below the left side of the upper tier of slabs (Sea of Slabs). Climb straight up these by a ribbon of grass-choked cracks and move left towards the Lower Tower, bypassed on the right. Continue up to The Fang, a rock tooth turned on the edge overlooking Labyrinth Direct. The Upper Tower lies above, and is passed on the right by a hidden chimney (crux). The finish is easier.

The White Elephant   300m   VII,6 *
N.D. Keir, D. Wright (Lower Tier)   February 1975
J. Anderson, A. Nisbet (Upper Tier)   31st March 1979
R. Anderson, R. Milne (Complete Ascent)   12th January 1980
A magnificent icefall, but the lower tier is reluctant to form and will be
thin at best. The upper tier can be gained by Labyrinth Edge (Grade
III) and climbed alone; this option is as good as the Hanging Garden
routes and at a similar grade (V,4). The upper tier forms in a left-curving
groove about 60 metres right of upper Labyrinth Edge. The lower tier
is a continuation, flowing down a shallow gully (**Dinosaur Gully**) and
hopefully over big overlaps near the base. In ideal conditions the grade
is VI,5.

Theseus Grooves   300m   III
J.T. Campbell, B.S. Findlay, G.R. Simpson, G.S. Strange
12th January 1969
Starting at the right end of the lowest rocks of the Central Slabs, a line
of grassy grooves and snow basins trends right onto Central Gully
Buttress. The first 10m is slabby but it is likely to be iced or banked
out. The rest is a fine narrow ice runnel or tedious wading in deep
ferns. There is minimal rock protection.

Central Gully Buttress   300m   II
T.W. Patey   March 1955
The easy-angled ridge bordering the left side of Central Gully. The crest
is straightforward but the first pitch, starting at the base of Central Gully,
will be tricky unless there is a good build-up.

Central Gully   300m   I ***
Miss McHardy, Miss Stewart   February 1933
This is the corridor running through the cliff, remarkable for its scale
and spectacular right wall. It is low-angled for the grade and the cornice
is usually avoidable on the left.

Sabre Cut   80m   IV,5
T.W. Patey, F.R. Malcolm   13th January 1957
On the right wall at the top of Central Gully is a short but very steep
section arrayed with sharp hanging aretes. Below this and separating
it from the main wall is a fault which fills with ice. Short and sharp.

Vertigo Wall   160m   VI,7 ***
A. Nisbet, A. Robertson (8PA)   3rd-4th December 1977
A. Cunningham, A. Nisbet (FFA)   November 1985
A truly mixed route with ice, turf and rock taking a stunningly exposed line out of Central Gully. A candidate for Scotland's best route, yet unrepeated free. Only the third pitch requires ice and it often holds enough. In the second half of the season the top wall receives sun and is stripped of snow. The route takes the huge recessed scoop below Sabre Cut. Start up from the true direct line where a grassy shelf leads right onto the face.
1. 30m   Traverse right onto the face and climb a turfy corner, then go up to a platform.
2. 35m   Move up right onto a big detached block, then go right and back left to climb a short hard section to stepped slabs which lead up right to a belay beside a chimney-icefall in the main corner line.
3. 30m   Climb the icefall until a line leads out right away from the steepest section. Return left above it and below a steep rock wall.
4. 25m   Climb the slab on the left to the impending headwall. Traverse right beyond a creaking flake into a shallow corner. Climb this steeply, traverse right again and pull up to belay.
5. 40m   The finish is easier but still steep.

North-West Gully   200m   II *
T.W. Patey, W.D. Brooker, J.M. Taylor, J.W. Morgan
29th December 1952
The obvious gully towards the right end of the cliff has a steep right wall, ice at the start and finish, but it is never steep. It is almost always climbable, but in lean conditions may be Grade III.

BROAD CAIRN BLUFFS

Funeral Fall   50m   IV,4 *
M. Freeman, N.D. Keir   3rd March 1974
The bluffs come into view on the left about 1km before the Dubh Loch on the approach from Loch Muick. This is a very prominent icefall on the left wall of an easy-angled snow gully, best seen when descending from the loch. It is a good climb for a short day, bad weather or change of plan, and also a good indicator of conditions on Creag an Dubh-loch.

EAGLES ROCK

These slabby rocks form a long discontinuous band of cliff set above 800m on the White Mounth escarpment, opposite Creag an Dubh-loch.

Weather and Conditions

The summer drainage lines ice up readily, so no snow is required. The routes face south so they are at their best early in the season after hard frosts; later on they can bank out and by late season they have melted. They provide a good alternative to the big cliff on the other side of the loch when ice or energy levels are low.

Layout

The most obvious feature is a big waterfall away to the left. Green Gully separates the Waterfall area from the rest of the crag. The Mid-West Buttress is the left-hand and largest of two zones of rock while the Mid-East Buttress is roughly triangular in shape and bounded by Diagonal Gully on the right. The smooth plaque of the Likely Story Slab is low down to the right of Diagonal Gully while the Plateau Buttress is high on the right and contains a prominent short icefall, **The Drool** (IV,4).

Access and Descent

Approach as for Creag an Dubh-loch. Descent is either well to the west of the Waterfall (easy), down Green Gully (usually easy Grade II) or, particularly for the Mid-East Buttress, down Diagonal Gully (Grade I).

The Waterfall   150m   II *
N.D. Keir, J. Taylor   2nd January 1974
Continuous low-angled ice forms to the left of the flow of water (only occasionally does it freeze completely). Escapes are available to the left.

Spectrum   110m   III **
D. Dinwoodie, J. Mothersele   1st December 1971
Climb the obvious line of corners and grooves right of the Waterfall and immediately right of black overhanging walls. The route is distinguished by the big groove near the top which gives a fine finish to a sustained climb on continuous water-ice (or finish more easily to the right).

Lethargy   120m   III *
J. Bower, G.R. Simpson   3rd January 1970
This is the obvious corner on the left of Mid-West Buttress. It has been graded for an early season ascent when it forms a continuous ribbon of ice, but it tends to bank out later. The Green Gully descent is immediately on the left. The direct finish (IV,5) is the prominent steep icefall above the corner.

Indolence   140m   III
A. Nisbet, A. Robertson   12th December 1976
The first groove line right of Lethargy forms a fine icefall, the best part of which does not bank out. A good combination very early in the season is the first pitch of Lethargy, an easy right traverse and the upper icefall of Indolence.

Sliver   150m   III
R.J. Archbold, G.S. Strange   15th December 1974
A fairly continuous line of water ice forms reliably between the Mid-East and Mid-West Buttresses.

GLEN CLOVA

Glen Clova provides easily accessible good winter climbing, particularly in the lower grades. Although the drive from the north and the west is long, it is a good option when conditions are poor in the higher Cairngorms and mild or stormy in the west. The two main corries are the Winter Corrie of Driesh and Corrie Fee on the north-east flank of Mayar.

DRIESH   947m   (Map Ref 272 736)

Winter Corrie is the obvious high corrie which overlooks the glen opposite Braedownie. Access is easy and obvious from the road.

The Waterfall   60m   II/III
Climb the icefall high on the left side of the face.

Central Gully   120m   II
This is the obvious deep gully right of The Waterfall and in the centre of the corrie.

Easy Gully   120m   I

The prominent straight gully has no difficulties and it provides a good approach to the summit of Driesh.

Right of Easy Gully is the highest section of cliff, Main Buttress. In its centre is a big snow patch, The Basin, where several of the routes meet.

Backdoor Gully   200m   II *

This gully cuts deeply behind Main Buttress, and slants right to emerge at the left side of The Basin. Either move left as soon as possible to reach easier ground or, usually easier, cross The Basin to its top right corner and finish up a gully on the right (near the finish of Diagonal Gully).

Direct Finish   80m   IV,4

Starting above the top left corner of The Basin, climb directly up ice steepenings in a gully to below The Deep Crack (an obvious feature). Traverse right, then go back left to climb the wall right of the crack. Continue slightly right to finish at the apparent summit.

Diagonal Gully   200m   III *

This is the most prominent feature of Main Buttress. In its centre is a 30m icefall coming from a right-sloping chimney; climb this to The Basin. From its top right-hand corner there is an easy finish on the right, often used by Backdoor Gully. Instead, climb the icefall above and continue until forced right to belay at a block. A chokestone chimney behind a pinnacle and right of the icefall is an alternative. Continue more easily to the top.

CORRIE FEE   *(Map Ref 255 745)*

This corrie is the finest in the glen for scenery and mountain atmosphere. It has two walls meeting at the Fee Burn waterfall at its head. The south wall extends inwards from the Shank of Drumfollow; the north wall from the headland of Craig Rennet. The south wall gives the best winter routes.

Descent

Gullies A and D are often used. In severe weather or white-out, follow a new fence south-east from the top of B Gully Chimney round to the Shank of Drumfollow, then descend the Kilbo path into the forest.

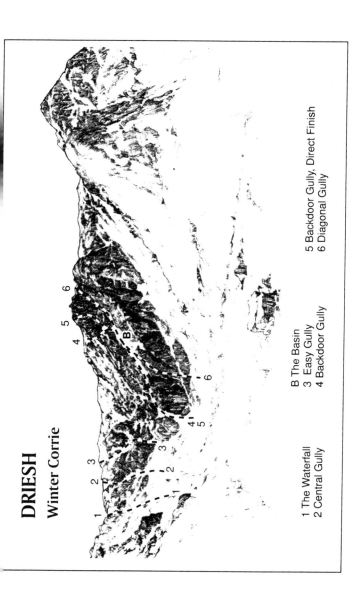

DRIESH
Winter Corrie

1 The Waterfall
2 Central Gully

B The Basin
3 Easy Gully
4 Backdoor Gully

5 Backdoor Gully, Direct Finish
6 Diagonal Gully

Layout
From left to right there are five gullies in the south wall; A, B, Look C, D and E. Most are well defined, but Look C is more of an icefall.

A Gully   200m   I
The gully on the left corner of the cliffs provides uniform snow slopes.

The deep-cut B Gully is the best defined of the gullies. About 60m up B Gully, B Gully Chimney breaches the left wall. B Gully Buttress is formed between the two; it culminates high up in a pinnacle with a great flake on the left shoulder at the top. The left branch of B Gully runs up to a col behind this pinnacle.

B Gully Chimney   150m   III,4 **
D. Crabb, D.F. Lang   29th December 1962
This good ice climb follows the chimney which breaks left out of B Gully. Some pitches bank out under heavy snow. It can be combined with Look C Gully; see below.

B Gully Buttress   150m   III
Climb the buttress direct from its base at the bottom of B Gully Chimney.

B Gully   200m   II *
H. Raeburn, W. Galbraith, W.A. Reid   May 1915
This gully generally contains at least one ice pitch, although it can be avoided by climbing up right. It is recommended by the left branch which is the obvious deep chimney high up which contains several chokestones.

Look C Gully   200m   IV,4 **
C.L. Donaldson, J.R. Marshall   15th February 1953
Probably the best route in the corrie, low in its grade, but it requires a good freeze to come into condition. The route follows the steep, shallow gully in the left section of the largest mass of rock, Central Buttress.
1.   Climb the left side up tiered ice to belay above a short chimney.
2.   Climb the left-hand gully line up into a basin, then ascend the rib on the right to belay below the main icefall.
3.   Climb the icefall direct, a classic pitch.
4.   Continue up short ice pitches to the gully bifurcation.

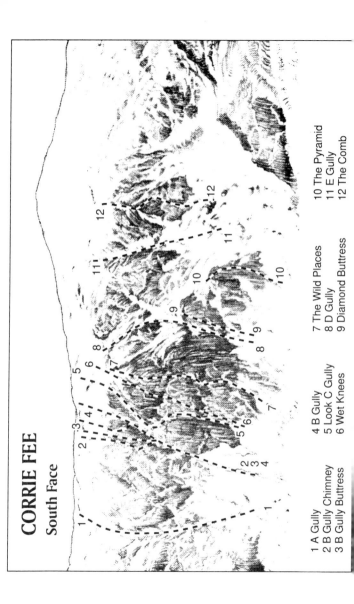

CORRIE FEE
South Face

1 A Gully
2 B Gully Chimney
3 B Gully Buttress

4 B Gully
5 Look C Gully
6 Wet Knees

7 The Wild Places
8 D Gully
9 Diamond Buttress

10 The Pyramid
11 E Gully
12 The Comb

The upper section of Look C Gully is easy-angled and uninteresting. By climbing the left fork and descending a small gully into B Gully, it can be combined with B Gully Chimney to give 200m of excellent and continuous climbing.

Wet Knees (200m IV,4) follows a direct but discontinuous line of chimneys breaching the steep rock bands immediately right of Look C Gully. Start up an ice smear at the base of Look C. The optional last chimney is the best.

The Wild Places (200m IV,4) follows a line of ice grooves leading to the obvious overhung niche in the centre of the face right of Look C Gully.

D Gully   200m   I
This gives a straightforward snow climb.

Diamond Buttress   60m   V,7
S. Stewart, B.A. Strachan   November 1985
On the right of D Gully are two pyramids; the upper and leftmost is the route, providing technical climbing. Start at an alcove on the right and climb a flake crack and a slab to a rib, then climb a groove to the top.

The Pyramid   60m   IV,5 *
A. Paul, G. Reilly, I. Reilly, W. Taylor   November 1975
This is the lower of the two pyramids.

E Gully   I
A short open runnel high up at the end of the face.

The Comb (60m IV,4) ascends the small isolated buttress high up on the extreme right of the face, just right of E Gully and some 300 metres left of the waterfall.

Ben Nevis and Lochaber

Fort William is the traditional base for Scottish winter climbing, largely because it is situated at the foot of Ben Nevis, whose icy North Face provides one extreme of the British mountain experience. Virtually the whole face can be plastered in ice to give the superb climbing so unique to Scotland. If this were the whole story, no-one would go anywhere else, but these wonderful conditions take a lot of production. A large amount of deep soft snow, which can sometimes last throughout January and February, followed by sleet and rain for which Fort William is well known, can ultimately bring perfect conditions later in the season. 'The Ben' in such good nick should not be missed, but with deep powder or rain, don't waste your time; save it for later.

Climbing here is steeped in history, from the epic ascents of the great ridges in the early days, through heroic attempts on Point Five Gully and Zero Gully in the fifties, Smith and Marshall's *blitzkreig* in the sixties, to the modern day playground. Here, step-cutting became such an obvious limitation that front-pointing and the use of curved picks produced an explosion of routes throughout the seventies, inspiring a revolution in Scottish ice climbing which has led to its international reputation.

Two days walking up The Ben taxes the legs, so most folk will seek a more accessible venue for alternate days. The obvious choice is Aonach Mor *via* the Gondola, and this recently developed mountain has rapidly become popular; Coire an Lochain is high and the routes are short. It also offers mixed climbing, particularly early in the season, for which the Ben is not well known. Glen Coe and Creag Meagaidh offer alternative options of a middle height range and about an hour's drive. With such a wide choice, it is easy to see why the Fort William area has become so popular; too popular for some, but information about conditions is more easily available.

Maps

The maps required for this area are the Ordnance Survey 1:50,000 Landranger Series, Sheet 41 for Ben Nevis and the Aonachs, and Sheet 34 for Creag Meagaidh. The Ordnance Survey Outdoor Leisure Mountain Master 1:25,000 Sheet 32 is probably the best map for Ben Nevis as it shows the summit at a scale of 1:10,000. Harveys publish two maps entitled Ben Nevis at scales of 1:40,000 and 1:25,000. The latter shows more detail of the crags and summit area of Ben Nevis.

BEN NEVIS
1344m   (Map Ref 166 712)

Ben Nevis is a mountain of superlatives. As the highest massif in the British Isles, with the tallest and most extensive cliffs, it attracts some of the most severe winter weather. This unique combination produces probably the best snow and ice climbing of its type in the world. Long recognised for its outstanding climbing, Ben Nevis is steeped in history, a crucible where influential climbers of past and present decades have forced new standards and techniques.

The sheer number of quality winter climbs, in all grades, is unequalled anywhere else in Scotland. Some have gained justified international recognition. Proximity to the western seaboard results in large and frequent variations in temperature which, coupled with high precipitation, leaves even the steepest faces plastered white. Deep thaw followed by rapid freeze transforms the hoar and powder to climbable neve, with runnels of white ice filling the grooves and cracks. Such conditions allow exhilarating climbing on very steep ground, and the consequent lack of easily accessible protection adds bite to the experience. In good conditions of plenty of ice, some of the descriptions may seem unnecessarily detailed. If you look up and see ice everywhere, simply choose the easiest line and feel pleased; this book may have fulfilled its role.

The Ben provides a wide variation in style of climbing. There are the snow and ice gully climbs, some straightforward, others complicated by bulges or long pitches on hard ice. These contrast to the face routes which are often long, bold and exposed, and much dependent on conditions and exact choice of line. Then there are the icefalls, some sweeping down unlikely walls of almost vertical rock. Finally there are the buttresses, not only the classic ridges (which are without equal in Britain), but also mixed climbs in the modern idiom, snowed up rock routes with high technical difficulty. This feast of opportunities provides climbs of all styles at all grades, but if you just feel like a walk, the traverse of the Carn Mor Dearg Arete gives a stupendous view of it all.

Opposite: The great ridges of Ben Nevis above the C.I.C. Hut
Photo: John Lyall

Next page: Astral Highway on the Orion Face   Climber: Neil Marshall
Photo: David Ritchie

Weather and Conditions

Records show that it can snow at any time of year on the summit plateau of Ben Nevis. However, good winter climbing conditions usually appear only from around early January onwards, and only then in the classic gullies. Unlike the Cairngorms or some of the crags on the nearby Aonachs, there is insufficient turf on the volcanic rocks to provide much early season climbing. The face climbs which require freeze-thaw may take until mid-February, or later. The ridges, however, can give enjoyable struggles on rocks plastered with powder as early as October. It is pertinent that the altitude of the foot of the Orion Face is higher than the summits of most other Scottish mountains, and that the whole of Indicator Wall and Gardyloo Buttress lies above 1200m. The commonest month for these latter faces to be in good condition is April. Once the major ice lines have formed, they are very resistant to thaw and some high routes may remain in good condition into May. In contrast, some of the lower routes, particularly the ice smears around Carn Dearg Buttress, require prolonged periods of frost to form, are most often in condition in January or February and they disappear very rapidly during a thaw.

Often the weather should be the deciding factor whether to visit the Ben. Once into mid-season, there will normally be a suitable route in condition somewhere on the mountain, provided the weather is not too stormy and the temperature is below zero. Walking in with a specific target should be reserved for those with local knowledge. Unless the wind is easterly, you will be lucky to have a view from the top. The commonest pattern is that January is stormy from the west (go elsewhere), February has high pressure over Scandinavia with easterly winds over Scotland (go for the classic gullies or lower ice routes), March is often stormy from the west with brief lulls (anything is possible if you're quick!) and April is settling down but warming up (the high faces are in their best condition, but start very early).

The Ben is not a good choice if avalanches threaten, as there are no safe routes. Clearly some will be safer than others but folk have even been killed by a huge avalanche while walking up the Allt a' Mhuilinn. Despite the justified notoriety of the Castle Area, Observatory Gully is perhaps the commonest site for avalanches, but the upper part of Coire na Ciste is also bad and snow conditions should be monitored on

Previous page: The Eastern Traverse, Tower Ridge   Climber: John Mackenzie
Photo: Steve Green
Opposite: The Great Tower from Observatory Buttress   Photo: John Lyall

approach. It is also worth mentioning that the approach slopes here are of a scale not found elsewhere in Scotland, and a slip is likely to be disastrous. It is best to don crampons and helmet, and get out both axes, soon after passing the C.I.C. Hut.

Troubleshooting Summary

The following is a brief list of suggestions on what to do when the weather or conditions are poorer than expected, or if big thaws have stripped most of Scotland, and the Ben is the last hope:

Poor weather or poor conditions options:

Go for routes at a lower level which avoid the summit plateau, but even these may be threatened by avalanche. Slingsby's Chimney; Green Hollow Route; Douglas Boulder and Douglas Gap West Gully; Vanishing Gully; Moonlight Gully Buttress (see Moonlight Gully); The Curtain.

In late season or after a big thaw and refreeze:

Go high! The classic ridges are dependable, although their lower halves may be snow-free (Alpine conditions); Observatory Buttress; Tower Scoop; Good Friday Climb; Indicator Wall; Smith's Route; the easier gullies, assuming safe cornices; the area around Raeburn's Easy Route; Number Three Gully Buttress area; Creag Coire na Ciste, although there may be huge cornices in late season.

Layout

Ben Nevis is situated 7km east-south-east of Fort William and has two subsidiary tops forming the massive bulk of the mountain and its extensive and wild summit plateau. The western and southern aspects of the mountain, overlooking Glen Nevis, consist of steep grass slopes and broken crags cut by long gullies. By contrast, the north-east face falls abruptly from the plateau to present a complex and magnificent series of cliffs overlooking the upper part of the Allt a' Mhuilinn glen. It is the most impressive and continuous mountain cliff in the British Isles, being over 3km in extent and reaching a height of 500m. The scale is so huge that it can be difficult to appreciate, particularly on first acquaintance.

The face can be divided conveniently into four sectors by Carn Dearg Buttress (with its vertical rock face), Tower Ridge (just above the C.I.C. Hut) and North-East Buttress (the skyline buttress), each of which descends low towards the approach:

1. Right of (below) Carn Dearg Buttress is the Castle Ridge and Castle Gullies area.

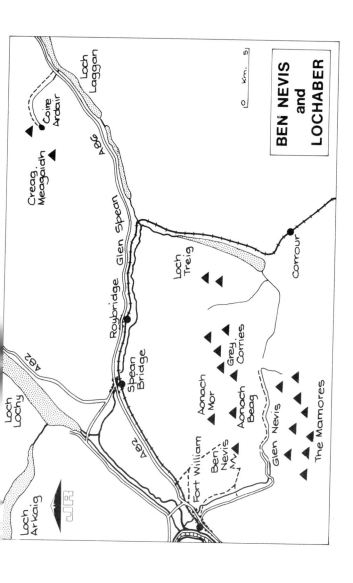

2. Between Carn Dearg Buttress and Tower Ridge are (from right to left) Number Five and Number Four Gullies, Creag Coire na Ciste, Number Three Gully, The Comb and Number Two Gully.

3. Between Tower Ridge and North-East Buttress is the massive slope of Observatory Gully, with Tower and Gardyloo Gullies at its head. Observatory Ridge descends part way down the slope, flanked by Point Five and Zero Gullies. Left again is the huge Orion Face.

4. Beyond North-East Buttress and unseen from the approach are Coire Leis and the Little Brenva Face.

Access

Approaches to the climbs on the north-east face of Ben Nevis all aim initially for the C.I.C. Hut (Map Ref 167 723), which is situated at 670m below The Douglas Boulder at the foot of Tower Ridge. The exceptions are the Castle Ridge and Castle Gullies area, where one should turn off rightwards below the Hut. The Hut is privately owned by the Scottish Mountaineering Club, but its walls afford a little shelter and a convenient place for refreshment and gearing up. There are three possible approaches to the Hut from the valley:

1. The Glen Nevis Approach via the Tourist Track:

Leave Fort William to the north, turn right into Glen Nevis and drive to the Youth Hostel (Map Ref 128 718). Arrive early to secure a parking spot. Cross the River Nevis by a footbridge and zigzag up steeply to join the track which traverses along the hillside. This point can be reached by a longer but more gentle approach which starts from Achintee Farm (Map Ref 126 730). Follow the track to the broad col between Meall an t-Suidhe and Carn Dearg. Leave the track above Lochan Meall an t-Suidhe (Halfway Lochan) and continue northwards, keeping almost level to the far slopes of the col. Here a path can be found which, after descending 30m, bears north-east to contour under the North Wall of Carn Dearg. The Hut is located some way beyond at a height of 670m, close to the Allt a' Mhuilinn, just above its junction with the burn from Lochan na Ciste (allow 2 to 2½ hours). The biggest advantage of this approach is the ease of the descent down the Tourist Path.

2. The Distillery Approach:

Start from the distillery near Victoria Bridge on the A82 (Map Ref 124 756). Walk through the premises of the distillery and cross the main railway line, where a well defined track leads to the line of a disused narrow gauge railway. Follow this to the left for a few hundred metres, cross a small bridge and climb eastwards up the slope on the right to reach the Allt a' Mhuilinn at a small dam (Map Ref 147 751). Cross the burn and follow the boggy track on its east bank to reach the Hut. Excellent views of the cliffs are obtained on this approach (1½ to 2 hours).

3. Golf Club Approach:
This is the shortest approach, but it may be necessary to park a few hundred metres before the Golf Club (Map Ref 136 762) unless the current restrictions are lifted. From the Golf Club carpark, walk under the main railway line, then go south-east across the golf course, taking care to keep off the greens, to reach a good path which keeps fairly close to the left side of the burn and is always to the right of a deer fence which rises straight up the hillside. At the time of writing, all identification features at the foot of this path seem to have been removed (although it is marked on the map), but once found, the way is obvious. The path leads to the dam where the distillery approach comes in from the right. Continue up the north-east bank of the Allt a' Mhuilinn to the Hut (1½ to 2 hours).

From the C.I.C. Hut to the Climbs
It should be realised that it may take over an hour to reach the foot of some routes from the C.I.C. Hut, and longer for Gardyloo Buttress and Indicator Wall, which are another 400m higher.
1. The approach to Coire Leis continues up the valley on a faint path.
2. Observatory Gully and Tower Ridge are reached by heading diagonally up the hillside.
3. For Coire na Ciste, go over the domed rock west of the Hut, then negotiate a short vegetated wall at the foot of the main corrie. The approach to the buttresses in the region of Number Five Gully, and Carn Dearg Buttress, starts up towards Coire na Ciste, then heads diagonally right below the short vegetated wall.
4. Castle Ridge, the Castle Gullies and the North Wall of Carn Dearg are all easily reached from the foot of Carn Dearg Buttress.

Descents
A navigation plan to the Tourist Path should be made before starting on a route in poor weather. A sensible decision is difficult if you arrive on the plateau in a storm, barely able to stand up or open your eyes. In poor weather, leave the rope on. It will only stop you falling over a cornice if your ropework is competent (apply techniques similar to

BEN NEVIS

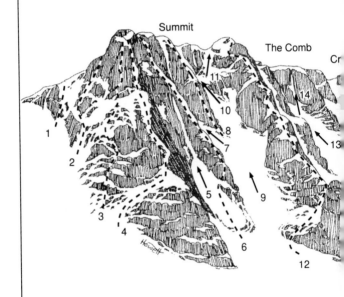

1 Bob Run
2 Cresta
3 Route Major
4 North-East Buttress
5 Zero Gully
6 Observatory Ridge

7 Point Five Gully
8 Observatory Buttress
9 Observatory Gully
10 Gardyloo Gully
11 Tower Gully

The North-East Face

re na Ciste

The Trident

Carn Dearg

The Castle

C.I.C. Hut

12 Tower Ridge
13 Number Two Gully
14 Comb Gully
15 Number Three Gully
16 Number Four Gully

17 Moonlight Gully
18 Number Five Gully
19 Ledge Route
20 South Castle Gully
21 North Castle Gully
22 Castle Ridge

Alpine glacier crossings), but at least it keeps the party in touch. The summit plateau is a large area with two main tops (the summit and Carn Dearg) linked by gentle slopes, but it is bounded to the north by the cliffs and to the south by endless craggy ground which plummets into Glen Nevis. The only easy route off the plateau is taken by the Tourist Track, sandwiched between Five Finger Gully and the Red Burn. This conspires to make descent from the climbs a tricky business and many accidents have occurred in descent; a detailed map of the summit plateau and the descent route is shown opposite. A good idea of the configuration of the mountain can be gained from the diagram; put a transparsealed copy in each pocket and remember that in the worst weather you won't be able to read it! Seriously, the most useful map is the O.S. Outdoor Leisure 32, Mountainmaster 1:25000, which has an enlarged 1:10000 detailed plan of the summit plateau.

Many routes finish near the summit and the best option may be to go there first. This particularly applies to the section to the east (near North-East Buttress and up to Point Five Gully). In a hard winter, the summit cairn and triangulation point can be completely buried by snow. However, the ruined Observatory, a few metres from the summit, is an unmistakable landmark, and it is topped by a survival shelter which can be used in an emergency.

Descent Routes
1. The Tourist Path and the Red Burn.
This is the safest and easiest descent. From the summit follow a bearing of 231 degrees grid for 150 metres (to a point just left of Gardyloo Gully), then continue downhill on a bearing of 282 degrees grid to reach the Tourist Track and the Red Burn area (after 800 metres). Continue on the same bearing down an easy slope for about 1km, then turn north towards Lochan Meall an t-Suidhe. From there descend the Tourist Track to Glen Nevis, or contour round and descend to the Allt a'Mhuilinn. It is essential to follow the bearings carefully, as there have been many accidents on this route in the vicinity of Five Finger Gully, when parties have headed towards Glen Nevis too early. The exact line of the Red Burn itself should be avoided in dubious conditions, as it can avalanche.

If completing a climb away from the summit area and the cornice edge is not visible (normal in the worst weather), then a modified version of navigation from the summit will be required. This involves a bearing directly away from the cliff edge for a short distance until the standard 282 degrees grid can be followed. The away leg will be between 50

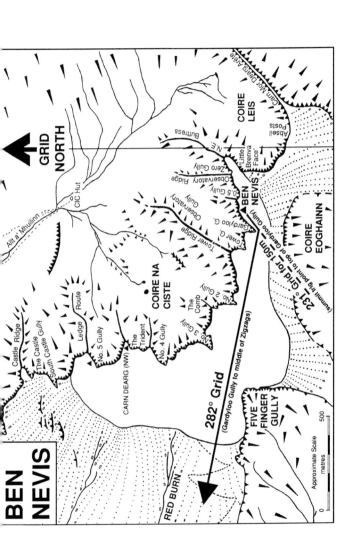

metres and 150 metres on a bearing of 220 grid (close to south-west, away from the north-east facing cliff). The diagram of the plateau will help on choice of distance. From the top of Number Two or Number Three Gullies, a direct 282 degrees is correct (these gullies cut in furthest). From Number Four Gully, 270 degrees grid leads directly to the Tourist Path. The top of Number Four Gully has a marker post, and it is also just at the point where the ground starts rising again towards Carn Dearg.

2. Number Four Gully.

This descent is commonly used by those returning to the C.I.C. Hut or the Allt a' Mhuilinn. Follow the line of the plateau, but only if the corniced edge can be distinguished, and remembering that Gardyloo and Tower Gullies are deeply incut, to reach the top of Number Four Gully. This is marked by a metal indicator post (Map Ref 158 717). Descend the gully into Coire na Ciste. Sometimes the cornice is impassable, but it may be possible to gain the gully by descending steeper ground immediately to the north, or by abseiling from a bollard or even the marker post (but two ropes are required). For a change of plan, descend by the Tourist Path (270 degrees from the top of Number Four Gully) and contour round into the Allt a' Mhuilinn from Lochan Meall an t-Suidhe.

3. The Carn Mor Dearg Arete.

Although this descent is the fastest means of losing height from the summit, it should only be used with care. There have been many fatalities to parties who have strayed too far north (left) from the summit, and the slopes leading down into Coire Leis from the arete itself are steep and often icy. It is not recommended in bad visibility and is therefore not described.

The climbs are described from left to right, starting with the Little Brenva Face.

COIRE LEIS

Coire Leis lies at the head of the Allt a' Mhuilinn under the crescent-shaped Carn Mor Dearg Arete, the well defined ridge extending from Carn Mor Dearg to Ben Nevis. There is a small emergency shelter on the floor of the corrie at Map Ref 173 714. It is often covered by snow in winter, so in an emergency it would be preferable to head for the C.I.C. Hut. Between the Carn Mor Dearg Arete and the east flank of North-East Buttress lies The Little Brenva Face, so-named due to its open Alpine character.

THE LITTLE BRENVA FACE

The climbs here are not technically hard, but they are generally long and, if visibility is poor, route finding may be difficult, with the routes open to variation. The face is exposed to the sun so there is a risk of falling ice in mid to late season. A good view of the face is obtained well back, so approach up the opposite side of the corrie, well away from the foot of North-East Buttress.

Bob Run   120m   II
I.S. Clough, H. Fisher, B. Small, D. Pipes, J. Porter, F. Jones
10th February 1959
The leftmost gully on the face is its easiest route, often banked up with snow. Climb easy-angled ice for 30m, then continue up snow to the bifurcation (30m). Either fork can be taken; each contains a short ice pitch. Finish up snow.

Cresta   275m   III **
T.W. Patey, L.S. Lovat, A.G. Nicol   *16th February 1957*
M. Slesser, N. Tennant (Direct Finish)   *18th February 1957*
This popular route is a climb of great character, and was the original route on the face. It follows a hanging snow gully which in its lower reaches ends at a rocky spur after 90m. Start well right of this spur and climb a left-slanting ice shelf for 75m to gain a small gully which runs up the right side of the rocky spur. Continue up the snow gully above for 185m to a large ice pitch, traverse right across steep rocks for 30m, then break through to easy ground above. **The Direct Finish** (IV,4) climbs straight up through the exit cliffs.

Route Major   300m   IV,3 **
I.S. Clough, H. MacInnes   *16th February 1969*
A fine and sustained mountaineering route with difficult route-finding, best climbed in good conditions. Start slightly left of the approach ramp to North-East Buttress and climb mixed ground to the top right corner of a large snowfield. Go diagonally right towards a rocky spur, then stay left of the spur (**Frostbite**, Grade III, crosses it and follows a shallow gully beyond) and follow a left-slanting gangway, broken by an awkward corner, into a snow bay (a distinctive feature high up on the face). Break out right to snow shelves near North-East Buttress, and follow these horizontally left for a short distance to reach a groove which leads to the upper slopes.

NORTH-EAST BUTTRESS

North-East Buttress, the first of the great ridges of Ben Nevis, extends east-north-east from near the summit cairn and divides Coire Leis from Observatory Gully. The lower rocks of the front face of North-East Buttress form a subsidiary buttress topped by the First Platform. Above this, the crest of the buttress rises in a great sweep to the summit plateau.

North-East Buttress   300m   IV,4 ***
W.W. Naismith, W. Brunskill, A.B.W. Kennedy, W.W. King, F.C. Squance   3rd April 1896
This varied route is quite simply one of the finest mountaineering expeditions in the country. Depending on conditions, all degrees of difficulty may be found, with success in the balance until past the Mantrap. The start of the climb proper can be reached from Coire Leis by a steep snow traverse right to the First Platform above the lowest buttress, or by an ascent of Slingsby's Chimney. After the First Platform the route takes the easiest line. Follow the easy ridge to a steepening of the buttress. Turn this by a shallow gully slanting up to the left, then trend right and left by steps and grooves to reach a snowfield on the left side of the ridge (90m). This is the Second Platform, which can also be reached by a ledge and gully on the right of the steepening. Climb the Second Platform snowfield easily to its top, where the way is barred by an overhanging wall. Turn this on the right by a corner and large step, and follow the ridge above to the notorious Mantrap. This can be extremely awkward when thinly iced, but it is short and well protected. Directly above, climb the '40ft corner' (or avoid it on the left by a small gully) to reach the summit snows. The Mantrap can be avoided on the right by taking the Tough-Brown Variant, stepping down and moving right into a groove which leads up to the foot of the '40ft corner'.

Slingsby's Chimney   125m   II
C. Donaldson, J. Russell   April 1950
Bounding the right side of the lower buttress of North-East Buttress and facing the C.I.C. Hut, this obvious gully provides an easy outing for a short day if combined with descent by the North-East Buttress approach ledge. However, it is often climbed as an alternative start to North-East Buttress. The lower gully gives a straightforward ascent on steep snow. The easiest line trends left where the gully fans out. If the top section is not snow-covered, it is a sustained mixed pitch (Grade III).

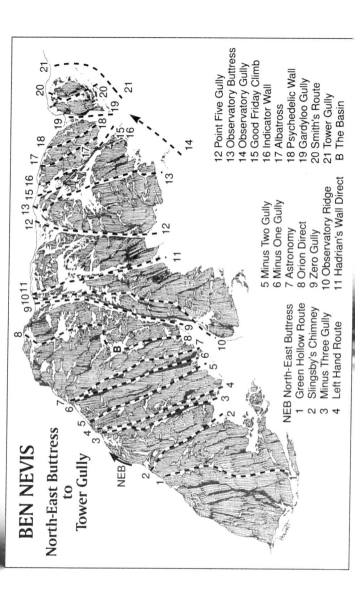

BEN NEVIS
North-East Buttress to Tower Gully

NEB North-East Buttress
1 Green Hollow Route
2 Slingsby's Chimney
3 Minus Three Gully
4 Left Hand Route

5 Minus Two Gully
6 Minus One Gully
7 Astronomy
8 Orion Direct
9 Zero Gully
10 Observatory Ridge
11 Hadrian's Wall Direct

12 Point Five Gully
13 Observatory Buttress
14 Observatory Gully
15 Good Friday Climb
16 Indicator Wall
17 Albatross
18 Psychedelic Wall
19 Gardyloo Gully
20 Smith's Route
21 Tower Gully
B The Basin

Green Hollow Route   200m   IV,4
J.R. Marshall, J. Moriarty   February 1965
A route which provides a good low level option on the buttress left of
Slingsby's Chimney. There are several similar options on the buttress.
Start at the lowest rocks and work diagonally rightwards to grooves,
from where one can exit rightwards into the Green Hollow (poorly
named for winter, as it becomes a snow-filled bay). Gain the arete on
the left and follow it to the First Platform.

OBSERVATORY GULLY

Contained within this broad amphitheatre are some of the finest and
most famous winter climbs in Scotland.

THE MINUS FACE
The Minus Face is the impressive wall of slabby buttresses and long
gullies between Slingsby's Chimney on the left and Minus One Gully
on the right. Minus Three Buttress is the shortest buttress immediately
right of Slingsby's Chimney, and is flanked on its right by Minus Three
Gully, which has an overhanging right wall. Minus Two Buttress is easily
identified by the huge undercut nose at about one-third height, and the
gully to the right is Minus Two Gully. Minus One Buttress is the slim
buttress between Minus Two Gully and the deeply-cut Minus One Gully.
All the routes finish on North-East Buttress (below the Mantrap), which
can be descended (at least Grade II) or followed to the summit.

Minus Three Gully   150m   IV,5 **
R. Smith, J.R. Marshall   7th February 1960
The shallow gully close under the left flank of Minus Two Buttress is
one of the best gully climbs of its grade on the mountain. The right wall
is overhung, but it is possible to escape leftwards at several points to
more broken ground. It comes into condition less readily than Minus
Two and Minus One Gullies. Climb to a deep cave (30m). Exit by a short
icicle on the left (crux) to gain a groove. The groove leads to easier
mixed climbing just below the crest of North-East Buttress.

Left-Hand Route (Minus Two Buttress)   275m   VI,6 **
S. Docherty, N. Muir (1PA)   30th January 1972
The big left-facing corner system on the left of Minus Two Buttress
gives a fine winter line up thinly iced slabs which require a delicate

touch. Climb the big corner on the right of Minus Three Gully (thin ice) until level with the overhangs on the right. Continue up the slab above, finding the best ice, until the difficulty eases below the crest of North-East Buttress.

Minus Two Gully   275m   V,5 ***
J.R. Marshall, J. Stenhouse, D. Haston   11th February 1959
A magnificent and classic climb - one of the finest of the Nevis gullies. Climb steep snow and ice to an overhang (45m) Turn the overhang by traversing left to enter the main chimney line. It is possible to avoid the left traverse by continuing directly over steep iced mixed ground, then stepping into the gully higher up (harder). Above is a steep ice pitch; turn this on the left, then continue more easily to where the gully forks. Climb the easy-angled chimney on the left, or make a difficult step right to finish up the right-hand chimney.

Minus One Gully   275m   VI,6 ***
K.V. Crocket, C. Stead   23rd February 1974
Another magnificent climb, the hardest of the Nevis gullies. It is not often in condition and consequently it is a much prized route. The conspicuous overhang at one-third height is the crux. Enter the gully and climb easily to an awkward ice wall which leads to a cave below the overhang. Turn this on the left, then regain the gully above. Continue up steep ice followed by a fine corner to reach a snow bay (The Meadow). A choice of two snowy grooves lies above. Either may be climbed, but the right-hand one is the more natural line. It leads to a groove which bears left to the final arete of Minus One Buttress.

THE ORION FACE

Shaped like an inverted wedge, the Orion Face fans out from Minus One Gully on the left to Zero Gully on the right. The depression in the centre of the face is known as The Basin. It holds snow well into summer, and is a place of intersection for many routes on the face. The name Orion is derived from a fancied resemblance of the original routes on the face to the configuration of the stars in the constellation Orion, with The Basin corresponding to Orion's belt. The short narrow chimney at the back left-hand corner of The Basin is Epsilon Chimney. This chimney, followed by a left-slanting line, gives the easiest exit from The Basin, and is also the best line for escape from the face in winter conditions (Grade IV,4).

Astronomy   300m   VI,5 ***
A. Fyffe, H. MacInnes, K. Spence (1PA)   March 1971
This first class winter route up the buttress right of Minus One Gully is never particularly hard, but it requires a good plastering of snow and ice, usually forming later in the season. Start just right of the toe of the buttress, immediately right of Minus One Gully. Climb up to twin cracks and onto sloping snow shelves slanting leftwards to a small snow bay. Climb up right by grooves to a large left-facing corner (the left-bounding corner of the Great Slab Rib). Follow the corner and exit right by a wide, shallow flake-chimney above the Great Slab Rib. Climb a thinly iced groove, then trend back left by walls and grooves until under the steep upper rocks near the top of the buttress. Make a short descent into the steep chimney at the top of Minus One Gully and climb this to the top.
Direct Finish   120m   VI,5
C. Fraser, M. Thompson   16th February 1986
This is a better finish, but less often in condition. At the top of the thinly iced groove trend slightly right to a belay below the steep upper section. Gain the crest on the right, then continue up an iced slab trending right to reach a fine ice groove near the crest of the buttress. Follow this steeply to an easier arete which leads to North-East Buttress.

Orion Direct   400m   V,5 ***
J.R. Marshall, R. Smith   13th February 1960
One of the finest winter climbs in Scotland, with all the atmosphere of a major Alpine face. The route is sustained, open, and exposed, but in good conditions is nowhere technically difficult, although both belays and runners can be hard to find (V,4). Start left of Zero Gully, where a broad ledge leads to the foot of a prominent chimney line leading up towards The Basin. Climb the chimney for two long pitches until a rising traverse leads left into The Basin. Traverse right across snow into a groove beside the Second Slab Rib, an obvious feature just right of The Basin. Descend a little, move round the right side of the rib, then climb up to and across a steep icy wall on the right (crux). Above, follow left-trending snow and ice grooves to the snow slope under the final tower. This is usually climbed by a steep icy chimney on the left to reach the plateau at the top of North-East Buttress. If conditions are poor on the upper section, it may be necessary to make a long traverse to the right in order to find a feasible route to the plateau.
Direct Start   75m   V,5
S. Docherty, N. Muir   March 1971
Steeper and more sustained than the original route. In good conditions a line of icy grooves forms on the front of the buttress between Orion

Direct and Zero Gully. Start just left of Slav Route and climb the grooves to reach The Basin in two pitches.

Astral Highway   240m   VI,5 **
C. Higgins, A. Kimber   28th December 1976
This excellent ice route takes a direct exit from The Basin up the steep line of grooves right of Epsilon Chimney. It is often in condition and is quite popular. Follow Orion Direct to The Basin and climb a shallow groove which trends left to the main groove line a few metres right of Epsilon Chimney. Climb the main groove over bulges (crux), then continue by grooves on the right to exit on the crest of North-East Buttress above the 40ft Corner.

Slav Route   420m   VI,5 **
D.F. Lang, N.W. Quinn   23rd March 1974
This is one of the longest winter climbs of its standard in Scotland. It climbs a somewhat featureless section of cliff; in very snowy conditions it can be technically straightforward but very lonely for the leader who might not find runners or rock belays for long sections. Indeed, the grade could be VI,4 apart from the optional lower icefall. Climb a groove immediately left of Zero Gully, then move up right into an iced groove to belay below a steep icefall (50m). Climb the icefall (crux), or avoid it on the left (easier), then continue up grooves to a snowfield (50m). Move up and right and belay below a snow arete overlooking Zero Gully (50m). Continue by steps and grooves for four long pitches, keeping close to but left of Zero Gully, to emerge on a snow slope below a wide square-cut chimney immediately right of a steep buttress. Trend right initially, then finish by corners on the left to emerge at the top of North-East Buttress.

Zero Gully   300m   V,4 **
H. MacInnes, A.G. Nicol, T.W. Patey   18th February 1957
This historic route was the first Grade V gully on Ben Nevis. It rarely achieves the character of a deep gully, being more of a great open groove. Although technically easy for the grade, it is a serious climb with poor belays and it is exposed to spindrift. Only the first two or three pitches are difficult. Climb icy grooves on the left of the main gully to a poor belay below a steep wall. Traverse right into the gully and climb this steeply to gain the easy upper gully. The gully can be climbed direct at the start; slightly harder.

Observatory Ridge   400m   IV,4 ***
H. Raeburn, F.S. Goggs, W.A. Mounsey   April 1920
The prominent steep ridge between Zero and Point Five Gullies gives a superb climb which can be very awkward under powder. It is the most difficult of the classic Nevis ridges, and climbers frequently find it harder than the big gullies on either side. The easiest line starts up the shelf on the left flank and works up obliquely rightwards to the crest. The crest is hard (turn the difficulties on the right) but the upper ridge is normally straightforward, although it can be time-consuming under heavy snow conditions. Many parties avoid it altogether and move left into the easier upper section of Zero Gully.

Hadrian's Wall Direct   300m   V,5 **
M.G. Geddes, G.E. Little (1PA)   April 1971
This popular ice climb comes into condition early and remains so until late in the season. It takes the large prominent icefall on the right flank of Observatory Ridge. Climb the ice smear, bulges and all, to a belay near steep rocks on the left. Continue very steeply for 10m, then trend slightly right on snow to a deep icy chimney, which leads to a snowfield. Continue more easily to finish by a scoop just right of Observatory Ridge, or by the ridge itself.

Sickle   300m   V,5 **
M.G. Geddes, B.P. Hall   29th December 1977
This excellent ice route takes the curving slabby groove right of Hadrian's Wall Direct. It is quite often in condition, but the start can be thin. Start a few metres right of Hadrian's below a small icefall. Climb over a steep ice step to gain a groove leading up and left close to Hadrian's Wall Direct, then curve back right to a steep icy corner and belay. Follow the icy corner and exit right up grooves to reach the snowy upper slopes.

Galactic Hitchhiker   300m   VI,5 **
M.G. Geddes, C. Higgins   14th April 1978
This serious route starts up a shallow corner system in the ice-glazed slabs between Sickle and Point Five Gully, then continues up the big right-trending and steepening corner system above. Start 15 metres right of Sickle below an icy corner.
1.50m   Climb the corner for 10m, step into another on the right and follow this over thinly iced slabs to an overhang. Exit right to a belay at a nose.

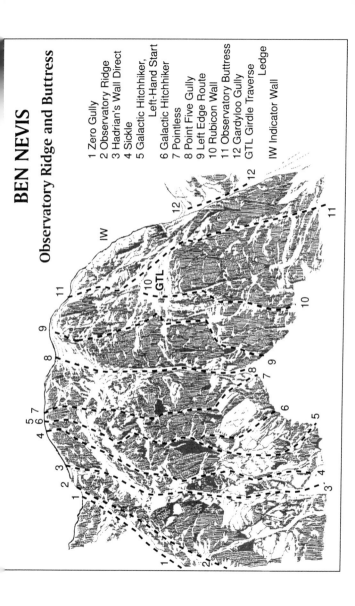

BEN NEVIS

Observatory Ridge and Buttress

1 Zero Gully
2 Observatory Ridge
3 Hadrian's Wall Direct
4 Sickle
5 Galactic Hitchhiker,
   Left-Hand Start
6 Galactic Hitchhiker
7 Pointless
8 Point Five Gully
9 Left Edge Route
10 Rubicon Wall
11 Observatory Buttress
12 Gardyloo Gully
GTL Girdle Traverse
   Ledge

IW Indicator Wall

2 and 3. 70m   Climb the continuation of the corner and snow shelves above to reach a snow bay up left, then traverse right past a distinctive pointed block to the base of the big corner (or reach this point by an icy corner on the right).

4. 45m   Climb the iced wall right of the corner with difficulty, then move back into the next corner and follow it to easier ground and the Girdle Traverse ledge.

5 to 7. 135m   Continue directly to the plateau.

Left-Hand Start   100m   V,5

Easier than the original way and more often in condition. Climb slabs and grooves just right of Sickle, then traverse right to the pointed block.

Pointless   330m   VII,6 **

N. Banks, G. Smith   19th February 1978

This serious thin face route, which follows slabs and an obvious corner trending left away from the base of Point Five, is guaranteed to provide a memorable experience. The climbing is hard and sustained, and protection is difficult to find; take care with this one. Start below an icy slab some 5 metres left of Point Five Gully.

1. 50m   Climb the slab to a groove, then break out right through a short overhang to reach the upper slab. Trend left across this to a large spike and peg belay. There is a variation nearer Point Five which goes higher across the upper slab.

2. 30m   From the top of the spike (peg runner on the left wall), climb the difficult corner above (crux), then move right into a small alcove and spike belay.

3. 30m   Climb an ice smear just to the left, and continue above to a narrow overhanging chimney.

4. 20m   Climb the chimney to easy ground.

5 to 8. 200m   Continue more easily to the plateau.

Point Five Gully   325m   V,5 ***

J.M. Alexander, I.S. Clough, D. Pipes, R. Shaw (6 days, fixed ropes) 16th January 1959

J.R. Marshall, R. Smith (first one day ascent)   10th February 1960

An outstanding climb, probably the most famous ice gully in the world! Belays are good and the route is often in condition. With the major difficulties concentrated in the first three pitches, the route is an excellent introduction to the Grade V classics and it is not uncommon for the gully to have several ropes of climbers stretching (often literally) from top to bottom. In windy conditions, the upper funnel collects vast quantities of spindrift which avalanches down the lower narrow section.

1. 40m   Climb easily up iced slabs to a steep ice wall, normally climbed on the left.

2. 45m   Climb the narrow ice-choked chimney in two sections (possible belay between them).

3. 30m   The Rogue Pitch. Continue up the gully and climb the bulging icy wall to the easier upper section.

4. etc. 210m   Follow the gully past an occasional short pitch to the plateau. The cornice is normally avoided on the right.

OBSERVATORY BUTTRESS

Observatory Buttress is the broad mass of rock extending from Point Five Gully on the left to Gardyloo Gully on the right. It rises steeply to a great ledge at half-height which narrows towards its left end and is taken by the Girdle Traverse. On the right, the ledge finishes at the foot of Gardyloo Gully at its junction with the top of Observatory Gully. The ledge is a useful but very exposed means of escape should conditions on the plateau make the prospect of a visit too daunting. Above the right end of the ledge and left of Gardyloo Gully is Indicator Wall; it is possible to link the lower and harder part of Observatory Buttress with a route on this upper section.

The buttress is characterised by the open left-facing corner of Rubicon Wall which separates the steep wall to the right of Point Five Gully from the easier-angled spur of Observatory Buttress route on the right. The high standard winter climbs to the right of Point Five Gully are most likely to be in condition towards the end of the season.

Left Edge Route   360m   V,5 **
D.F. Lang, N.W. Quinn   9th March 1974
A climb of great character, especially if followed by the Direct Finish. Start at the foot of Point Five Gully and climb the rib on the right to a snow patch. From its right end, climb the left-hand of two grooves to a hidden traverse line leading right to beneath twin icefalls. Climb the left-hand icefall to the easy terrace. Move right along the Girdle Traverse ledge and finish as for Observatory Buttress.
Direct Finish   200m   V,5
D. Wilkinson, M. Burt   8th March 1980
Instead of traversing right along the terrace, climb directly up a series of sustained icy grooves just right of the crest overlooking the upper section of Point Five Gully.

Rubicon Wall   150m   VI,5 *
N. Muir, A. Paul   14th April 1977
In good conditions a prominent icefall forms down the left-facing corner
which divides centrally the smooth left side from the spur on the right
(about 20 metres from the left edge of the buttress). Climb the icefall
in three pitches to the Girdle Traverse ledge. With good snow-ice
conditions, the grade can be V,4. Finish by one of the other routes, or
traverse right to Indicator Wall.

Observatory Buttress   340m   V,5 **
J.R. Marshall, R. Smith   9th February 1960
A fine and interesting climb, with one short hard section just before the
chimney. Start in the centre of the spur, well right of Rubicon Wall, at
an iced depression below a chimney. Climb a short snow runnel and
continue on steep snow with short ice steps, following the shallow
depression to the chimney (normally well choked with ice), then
continue up an easier groove to the Girdle Traverse ledge. It is possible
to traverse right from here into Observatory Gully, but it is preferable
to continue up and slightly left to the crest of the buttress, which leads
with little difficulty to the plateau.

INDICATOR WALL
The steep slabby face above and to the right of the Girdle Traverse
ledge extends from the narrow gully of Good Friday Climb on the left
to the deep cleft of Gardyloo Gully on the right. In winter, after an
extended cycle of freeze-thaw, the slabs become coated with a thin
layer of ice and provide a number of excellent routes, which are mostly
hard and serious with infrequent belays and limited protection. Starting
at an altitude of 1200m, they are the highest ice climbs in the British
Isles, and are often in condition late into the season.

Good Friday Climb   150m   III **
G.G.Macphee, R.W.Lovel, H.R.Shepherd, D.Edwards   7th April 1939
This enjoyable and popular climb is especially good early in the winter
before snow banks much of it out. Sometimes it is the last route to
remain iced at the end of the season. From the foot of Gardyloo Gully,
traverse left along the easy terrace to the foot of a narrow gully. Climb
this for 60m to a steep rock wall. Traverse right on ice to a small gully,
then climb up and slightly left to easier ground leading to a further small
gully. Climb this for 15m, before moving up and right to the summit

cornice. The indicator post no longer exists, but tradition still dictates taking the highest belay in the country, round the triangulation pillar on the summit.

Indicator Wall   165m   V,4 **
G. Smith, T. King   February 1975
This excellent climb is often in condition, and takes the easier line up the prominent ice sheet on the left side of the face. **Indicator Right-Hand** (V,5) takes a more direct line just to the right. Start at the base of a groove not far right of the gully of Good Friday Climb.
1. 30m   Climb an icy chimney-groove on the right of a prominent rib over ice bulges to a small snow scoop.
2. 45m   Choose the best line through a steep ice bulge and ramp, then move up and right to the base of a short chimney.
3. 45m   Climb the chimney and follow a line leading out left through bulges to the snow slope above.
4. 45m   Either climb straight up, or bear left on steep snow and ice to the cornice. An easy pitch in a superb situation.

Albatross   170m   VII,6 ***
M.G. Geddes, C. Higgins   21st January 1978
An excellent route up thinly iced slabs – a modern classic. The line follows the prominent shallow corner in the centre of the wall which runs the full height of the crag. There are three separate starts, but the original central line is usually followed. Start left of the centre of the open bay to the left of Psychedelic Wall, about 25 metres right of the rock spur on the left.
1. 30m   Follow a shallow ramp trending up and right into the main line, which leads to a rock spike where the corner runs into an overlap.
2. 50m   Climb the twinned groove above and make an interesting move left onto the top of the overlap. Continue above on steep slabs, avoiding an overhang on the right, to reach a snow bay and belay.
3. 50m   Exit from the bay on the right by a ramp, then traverse left into a shallow corner and follow this over an icy bulge to a snowfield below the cornice.
4. 40m   Continue easily to the cornice.

   Stormy Petrel (170m VII,6) is a thin face route which starts close to and on the right of Albatross and slants up right of a big right-facing and roofed corner before finishing directly.

Psychedelic Wall   165m   VI,5 ***
N. Muir, A. Paul   22nd January 1978
A popular route, the established classic on the wall, which takes a direct line starting from the lowest rocks opposite the left edge of Gardyloo Buttress.
1. 50m   Start up icy slabs to reach a snow bay, then continue up steeper ice to a left-trending snow ramp leading to a large plinth. Belay below and to the left.
2. 40m   Climb slabs to an open corner which leads onto a large area of thinly iced slabs. Climb these slightly right to a corner high on the right. (A direct finish goes straight up the slabs and steep ground above; VI,5.)
3. 45m   Continue up the corner and short chimney above to below a steep wall. Step left through bulges and climb the rightmost of three corners to an easy snow slope.
4. 30m   Follow the snow to the cornice, which is best breached on the left.

Gardyloo Gully   170m   II *
G. Hastings, E.L.W. Haskett-Smith   26th April 1896
Originally called Tin Can Gully, this deep cleft was used as a rubbish chute for the old observatory. The difficulty largely depends on the amount and condition of the snow. Start up a uniform snow slope above the narrows in Observatory Gully to reach an ice pitch. Climb this, and continue up steep snow to the cornice which can be very large, and is often double. The gully can almost totally bank out in a winter of heavy snow, but lying high on the mountain and being a natural drainage line, it is one of the first routes to freeze up. Under these conditions it provides an interesting passage under a huge chockstone to a steep ice pitch (III,4).

GARDYLOO BUTTRESS

This steep and compact buttress dominates the head of Observatory Gully, and consists of two ridges with a shallow depression between them. The left-hand ridge is well defined, and the upper part of the depression opens out into a wide funnel. In winter the funnel takes the form of a snow chute, which drains into two icefalls. The most prominent by far is the left-slanting icefall of Smith's Route. The steeper line to the left is taken by **Kellett's Route** (VI,6).

Smith's Route   125m   V,5 ***
R. Smith, J.R. Marshall   8th February 1960
A very popular ice route. Although short, it is a sustained climb with impressive exposure and is often in condition from December until May. The Icicle Variation is slightly easier and better protected than the original route, but less often in condition. Start directly below the lower end of the slanting grooves.
1. 30m   Follow the ice groove to a good belay in the groove below a roof.
2. 50m   A serious pitch. Move up to below the icicle, then traverse out left to steep grooves on the edge of the buttress. Break out right on steep ice to gain the left edge of the upper funnel. Snow or ice belay.
3. 50m   Continue easily up the gully above and exit on the left.
Icicle Variation   40m   V,5
K.V. Crocket, C. Gilmore   February 1975
From the belay at the top of pitch 1 climb the icicle on its left side, then continue up the brilliant ramp above into the funnel.

Three-quarters of the way up Observatory Gully, just below and to the right of Gardyloo Buttress, a rock barrier extends across the right side of the gully, joining the steep east wall of Tower Ridge. On the ascent of Observatory Gully, this barrier is easily passed on its left, and above it a rising traverse rightwards leads into Tower Gully.

Tower Scoop   65m   III *
I.S. Clough, G. Grandison   4th January 1961
This short and very popular ice route climbs the obvious icy scoop in the rock barrier. It is almost always in condition, although not necessarily safe. It can be used as a good warm-up on the way to the higher routes if time allows. Climb an ice pitch to gain the scoop, and finish by an awkward corner to reach the slopes below Tower Gully. Some variation is possible depending on conditions.

Tower Cleft   75m   III *
C. Pratt, J. Francis   19th February 1949
This interesting route follows the deep cleft in the angle formed by the cliff containing Tower Scoop and the east flank of Tower Ridge. The difficulty depends largely on the quantity of snow present. Alternatively, climb the steep icy left wall to break out left to easy ground.

TOWER RIDGE

Probably the best known feature on Ben Nevis, Tower Ridge is the third of the great buttresses on the mountain, projecting northeastwards from the main line of the cliffs towards the Allt a' Mhuilinn. Starting a short distance above the C.I.C. Hut at a level of 700m, the ridge rises for 200m to the top of the Douglas Boulder, a gigantic rock pinnacle separated from the main ridge by the deep cleft of the Douglas Gap. The Gap has a gully either side with the East Gully on the left. The ridge then narrows and after an almost level section rises to the Little Tower. A short distance above this is the Great Tower, which rises steeply for some 30m. From its top a short descent leads to the Tower Gap, after which easy rocks lead to the plateau at a height of almost 1340m.

Tower Ridge   600m   III ***
J.N. Collie, G.A. Sollie, J. Collier   30th March 1894
Another of the finest mountaineering expeditions in the British Isles. Depending on the conditions, all degrees of difficulty may be encountered, with many of the major obstacles being met high on the route. The Ridge has repulsed strong and experienced parties, and should not be under-rated. Benightments occur with monotonous regularity and 6 to 10 hours should be allowed for an ascent. It is important to be quick on the easier lower sections, and this may mean moving together in Alpine style. Early in the season, when coated in powder snow and verglas, the Ridge may be very time consuming and possibly a grade harder. It is important not to traverse left too soon, mistaking the Little Tower for the Great Tower.

The normal approach is to follow East Gully to the Douglas Gap. The chimney on the left leaving the Gap can be tricky, but thereafter the ridge is quite straightforward, with one steepening, as far as the Little Tower. In dry or good icy conditions this is best climbed on the left, but under heavy powder variants further right may be easier. Above, easy but spectacular ground leads to the foot of the Great Tower. The best route is to take the Eastern Traverse, a narrow ledge on the left which is sometimes banked out to an alarming angle. This leads to the sometimes buried fallen block chimney, above which tricky short walls lead to the top of the Great Tower. Follow the knife edge ridge to Tower Gap. The descent into the Gap involves a tricky move. The climb out the other side can be a little easier with good ice on the left or a little harder if taken direct. Above there the ridge eases until the final steepening, which is best taken by a groove on its right-hand side.

If time, energy or proficiency run short, there are escape routes. The ascent of the Great Tower can be avoided by a devious continuation of the Eastern Traverse, with a tricky move at the start, which leads into Tower Gully below Tower Gap. Alternatively, it is possible to escape into Tower Gully from Tower Gap (Grade II, or one abseil and a small traverse), but remember that the slopes leading across to Observatory Gully are steep (Grade I) and below lie the cliffs of Tower Scoop.

THE DOUGLAS BOULDER

The Douglas Boulder is often clear when the rest of the mountain is shrouded in mist. In winter there are a number of good mixed lines, which can provide absorbing climbing if there is avalanche risk after a heavy snowfall, or before the higher routes have come into condition. From the top of the Boulder it is necessary to either climb down or abseil to reach the Douglas Gap. Route finding can be awkward, and it is easiest to descend to the right as one looks into the Gap.

Direct Route   215m   IV,4
J.R. Marshall and party   1958
This fine climb takes the great groove in the centre of the front face of the Boulder. It can be used either as a start to Tower Ridge (but only by a fast party) or as a route in its own right. Start at the foot of the lowest rocks, well left of a smooth slabby wall which is an obvious feature of the lower section of the face. Climb up easily by a large shallow groove to a point where the groove steepens to form an open chimney. Climb the chimney for some 60m to a well defined ledge. Traverse right along this and climb steep but broken rocks to the top.

Douglas Gap West Gully and Traverse   300m   I *
West Gully rises to the Douglas Gap from the Coire na Ciste side. It is a good snow gully with fine scenery, and it can be used as an alternative start to Tower Ridge. An interesting poor weather option is to climb West Gully to the Gap, then descend *via* East Gully.

SECONDARY TOWER RIDGE

Secondary Tower Ridge lies on the west flank of Tower Ridge, some distance below its crest. For the most part it rarely attains the status of a distinct ridge but takes the form of a parallel slanting shelf, which is separated from the main ridge by a well defined depression which holds snow until late in the season and into which the routes finish.

On completion of a route on this part of the mountain, one can ascend or descend Tower Ridge but, apart from Vanishing Gully, it is shortest and most common to traverse right and descend Broad Gully, a snow gully which leads to the platform of Garadh na Ciste. Thereafter, walk off right into Coire na Ciste. This is a useful option to avoid being exposed to bad weather (or queues) on Tower Ridge and the summit plateau.

Vanishing Gully   200m   V,5 **
R. Marshall, G. Tiso   15th January 1951
The next obvious gully well right of Douglas Gap West Gully gives a classic ice climb with good belays and protection. It can be combined with The Curtain to give a low-level ice day. It is deep and well defined in its upper reaches, but lower down it narrows, eventually becoming a crack before finally disappearing. It forms ice well, and under normal conditions it presents a steep ice runnel for the lower 70m. Lying low on the mountain however, it can be quickly stripped after a thaw. Gain and climb the deepening gully to belay in an ice cave. Continue above by the bulging ice wall to easier ground. Either continue up the easier upper gully to the crest of Tower Ridge, or satisfied with the completion of the difficulties, traverse left and descend a shallow snow gully (**1934 Route**, Grade II) to reach Douglas Gap West Gully.

Italian Climb   180m   III
J.R. Marshall, A. McCorquodale, G.J. Ritchie   January 1958
The deeply cut gully which defines the right flank of the steep two tiered buttress right of Vanishing Gully provides a popular winter climb. Care should be taken assessing snow conditions before attempting this route, since the large snowfield at the head of the gully lies on slabs, and is avalanche prone. The lower gully normally contains two good ice pitches, above which the angle eases to snow slopes and occasional ice, leading to the crest of Tower Ridge below the Little Tower. Alternatively, before reaching Tower Ridge, traverse right and descend on snow into Broad Gully.

Italian Right-Hand   IV,4 **
I. Fulton, S. Belk   February 1973
Better climbing than the original line, but harder. Follow the first pitch of the original route, climb the icefall on the right, and rejoin the original route on the easier upper section. Descend as for the original route.

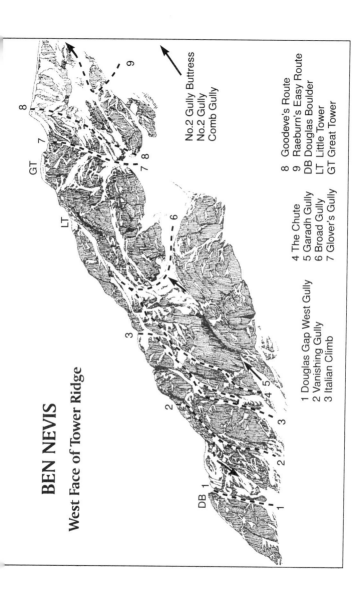

BEN NEVIS

West Face of Tower Ridge

1 Douglas Gap West Gully
2 Vanishing Gully
3 Italian Climb

4 The Chute
5 Garadh Gully
6 Broad Gully
7 Glover's Gully

8 Goodeve's Route
9 Raeburn's Easy Route
DB Douglas Boulder
LT Little Tower
GT Great Tower

No.2 Gully Buttress
No.2 Gully
Comb Gully

The Chute   220m   V,4 *
J.R. Marshall, R.N. Campbell, R. Holt   February 1965
This excellent route starts 30 metres right of Italian Climb and follows a prominent line of icy grooves directly up the face. Unusually heavy snow conditions are required for the steep initial icefall to form. On the first ascent it was avoided by a rising traverse, first left then right, to gain entry to the grooves above (IV,4).
1. 30m   Climb the icefall to the start of the grooves.
2. 45m   Move into an icy groove on the right and follow this to a horizontal ledge which leads across a steep wall into a small gully.
3. 30m   Traverse up and right to a stance below a steep ice wall.
4. 25m   Climb the ice wall to the snow gully above.
5 and 6. 90m   Continue above to a steep rock buttress and follow an easy snow shelf rightwards to the top of Broad Gully.

GARADH NA CISTE
To the right of Italian Climb is a subsidiary buttress separated from the main mass of Tower Ridge by the wide Garadh Gully. The buttress is crowned by a spacious platform known as Garadh na Ciste.

Garadh Gully   95m   II
I.S. Clough, M. Bucke   16th February 1958
Although this gully is sometimes climbed for its own sake, it is often used as an interesting approach to routes starting higher up on the west flank of Tower Ridge. Under normal conditions the gully gives a straightforward climb with two short, steep ice pitches. Later in the season it may bank out to a uniform snow slope. The **Indirect Finish** (Grade III) breaks out left from above the second ice pitch and crosses slabs on the headwall to reach the foot of Broad Gully.

Glover's Chimney   140m   III,4 *
G.G. Macphee, G.C. Williams, D. Henderson   17th March 1935
Dropping directly from Tower Gap to the right-hand end of the Garadh is a narrow gully which provides a fine and very popular winter route. Climb the initial icefall from left to right to a stance (35m), then take mixed snow and ice back left into the gully. Follow this easily on snow to the final chimney, and climb this to Tower Gap. This spectacular mixed pitch is seldom easy, but it is well protected.

Goodeve's Route   140m   III *
T.E. Goodeve, C.I. Clark, J.H.A. McIntyre   *28th December 1907*
This excellent winter climb comes into condition early and remains so throughout the season. Either start up the initial icefall of Glover's Chimney, or climb the icefall to its right, then cross a snow ramp and continue just right of Glover's Chimney to gain a snow ledge leading up right. Climb an icefall (difficult to start) to a snowfield. From its top, continue up a short chimney, then take a shallow gully which leads to open snow slopes which finish at the top of Tower Ridge. Several variations are possible in the upper section.

Raeburn's Easy Route   250m   II ***
SMC party, names not recorded   *April 1920*
The long but somewhat featureless headwall between Tower Ridge and Number Two Gully holds ice very late in the season and provides this superb and reliable climb. From the foot of Number Two Gully, traverse left under a steep wall (part of Number Two Gully Buttress) to a large but easy-angled icefall. Climb this for 30m to a snow slope which leads to a long right traverse below the upper wall. At its far end, gain the plateau by a shallow gully. The cornice is not usually too large at this point. A good direct finish leads from the icefall to finish near the top of Tower Ridge (Grade III).

COIRE NA CISTE

The following buttresses and gullies lie between Tower Ridge and Number Five Gully, and are best reached by skirting Garadh Buttress to its right. However, it is also possible to climb Garadh Gully as a warm-up on the approach to the climbs in the left-hand part of the corrie.

NUMBER TWO GULLY BUTTRESS

At the right-hand end of the headwall containing Raeburn's Easy Route is a scimitar-shaped buttress, defined on the right by the wide and deeply cut Number Two Gully. This is Number Two Gully Buttress. The bottom third of the buttress is set at a low angle, with only the upper section giving continuous climbing. There are several short but very worthwhile climbs here, which are often in good condition.

Five Finger Discount   135m   IV,4 *
M.G. Geddes, C. Higgins   4th February 1978
Between the slabby face of Raeburn's Easy Route and the projecting
spur of Number Two Gully Buttress are two grooves. This is the
left-hand one, defining the left edge of the buttress.

Burrito's Groove   135m   IV,5 *
M.G. Geddes, C. Higgins   8th April 1978
This good climb takes the right-hand groove system. Climb the groove
throughout, passing an overhang at 45m on the left, or continue
straight up if it is well iced.

Number Two Gully Buttress   120m   III **
J.R. Marshall, L.S. Lovat, A.H. Hendry   23rd March 1958
A popular and enjoyable route. Climb easy-angled mixed rock and ice
to a large snowfield where the buttress steepens. About 20 metres left
of the buttress crest, climb a steep ice groove for 20m, then trend right
on snow and ice to reach the crest a little below the plateau.

Number Two Gully   120m   II ***
J. Collier, G. Hastings, W.C. Slingsby   April 1896
This is the finest of the easy gullies on the mountain, passing through
good scenery. The gully fills up well and is normally a steep snow slope
with perhaps a short ice pitch at the narrows. The cornice is often large
and difficult, and is best passed on the left. Early in the winter the route
can be very interesting and significantly harder (Grade III).

COMB GULLY BUTTRESS
The wedge-shaped buttress to the right of Number Two Gully has an
easy-angled crest which leads to the broad middle section topped by
a steep headwall.

Comb Gully Buttress   125m   IV,5 *
I.S. Clough, J.M. Alexander   8th January 1960
I. Fulton, D. Gardner (Variation Finish)   3rd January 1971
This good route is normally combined with the Variation Finish which
is more often in condition. Either start from just left of the lowest rocks

Opposite: Comb Gully   Climber: Chris Anderson
Photo: Rab Anderson

Next page: The steep icefall of Mega Route X on Central Trident Buttress
Climber: Neil Marshall   Photo: David Ritchie

and gain the central snowfield or, harder, climb directly up the lower chimney a little to the left (IV,4). Follow a groove on the left edge of the buttress. The Original Route makes a rising traverse right to the foot of a chimney in the steep final rocks. This chimney is rarely in condition so the variation is usually followed. After the groove, go left to an ice column. Climb this to an ice-filled groove which narrows and steepens and leads to the top.

Comb Gully   125m   IV,4 **

F.G. Stangle, R. Morsley, P.A. Small   12th April 1938

The prominent gully which separates Comb Gully Buttress from The Comb provides a splendid climb which is in condition for most of the winter (but it is hard very in early season when there is a cave pitch). The belays are good when found, but protection can be sparse. Follow easy snow to the narrows where a long pitch leads to a belay. Climb a short steep ice wall on the right (crux) to easy ground and the top.

THE COMB

This great wedge-shaped buttress dominates the southerly part of Coire na Ciste. On each flank steep gullies define the buttress. To the left is Comb Gully and to the right is Green Gully, which separates The Comb from Number Three Gully Buttress. It is girdled by three prominent sloping fault lines which rise from left to right. Below the lower fault, which is taken by Piggott's Route, the buttress is easy-angled and slabby, whereas above it is protected for most of its length on the northern side by considerable overhangs. The middle fault starts at the entrance to Comb Gully and crosses the buttress at one-third height. The upper fault, which is not visible from below, is known as Hesperides Ledge.

Hesperides Ledge   200m   III *

J.R. Marshall, J. Stenhouse, D. Haston   12th February 1959

An exposed and exciting route taking the highest prominent shelf leading out right. Climb Comb Gully for 70m to the obvious snow ramp leading out right onto the crest of the buttress. Follow this, with a difficult and exposed step, for two pitches to reach the crest. Continue up the crest in a fine position to the top.

Previous page: The Curtain, Carn Dearg Buttress   Climber: John Peden
Photo: David Ritchie
Opposite: Looking down the crux pitch of Castle Ridge   Climber: Lou Kass
Photo: Grahame Nicoll

Tower Face of the Comb   230m   VI,6 ***
R. Smith, R.K. Holt   1st January 1959
This route deserves much more attention; it is often in condition and is one of the best mixed routes on the mountain. It remained unrepeated until the mid-eighties. The route finding is intricate and variations have been climbed which in general are harder than the original. Notably, after the groove, instead of traversing right, continue up the forked chimney line above. Start a little way up Comb Gully where an obvious ledge splits the buttress diagonally at one third height.
1. 30m   From the bottom left end of the ledge move up to another parallel ledge.
2. 25m   Go right to the foot of an obvious groove.
3. 50m   Climb the groove to a collection of broken blocks. Turn the steep wall on the left with difficulty (crux) and move up to a further ledge. Belay on the right. A fine and sustained pitch.
4. 45m   Traverse right by walls and steep snow to the buttress crest.
5 and 6. 80m   Continue more easily up the crest to the plateau.

Green Gully   180m   IV,4 ***
H. Raeburn, E. Phildius   April 1906
The prominent gully defining the right flank of The Comb is a popular classic and a fine companion to Comb Gully. It is often in condition; a good choice early in the winter because, unlike Comb Gully, no surprises appear in thin conditions. It has good belays, although they can be difficult to find on the central section of the route. Climb a steep ice pitch (which can vary depending on the snow build-up) to a peg belay on the left wall (45m). Continue up the gully for two or three ice pitches with peg belays on the right wall. Above, the gully fans out and there is a choice of finishes. The easiest options are to traverse left to the ridge at the top of The Comb, or bear right up easy snow. The best finish is straight up *via* a fine direct ice pitch, but a large cornice can make this problematical.

NUMBER THREE GULLY BUTTRESS
Number Three Gully Buttress extends rightwards from Green Gully, and presents first a broad slabby wall, then a very steep buttress. A huge open left-facing corner, taken by Quickstep, defines the junction between the two sections of the buttress, which is bounded on its right edge by Number Three Gully.

BEN NEVIS

Number Three Gully Buttress

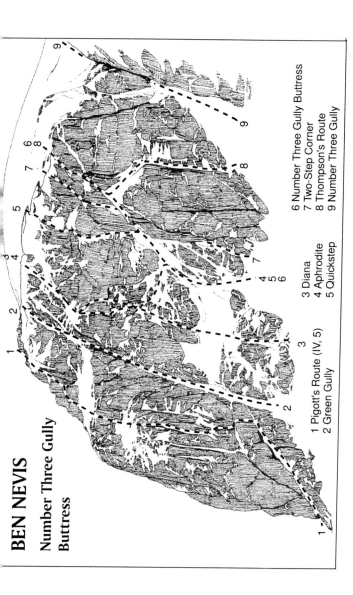

1 Pigott's Route (IV, 5)
2 Green Gully
3 Diana
4 Aphrodite
5 Quickstep
6 Number Three Gully Buttress
7 Two-Step Corner
8 Thompson's Route
9 Number Three Gully

Diana   190m   V,5
M. Duff, J. Tinker   16th February 1985
This route takes a direct line on ice, crossing Aphrodite. Start at the foot of the icefall to the right of Green Gully.
1. 50m   Climb the icefall, then snow, to belay at a steep rock wall.
2. 45m   Climb the chimney-groove in the centre of the steep wall. Pull over a large chockstone to reach another snow band and a huge block stance. Aphrodite crosses near here and finishes on the left.
3. 25m   Follow corners to below a huge right-facing corner.
4. 45m   Pull over an overlap onto the right wall and continue up steep thin ice to easier ground.
5. 25m   Follow the obvious line up snow to the top.

Aphrodite   200m   IV,4 *
M.G. Geddes, J.C. Higham   15th March 1971
This good but wandering route traverses left along the second snowy ledge system at half-height on the face to finish up mixed ground to the right of Green Gully. Start in a snowy depression just right of the centre of the base of the buttress (as for Number Three Gully Buttress). Climb to the foot of a slabby wall, then traverse up and left on snowy ledges until it is possible to make a hard move down and left to the foot of an open groove which is undercut by a large rock wall. Climb the groove and its continuation on the crest beside Green Gully. Move up right across snow to the cornice, which can sometimes be difficult.

Number Three Gully Buttress   130m   III **
L.S. Lovat, D.J. Bennet   18th February 1957
One of the finest medium grade winter climbs on the mountain. The route is somewhat exposed in places, and the upper section can be time-consuming if the snow is not consolidated. Start as for Aphrodite in a snowy bay just right of centre of the lower part of the buttress. Climb up to a snow shelf and follow it up to the right. From its highest point traverse right over snow and ice to a large platform. Either traverse left to the Chimney Variation and climb this on steepish ice to the top, or follow the original summer route, slabby rock trending right to the plateau. Both lines are exposed.

The open slabby corner which splits the buttress into two distinct sections is interrupted by the traverse line of Number Three Gully Buttress. Quickstep follows the corner, and the obvious fault line to the right is taken by Two-Step Corner.

Quickstep   130m   V,5 *
T. Bray, R. Townsend   26th March 1983
This excellent steep ice climb takes the huge left-facing corner directly above the start of Number Three Gully Buttress. The corner ends at a basin below the cornice, which can be bypassed on the right.

Two-Step Corner   130m   V,5 **
D. Kirtley, D. Montgomery   March 1975
This route with a reputation (being considerably steeper than it looks) is another good ice climb which is often in condition. Start 20 metres right of the snow bay at the foot of Number Three Gully Buttress below an icy groove. Climb the groove to the prominent ledge on which Number Three Gully Buttress crosses rightwards, and continue up the very steep corner to the top. There is often a large cornice which can be avoided by a traverse to the right.

Thompson's Route   110m   IV,4 **
R. Marshall, J.R. Marshall, J. Stenhouse   December 1963
The steepest section of the buttress is bounded on the right (near Number Three Gully) by a line of icy chimneys. These provide a good and sustained route which has a well deserved reputation for quality. Climb the chimneys in two or three pitches to the large platform above the lower buttress. Easier climbing leads to the plateau.

Number Three Gully   90m   I *
J.N. Collie, M.W. Travers   April 1895
This is the large gully situated at the back of Coire na Ciste, separating Number Three Gully Buttress from Creag Coire na Ciste. Walking directly up the Tourist Path leads to the top of this gully. It can be easily identified from above by a pinnacle standing as a flat-topped blade of rock at the head of the gully. This is a useful landmark for trying to locate the gully when the plateau is shrouded in mist. The gully is a straight-forward snow slope, although the final 10m may be quite icy. If using the gully for descent, start to the right of the pinnacle.

CREAG COIRE NA CISTE

The series of buttresses which lie between Number Three and Number Four gullies is known as Creag Coire na Ciste. The left end of the cliff is set at a high angle, and is seamed by a number of steep gullies. The cornices may present a formidable problem.

South Gully   120m   III *
G.G.Macphee   10th April 1936
Start from the foot of the narrow section of Number Three Gully, level with the lowest rocks of Number Three Gully Buttress. Climb an obvious slanting ledge leading right to the foot of a steep gully which turns back left. Normally there will be a couple of ice pitches, although they can bank out under heavy snow.

Central Gully Right-Hand   120m   IV,4 **
I.A. MacEacheran, J. Knight   date unknown
Start at the lowest rocks and climb *via* a series of snow patches left of a rib to reach the foot of two parallel ice gullies. Climb the right-hand chimney throughout; an excellent sustained ice pitch with good belays.

North Gully   110m   II **
J.Y. MacDonald, H.W. Turnbull   24th March 1934
The obvious narrow gully close to the entrance to Number Four Gully gives a great little climb. The first section is often full of ice, and the route is reliably in condition early in the season. Climb the initial gully, then traverse up and right to a large snow fan leading to the plateau. Beware of avalanche danger on the final slopes. A scoop and steep ice groove on the left give an alternative Grade III last pitch.

Number Four Gully   100m   I
A.E. Maylard, W.W. Naismith, F.C. Squance   April 1895
The most straightforward of the Nevis gullies, and the best descent route from the plateau. There is a marker post at the top. The gully is a simple snow slope, and the cornice can always be turned on the right towards the upper slopes of Number Four Gully Buttress. About halfway up the gully, a chimney splits the left wall; it is Grade III.

TRIDENT BUTTRESSES

The triple buttresses right of Number Four Gully are the South, Central and North Trident buttresses. The most southerly (topmost) and best defined of the three is composed of three tiers and is bounded on the left by Number Four Gully, and on the right by **Central Gully** (Grade III). Between South and Central Trident buttresses is a narrow diamond-shaped buttress (Jubilee Buttress) formed between Central Gully and its right-slanting branch of **Jubilee Climb** (Grade II). The following route climbs this buttress.

BEN NEVIS
Creag Coire na Ciste

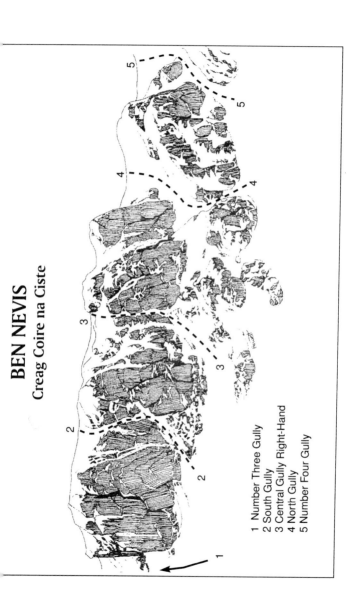

1 Number Three Gully
2 South Gully
3 Central Gully Right-Hand
4 North Gully
5 Number Four Gully

Jubilation   240m   IV,4
R. Marshall, J.R. Marshall, J. Stenhouse   December 1963
On the approach this climb is seen to lie just beyond the steep wall at the base of Central Trident Buttress. Follow Jubilee Climb for 75m, then traverse left to an icefall and climb steep ice to a snow bay. Move left into a chimney which leads to the final arete of the buttress.

To the right of Jubilee Climb is Central Trident Buttress, easily picked out on the approach as an extremely steep, rounded wall hopefully with a prominent icefall.

Mega Route X   70m   VI,6 **
J. Murphy, A. Cain   18th December 1982
This very steep icefall has a substantial reputation, but it was made to look almost ridiculously straightforward by Dave 'Cubby' Cuthbertson during a filmed ascent for the BBC series *The Edge*. The lowest 5m takes a long time to form, and the icefall sometimes crashes to the ground at about the point it becomes climbable.

North Trident Buttress is smaller and right of the steep wall. It is split by the S-shaped **Neptune Gully** (Grade III). The crest right of this is the line of the following route:

North Trident Buttress   200m   III *
J. Maclay, H. Raeburn, C.W. Walker, H. Walker   1904
A good mixed climb up the buttress which overlooks Moonlight Gully. The final tower is bypassed, and much variation is possible.

Moonlight Gully   150m   II
W. Inglis Clark, T. Gibson   3rd January 1898
This pleasant snow gully, the next gully left of Number Five, separates North Trident Buttress from Moonlight Gully Buttress. It is narrow and straight and ends in the wide upper funnel of Number Five Gully.

Moonlight Gully Buttress, between Moonlight Gully and Number Five Gully, offers a number of options for poorer conditions. The best two take the two chimneys in the lower buttress and their continuations. **Diagonal Route** (easy Grade III) is on the left and **Right-Hand Chimney** (hard Grade III) is on the right.

Number Five Gully   450m   I
J.N. Collie and party   April 1895
The gully immediately left of Carn Dearg Buttress is wide and shallow
in its lower reaches, and higher up it opens out into a small corrie. The
cornices can be massive, but the rim is extensive and an exit should
always be possible. There is often a large cone of debris at the foot of
the gully which testifies to its tendency to avalanche.

Ledge Route   450m   II ***
SMC party   Easter 1897
This is probably the best route of its grade on the mountain, with
sustained interest and magnificent situations. Start up Number Five
Gully, but leave it by a right-slanting ramp soon after it becomes a gully
proper. Follow the ramp over the top of The Curtain to a broad almost
horizontal ledge which fades out on the right. Before the ledge narrows,
leave it by a left-slanting gully which comes out on a broad snow shelf.
Go right past a large pinnacle block and round the corner to reach a
platform. Continue up the ridge, narrow in places, to the north-west
summit of Carn Dearg. In good visibility, Ledge Route can be used for
descent. From the top, follow the narrow ridge down to the top of Carn
Dearg Buttress, then take the broad highest shelf (marked by the
pinnacle block) to reach Number Five Gully. Instead of descending the
gully (which may contain a short ice pitch), continue to the far side
where another broad shelf leads gradually down from the large ledge
at the top of Moonlight Gully Buttress towards Lochan na Ciste.

CARN DEARG

The Great Buttress of Carn Dearg lies to the right of Number Five Gully.
The rock architecture of its magnificent front face, consisting of over-
lapping slabs, huge corners, and sweeping overhangs, is unequalled
in the British Isles. The right-hand of the buttress is defined by an
impressive vertical wall, with a long gully to its right (Waterfall Gully).
The best descent is down Ledge Route into Number Five Gully.

    Carn Dearg is an awe-inspiring place in winter and the routes tend
to be hard mixed climbs with sections of ice. Most of the climbs are of
high quality, but they are not often in condition. Optimum conditions
occur usually in mid-season, after a heavy snowfall, followed by a
sustained freeze. Much of the ice here is stripped quickly by thaw.
However, The Curtain (the huge icefall down the left hand side of the
buttress) is often in condition.

CARN DEARG BUTTRESS

The Curtain   90m   IV,5 **
J. Knight, D. Bathgate   February 1965
This magnificent exercise in ice climbing is an excellent introduction to
the steeper routes. It probably receives more ascents than any other
route of its grade on the mountain. Start at the foot of the huge iced
slab left of the buttress. For confident leaders, the last pitches can be
combined and the top belay reached on the rope stretch.
1. 40m   Climb the slab to a cave belay at its top.
2. 20m   Move left and climb the bulging wall above to reach an
exposed stance under a rock wall, immediately left of a steep iced wall.
3. 30m   Climb the wall trending right to gain an icy groove which leads
to Ledge Route. Belay well back.

Route I   175m   V,6 **
D. Knowles, D. Wilson   1972
Near the left-hand side of the cliff (but right of The Curtain) and above
a curving subsidiary buttress, there is a long deep chimney which runs
up to join Ledge Route. This is the line of Route I. From the foot of The
Curtain, follow the obvious ledge right over the top of the subsidiary
buttress for 60 metres to the foot of the chimney. The first pitch is
difficult, and the final chimney may call for some cunning. If it proves
too tight a squeeze, it is possible to avoid it by steep moves on the right
wall.

Direct Start   80m   VI,6
D. Cuthbertson, J. Sylvester   March 1984
Start just right of the toe of the subsidiary buttress below a right-facing
corner. Climb the corner, first by its right wall then its left, to gain the
crest of the buttress. Follow this to the ledge leading right to the upper
chimney.

Route II Direct   265m   VI,6 ***
M. Geddes, A. Rouse (3PA)   12th February 1978
G. Smith, I. Sykes (Direct)   15th February 1978
This magnificent climb is one of the finest mixed routes on the mountain. It is graded for good conditions, with ice on the slabs, otherwise
the grade might be higher and tension used, as on the first ascent.
Immediately right of the subsidiary buttress taken by the Direct Start
to Route I is a right-facing corner. Start below the deep corner next to
the right. Climb the corner, traverse left below an overhang, move up
to a large block and continue up the groove above. Traverse right round

an arete and climb the bulge above to reach the traverse ledge. Take a diagonal line across the slabs close under the overhangs to reach a groove on the far edge of the buttress. Follow this up the crest to easy ground. It is possible to avoid the lower section of the buttress altogether and reach the top of the Direct Start by traversing in from the foot of The Curtain, but this is definitely inferior.

The Shield Direct   285m   VII,7 ***
M. Fowler, A. Saunders   15th March 1979
The Shield is the line of chimneys formed by the junction of Titan's Wall (the big vertical wall on the right side of the buttress) and the huge flake on its right. This outstanding route combines very steep ice with sustained and technical mixed climbing. It is rarely in condition, and the initial groove is often bare. Start at an ice groove directly below the chimney of The Shield.
1. 50m   Climb the ice groove and continue over two bulges to gain a large ledge on the right at the foot of the chimney section of The Shield.
2. 30m   Climb the ice chimney and continue up steep ice to a cave stance on the left.
3. 35m   Follow the line of icy grooves to easier climbing in the now wider chimney.
4. 40m   Continue in the same line to the top of the chimney-flake.
5. 45m   Move up left onto a flake, cross the bulge above trending right and continue by the easiest line to ledges.
6. 35m   Climb up and right to a left-slanting ledge line. Follow this to the crest of the buttress.
7. 50m   Follow the arete to its top and a junction with Ledge Route.

Gemini   300m   VI,6 ***
A. Paul, D. Sanderson   23rd March 1979
A. Kimber, A. McIntyre (direct start, as described)   1st April 1979
One of the most interesting and atmospheric ice climbs on the mountain. The steep ice smear, if in condition, is prominent from the Allt a' Mhuilinn. Climb a steep ice groove just left of the first pitch of Waterfall Gully to join a right-trending groove after 70m. Follow this to an enormous detached flake. Climb the very steep ice smear on the left wall of the flake to reach a ledge below some right-sloping grooves. Follow these for 60m to the foot of obvious twin grooves. A possible left-hand finish starts from here. For the normal route, climb either groove to a broad ledge. Traverse right along the ledge for 15m and climb iced slabs for 45m to easier ground.

Waterfall Gully   215m   IV,4 *
D. Pipes, I.S. Clough, J.M. Alexander, R. Shaw, A. Flegg   8th January 1959

The prominent gully which defines the right flank of Carn Dearg Buttress provides a good and varied winter climb, but unfortunately it becomes much easier after the initial icefall. Climb the 40m icefall to its top where the angle eases. Follow the bed of the gully for 200m to a cave or possible through route on the right. Exit right (sometimes difficult) onto mixed ground and follow this up left for three pitches to join Ledge Route. Care should be taken on the slabby rocks in the exit area which may present a hazard in avalanche conditions.

True Finish   VI,6
D. Cuthbertson, C. Fraser   3rd March 1984

Although the difficulties are short-lived, this is a very worthwhile finish. At the point where Waterfall Gully swings right, climb the steep crack on the left wall and continue up the narrow chimney above to a small snow basin (40m). Either finish by the line of the crack or exit left onto easier ground to join Ledge Route.

The North Wall of Carn Dearg is the name given to the northern flank of Carn Dearg Buttress, right of Waterfall Gully. Above and to its right is a hanging corrie, from the base of which dangle some impressive icicles. In two recent winters they have connected with the ground and provided **The Shroud** (VII,6), arguably Scotland's finest ice feature.

Cousin's Buttress is next right and has the appearance of a huge flake or pinnacle some 60m high, butting against the North Wall of Carn Dearg, and separated from it by a deep chimney. This chimney, close on the right of The Shroud icicles, provides the following route:

Harrison's Climb Direct   275m   IV,4 ***
K.V. Crocket, C. Gilmore   7th February 1976

This superb climb gives some of the best ice climbing of its grade on the mountain. Start below the deep chimney described above. Climb a steep ice pitch (The Chimney Start), then continue up the icy corner to reach the saddle behind the top of Cousin's Buttress. Traverse left to a 30m icefall, then take a rising line up the buttress on the right to gain the edge overlooking Raeburn's Buttress. Follow the edge for two pitches to the upper corrie, where a selection of routes leads to the top.

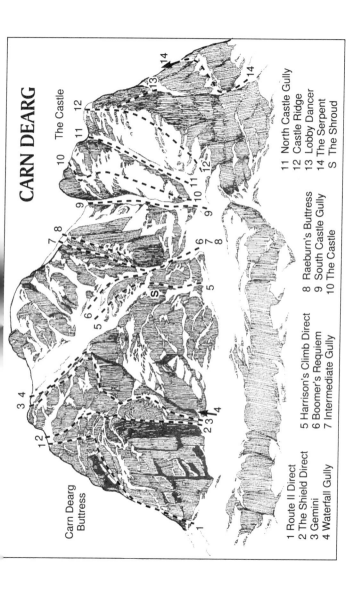

CARN DEARG

Carn Dearg Buttress

The Castle

1 Route II Direct
2 The Shield Direct
3 Gemini
4 Waterfall Gully

5 Harrison's Climb Direct
6 Boomer's Requiem
7 Intermediate Gully
8 Raeburn's Buttress

9 South Castle Gully
10 The Castle

11 North Castle Gully
12 Castle Ridge
13 Lobby Dancer
14 The Serpent
S The Shroud

RAEBURN'S BUTTRESS

Between Carn Dearg and The Castle lies a tall slender buttress which appears as a pinnacle from some angles. This is Raeburn's Buttress. The left side of the buttress is defined by a gully system which splits into two chimneys, and its right side is bordered by South Castle Gully.

Boomer's Requiem   180m   V,5 **
C. Higgins, D. MacArthur   February 1973
This route starts up the left branch of the gully system to the left of Raeburn's Buttress to reach the icefall which plunges from the hanging corrie to meet the lower section of the buttress. It has a daunting crux on very steep ice, and was originally graded IV and regarded as the test piece for the grade. Follow the initial gully of Raeburn's Buttress to the bifurcation, where the left-hand fork is barred by an impressively steep icefall. Climb this in two pitches and continue up snow slopes into the hanging corrie. Either descend Ledge Route or finish up one of the routes on Carn Dearg Summit Buttress. Of these, the left-hand and right-hand gullies are Grade II and the central gully is Grade I.

Raeburn's Buttress   230m   IV,4 **
W.D. Brooker, J.M. Taylor   31st January 1959
R. Ashley, G.G.I.S. Clough, C.H. Oakes (Intermediate Gully Finish)
14th April 1938
An excellent and sustained mixed climb. Start as for Boomer's Requiem and climb the introductory gully to the bifurcation; then follow the right branch to the cave. The original route climbed the right wall of the cave, then the gully on the right and the buttress crest above. The Intermediate Gully Finish is easier and more often in condition. Instead of climbing the right wall of the cave, continue up the gully to a steep exit at the top. Finish up grooves on the left of the final arete.

THE CASTLE

The deep recess of Castle Corrie contains the buttress of The Castle, which is well demarcated by South and North Castle gullies.

South Castle Gully   210m   I *
W. Brunskill, W.W. King, W.W. Naismith   1st April 1896
This gully divides Raeburn's Buttress from the recessed buttress of The Castle on the right. Extreme care should be taken after a heavy

snowfall, as the outward sloping rock strata makes the gully avalanche prone. The gully is normally an uncomplicated snow ascent. However in very lean conditions at the start of the season it can give a fun climb (Grade III).

The Castle   210m   III
W. Brown, J. MacLay, W.W. Naismith, G. Thomson   April 1896
An atmospheric route, largely because of its reputation for huge avalanches (be warned!). A steep pitch at the toe of the buttress between the two gullies, often well banked, leads to a central snowfield. Go up the centre, then trend left and climb a steep groove until beneath the final steep wall. Exit right on slabs.

North Castle Gully   230m   II *
J.H. Bell, R.G. Napier   4th April 1896
The gully to the right of The Castle contains several short chockstone pitches which are normally completely covered, giving an uncomplicated snow ascent. The cornice is seldom large.

CASTLE RIDGE

Castle Ridge is the final great ridge on the north face of Ben Nevis. It is the easiest of the four ridges, and while not in the same class as the others, it does have a distinct quality of its own, mainly derived from the tremendous views out over Lochaber. The huge north wall of Castle Ridge has yielded some excellent winter climbs. An easy descent can be made down the extensive boulder field on the north side of Carn Dearg to reach Lochan Meall an t-Suidhe. From the top of Castle Ridge it is important to first head due west for 300 metres before descending, to avoid the North Wall of Castle Ridge.

Castle Ridge   275m   III **
J.N. Collie, W.W. Naismith, G. Thomson, M.W. Travers
12th April 1895
A good climb which is possible in most conditions, although it should be avoided after heavy snowfall as the approach slopes can be swept by huge avalanches from above. Gain the ridge from below the Castle gullies, and follow the easiest line until the crest is blocked by a steep wall. Traverse up and right, and climb an awkward flaky chimney to a good ledge. Climb another difficult pitch to gain the upper part of the ridge, which leads to the top with no further difficulty.

NORTH WALL OF CASTLE RIDGE

To the right of Castle Ridge, a huge broken face extends for about 600 metres to the west until the cliffs merge with the hillside. There are many winter climbs here, but their lines are not outstanding, apart from the prominent curving shelf of The Serpent which slants diagonally across the wall from left to right and is easily seen from the Allt a' Mhuilinn path. Lobby Dancer is on the steep buttress high up on the left side of the face.

The Serpent   300m   II
I.S. Clough, D. Pipes, J. Porter   12th February 1959
This steep snow climb is the easiest route on the face, but it is quite committing and has difficult route finding. Start near the left edge of the face at a small gully above a prominent boulder called the Lunching Stone. Climb the gully, then follow a curving shelf leading right to reach the lower section of a second gully (150m). Climb this to the shoulder of Carn Dearg.

Lobby Dancer   280m   VI,6 **
C. Higgins, A. Kimber (1PA)   28th February 1977
This climb follows the prominent groove to the right of the large roof at the right side of the wall. Although it has seen few ascents, it is of very high quality. Climb directly up to the foot of the groove by a series of ice pitches, or traverse in from the left along the diagonal ledge line of The Serpent. Follow the groove for three pitches to belay below the barrier wall. Gain the continuation of the groove above the wall (1 peg for aid), then climb up to a block belay on the right. Move left to finish on the crest of Castle Ridge.

Nordwand   430m   III *
I.S. Clough, D. Pipes, B. Small, F. Jones, J. Porter   11th February 1959
A worthwhile and well named mixed climb. Start in a small gully towards the right side of the face. After 25m, break out left onto the buttress, or alternatively continue by an ice pitch in the gully. Traverse left to gain the natural line of ascent and follow this until about 200m up the face. At this point the rising shelf of The Serpent comes in from the left. Cross this and continue up steep snow to the foot of the summit rocks. Climb these by a series of walls and traverses leading to the left, to gain the final rocks of Castle Ridge.

AONACH MOR
1221m   (Map Ref 193 730)

At first glance, the great rounded bulk of Aonach Mor would seem to be an unlikely climbing ground, since the crags on the east and west faces of the mountain are hidden from many viewpoints. The cliffs of Coire an Lochain can be seen from Spean Bridge, but they are dwarfed by the vast scale of the mountain's eastern aspect. Lying close to Ben Nevis, development of these crags has been slow, and it is only in the late 1980s that they were systematically explored.

Coire an Lochain, on the east face of Aonach Mor, presents a long line of granite cliffs up to 150m high. These used to be the sole preserve of the mountaineer who favoured solitude and long walks, but completion of the Gondola and ski development in 1990 made Coire an Lochain one of the more accessible winter cliffs in Scotland. For those with skis, it is now a mere 150 metres walk from the top ski tow to the descent gully, and the promise of a winter route or two followed by an exhilarating ski descent at the end of the day has added an extra attraction to climbing in the corrie. Even without skis, the approach is short and conditions reliable, and the corrie has become very popular. Convenient descents at either end of the cliffs allow two or more climbs to be done in the day, and the general feel of the place is similar to Coire an t-Sneachda in the Northern Corries of Cairn Gorm.

The rock is excellent fine grained granite that has been fractured along a vertical plane, resulting in many cracks, chimneys and gullies. The buttress routes are generally well protected, but the rock on the side walls of the major fault lines is often quite compact, so belays in the gullies can be harder to find.

Weather and Conditions
The cliff base, above 1000m, and the vegetated rock means that the routes come into condition rapidly and provide good climbing when other crags in the west are too low to be properly frozen. Early in the season they can provide the perfect complement to Ben Nevis, especially before there is sufficient ice for good climbing. Indeed, the best conditions are often early in the season before heavy snow banks up the bases and shortens the routes. Facing east, and sheltered from southerly and westerly gales, the crag receives the morning sunshine and readily forms ice.

Under heavy snow conditions, and with the frequent westerly gales, the corrie cornices easily. Late in the season the cornices can reach monstrous proportions and make direct exits from some of the routes impossible. However, many of the climbs finish on relatively easy ground, across which it is possible to traverse to places with less pronounced cornices.

All the approaches involve traversing steep avalanche prone slopes beneath the routes. In freshly deposited snow conditions, when a high category avalanche warning report will usually have been issued, climbing should be avoided in the corrie. It is worth noting, however, that avalanche conditions may occur here even in November, before the regular avalanche warning reports have started for the winter.

Access

An approach on foot from the valley (3-4 hours total) may be necessary in November. Start from the Gondola car park and follow a rather indistinct path up through the cleared area under the cables. This joins a forestry track which takes a sharp right turn and leads to a small dam. Now head uphill on a rather better path and follow it to the Gondola station. Obviously the same point can be reached rather more quickly by mechanical means, but note that the Gondola does not run in high winds; check by phoning Nevis Range at Fort William (01397) 705825.

The easiest way to the cliffs from the Gondola station is on ski by the chairlift and tows. On foot, the quickest way is to follow the line of the ski tows directly up the side of the main ski run, then alongside the summit ski tow to its end (1½ hours). This point, marked by a small shack and a large cairn, is 150 metres south from the rim of Easy Gully (grid bearing 185 degrees). Don't be confused by another tow further left and lower, which also ends at a shack, but below the north bounding ridge of the corrie. In poor visibility it may be difficult to locate the top of Easy Gully, and extreme caution should be exercised as the cornices can be very large. It is normally possible to enter the gully by its northern edge, which appears to escape much of the cornicing. It may be necessary to abseil from a snow bollard (or from your skis!). For climbs on North Buttress, it is usually possible to descend just to the north of the north-bounding ridge of the corrie.

In doubtful weather or snow conditions, a more circuitous but safer approach is to contour east below Aonach an Nid, then to take a gently rising line southwards to reach a minor col high on the ridge which bounds the north side of Coire an Lochain.

Descent
The best way off the mountain after finishing climbing is to descend the ski slopes to the Gondola station, then continue down by the method of choice. To return to the corrie, repeat the approach *via* Easy Gully or the north-bounding ridge (see Access).

COIRE AN LOCHAIN

The corrie forms part of an almost perfect spherical bowl, centred around the lochan at Map Ref 198 739. The apex of the corrie rim is cut by a broad snow gully, Easy Gully, which lies almost due east of the lochan, and is a convenient reference point for describing the climbs.

Left of Easy Gully, the south side of the corrie contains a series of north-east facing buttresses, which, although shorter than those further to the north, are less exposed to the sun and stay in condition later into the season. The most prominent of these is called The Prow.

Right of Easy Gully the climbs can be divided into four main sections. First are the Ribbed Walls, which are divided into a series of grooves and ribs and are separated from Central Buttress by the deep gully of Tunnel Vision.

Further right are two narrow buttresses separated by three deep gullies. This is the Twins Area. The left-hand buttress can be recognised by the deep cleft of The Split, which is a useful landmark in poor visibility. Further right is North Buttress, which terminates with a wide gully left of the ridge bounding the north end of the corrie.

NORTH-EAST FACE

Hidden Gully   120m   II *
R.G. Webb, C. Rice   21st January 1989
An attractive-looking route up the narrow twisting couloir in the centre of the slabby buttress which defines the southern edge of the corrie. It may bank out under heavy snow conditions.

The following climb is located on The Prow, which is approximately 100 metres left of Easy Gully. This distinctive buttress, which lies left of a deep gully (suitable descent late in the season), is characterised by a rock prow high in the centre. The obvious line of Stirling Bridge takes the right-angled corner near the right edge.

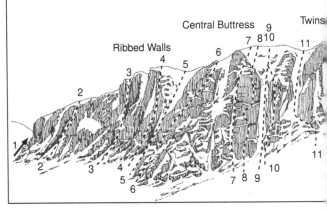

AONACH MOR

Coire an Lochain

Central Buttress

Twins

Ribbed Walls

Stirling Bridge   70m   VI,7 **
S. Kennedy, D. Ritchie   4th April 1990
An excellent route with a memorable first pitch. Climb the prominent
right-angled corner (steep and strenuous) close to the right edge of
the buttress, and pull out right near the top. Continue up a short groove
to a large block belay on the left. Easier ground leads to the cornice.

Easy Gully   100m   I
This broad snow gully cuts deep into the plateau, and gives the best
descent route back to the corrie. The cornice can normally be avoided
on the right (north).

THE RIBBED WALLS

This section is characterised by a series of vertical ribs seamed by
grooves. The most obvious feature near the left end of the face is the
deep cleft of Temperance Union Blues and further right are several
icefalls which provide the best pure ice climbing on the mountain. Just
left of the broad gully of Tunnel Vision is a prominent tower taken by

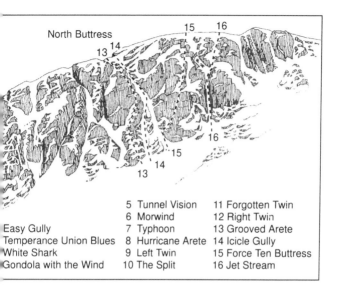

	5 Tunnel Vision	11 Forgotten Twin
Easy Gully	6 Morwind	12 Right Twin
Temperance Union Blues	7 Typhoon	13 Grooved Arete
White Shark	8 Hurricane Arete	14 Icicle Gully
Gondola with the Wind	9 Left Twin	15 Force Ten Buttress
	10 The Split	16 Jet Stream

Gondola with the Wind. Late in the season the first pitch of many of the routes can bank out, and a large cornice often forms over the entire length of the cliff. This is best avoided at its right-hand end, just left of the final tower of Gondola with the Wind.

Temperance Union Blues 90m III
S. Richards, G. Armstrong, C. Millar, J. Owens 18th February 1989
The cliff is split by a deep cleft at half-height about 50 metres right of Easy Gully. Take either of two converging lines to the bottom of the cleft (45m). Climb the cleft to where it steepens, then exit by a ramp to reach the cornice (45m).

White Shark 110m IV,4 **
C. Millar, R.G. Webb 27th January 1990
To the left of the prominent tower of Gondola with the Wind are twin icefalls. The right-hand icefall gives an excellent route. Climb the shallow gully, characterised by a steep slabby corner at half-height, to a ledge. Continue up the steep icefall which forms down the corner to an exit onto easier ground. The left icefall is **Aquafresh** (IV,4).

Gondola with the Wind   125m   IV,5 *
S. Kennedy, S. Thirgood   30th December 1989
A good mixed climb up the right side of the buttress, just left of Tunnel Vision. The steep tower immediately below the plateau provides an exciting finish.
1. 45m   Start up a short groove 10 metres left of Tunnel Vision. Climb to a small amphitheatre, then exit on the right.
2. 35m   Follow a system of shallow grooves close to the edge of the buttress and spiral right around the side of the tower to reach a steep corner.
3. 45m   Climb the corner (hard) and continue up the snow slopes above.

Tunnel Vision   120m   III
S.M. Richardson, R.D. Everett   22nd January 1989
S. Kennedy, S. Thirgood (Left Branch)   1990
The wide gully between the Ribbed Walls and Central Buttress. An initial narrows leads to a snow bay with three possible exits. The Central Finish climbs ice smears up the back wall in an exposed position to a steep cornice finish. In full conditions this wall may bank out to a frightening angle with an impassable cornice. The Left Branch provides a steep and technical alternative (III,4), and it should always be possible to climb the Right Branch to reach the upper easy section of Morwind.

CENTRAL BUTTRESS

This buttress lies between the gullies of Tunnel Vision on the left and Left Twin to its right. It is the highest section of crag in the corrie, and it provides some of the finest mixed routes on the mountain. The two most prominent lines are Morwind, which takes the fault line up the left crest of the buttress, and Typhoon, which climbs the left-facing corner system on the right side of the front face. The cornices on this buttress are often large and unbroken, but a vague snow arete on the final snow slopes can normally be relied on to provide a safe way through. If the cornice is impassable, it is possible to traverse right for 50 metres and descend the gully of Forgotten Twin.

Morwind   150m   III,4 **
R.D. Everett, S.M. Richardson   10th January 1988
This fine mixed route was the first to be recorded in the corrie, and has rapidly become a classic. Start at the toe of the buttress and climb a

short gully to enter a shallow chimney line. Follow this for two pitches to a small bay beneath a cave. Exit right up mixed ground to reach snow slopes and the summit cornice.

A good variation to Morwind is **Turf Walk** (III, 4*) which takes the fault slanting right across the front face of the buttress, then up grooves and a steep prow left of the central depression.

Typhoon   130m   IV,4 **
R.D. Everett, S.M. Richardson   14th January 1989
This excellent climb takes a direct line up the left-facing chimney-groove on the right side of the front face. Start 15 metres left of the deep gully of Left Twin. Just in case you're wondering about the windy names of the climbs around here, the first ascent of this one was on a day when 220kph winds were recorded.
1. 40m   Climb the lower slabby grooves to belay at the base of a chimney.
2. 30m   Climb the chimney and groove past an overhang.
3. 40m   Continue straight up on steep ice to reach the final snow slopes.
4. 20m   Easy climbing leads to the cornice.

Hurricane Arete   140m   VI,7 *
S.M. Richardson, R.D. Everett   4th March 1989
This technical mixed climb weaves an intricate and unlikely line through the overhangs just left of the right arete of Central Buttress. Start midway between Typhoon and Left Twin.
1. 50m   Take iced slabs for 30m to reach a short left-slanting gully. Climb this, then move up right along a narrow ramp to a small ledge. Belay beneath a prominent overhang, just left of a right-facing corner that is capped by yet another overhang.
2. 20m   Pull over the roof directly above the belay onto a steep slab, then follow a left-slanting crack to a prominent spike. Move right below an overhanging wall, then climb very steeply into a small snow bay. A difficult and sustained pitch.
3. 50m   Climb the groove on the left to the final overhangs. Bridge up and exit on the left and continue up easier ground.
4. 20m   Snow slopes lead to the cornice.

TWINS AREA

To the right of Central Buttress are two steep and narrow buttresses, Split Buttress and Siamese Buttress, which are bordered by three deep gullies. The gullies are rather confusingly known as 'The Twins'. The left side of Split Buttress is cut by the deep chimney of The Split. This is a useful point of reference in poor visibility which can be easily recognised by its large jammed blocks.

Left Twin   120m   III **
R.D. Everett, S.M. Richardson   22nd January 1989
The deep gully immediately right of Central Buttress is the best traditional gully climb in the corrie. It is similar in difficulty and quality to SC Gully on Stob Coire nan Lochan (Glen Coe).

The Split   130m   III,4 *
S.M. Richardson, R.D. Everett   19th February 1989
The prominent chimney, which almost slices Split Buttress in two, provides a climb of character and interest.
1. 25m   Start at the foot of the buttress and climb the introductory gully to enter the chimney.
2. 45m   Climb the chimney passing beneath several large jammed blocks until it is possible to exit left, just below the capping roof. Continue up the arete to belay.
3. 60m   Easy snow leads up and left to finish as for Left Twin.

Forgotten Twin   120m   II
R.D. Everett, S.M. Richardson   22nd January 1989
The gully between Split Buttress and Siamese Buttress provides the easiest climb on the face. Start *via* a short ramp leading left from the foot of Right Twin.

Right Twin   120m   II **
S.M. Richardson, R.D. Everett   22nd January 1989
A good traditional gully, narrow and well defined, with steep sections at the bottom and at mid-height. Exit left at the top.

NORTH BUTTRESS

The last continuous section of crag at the northern end of the corrie is separated from the deep gully of **Molar Canal** (III) by two narrow ribs.

It is made up of three distinct buttresses, divided by the deep Icicle Gully on the left and the clean-cut ice groove of Jet Stream on the right. The routes here are among the finest in the corrie.

Grooved Arete   130m   IV,5 **
S.M. Richardson, R.D. Everett   26th November 1988
A superb mixed route up the narrow buttress immediately left of Icicle Gully. Technically hard for the grade, but well protected. A little gem!
1. 45m   Start at the foot of the gully and gain the arete to the left. Follow this, easily at first, then with increasing difficulty up grooves on its left side. Move back right to belay below a steep tower.
2. 35m   Climb a series of grooves on the crest of the tower, step left to a ledge and continue up a vertical corner. An excellent pitch.
3. 50m   Easy climbing on the crest leads to the plateau.

Icicle Gully   130m   III
R.D. Everett, S.M. Richardson   26th November 1988
The gully between Grooved Arete and Force Ten Buttress.
1. 50m   Climb the gully to a belay on the right.
2. 50m   Continue up the wider right-hand line to where it narrows. Climb the icicle to a snow bay.
3. 30m   Follow mixed ground to the cornice.

Force Ten Buttress   140m   III,4 *
R.D. Everett, S.M. Richardson   3rd December 1988
An excellent mixed route up the buttress between Icicle Gully and Jet Stream. It tackles some surprising ground for the grade, but it is well protected.
1. 45m   Start up mixed ground just left of the crest, then move right to a belay at the foot of a steep chimney where the buttress steepens.
2. 30m   Climb the chimney, then step right and climb a short difficult crack.
3. 40m   Continue up interesting mixed ground to the right of the crest to join a gully. Follow the gully to a col where the buttress merges into the final snow slopes.
4. 25m   Easy snow leads to the cornice.

Between Force Ten Buttress and North Buttress is a small bay which contains two prominent gully lines. They form ice readily, lie in the shade until late in the season, and are often in condition throughout the winter. The left-hand line is **Solar Wind** (IV, 4*).

Jet Stream   100m   IV,4 **
R.D. Everett, S.M. Richardson   3rd December 1988
C. Grant, C. Rice (Direct Finish)   27th January 1990
The striking right-hand chimney immediately left of North Buttress
Route is one of the finest ice routes on the mountain, especially early
in the season before the first pitch banks out.
1. 45m   Climb the chimney over several steep sections to a snow
ledge.
2. 45m   Either exit right up a steep wall to reach easier ground, or
better, take the Direct Finish (IV,5) directly up the headwall above.
3. 10m   Easy climbing leads to the cornice.

WEST FACE   (Map Ref 189 729)

For those seeking solitude away from the bustle of Coire an Lochain
and the ski area, the crags on the west face of Aonach Mor are in a
truly wild and remote setting. They consist of a number of long granite
ridges, the steepest of which lie directly below the summit. The routes
are over 500m long and finish just by the summit cairn. They provide
enjoyable mountaineering expeditions that are possible in a variety of
conditions. There are four main ridges, the most distinctive being the
third from the left which contains a prominent slab at half-height.

The quickest approach is to contour round into the Allt Daim from
the Gondola station (1½ hours). The routes lie in a slightly recessed
bay and are not visible until just past the prominent east ridge of Carn
Dearg Meadhonach. Alternatively, approach as for the west face of
Aonach Beag, but continue to the col between Carn Mor Dearg and
Aonach Mor and traverse to the foot of the routes (2½ hours).

Western Rib   500m   II/III *
S.M. Richardson   17th December 1988
From below, the second buttress from the left appears as a flying
buttress to the one on its right. It is in fact distinct and gives the best
route on the face.

Daim Buttress   500m   II/III
R.D. Everett, N. Barrett, S.M. Richardson   25th February 1989
The third buttress from the left. Follow snow and rocky corners for
200m to the base of the prominent slab. Move left and climb cracks on
the left edge of the slab to a platform (50m), and continue up the cracks
and corners above (50m). Scrambling for 200m leads to the top.

AONACH BEAG
1234m   (Map Ref 197 714)

Situated between Aonach Mor and Carn Mor Dearg, this secluded and rather secretive mountain is the second highest in the Central Highlands. It boasts several crags, which retain an air of remoteness despite the nearby ski development on Aonach Mor. The three principal climbing grounds lie on the north, east and west faces.

NORTH FACE   (Map Ref 196 718)

The large triangular face between the Aonach Mor-Aonach Beag col and the North-East Ridge provides several excellent ice routes in a remote setting. In contrast to Aonach Mor, the rock on Aonach Beag is schist rather than granite, and the routes are generally more serious, particularly true of the north face. A good selection of pegs and ice screws should be carried on the harder routes.

Weather and Conditions
A serious place; high, snowy and remote, but this is its attraction. Good conditions are likely to be found here when the Psychedelic Wall area on Ben Nevis is well iced, although it is rare for good ice to remain after March. If ice conditions are poor, and this should be visible on the descent from Aonach Mor, the alternative is either to climb the North-East Ridge or descend west from the col to the West Face (briefly described after this section).

Access
The Aonach Mor-Aonach Beag col is the key to approaching many of the routes on the mountain; this can be reached from the summit of Aonach Mor in about 15 minutes. Some organisation, or speed, is required to fit in with the Gondola's opening times. The ideal is a second car at the top of Glen Nevis, allowing a round trip. An approach from Glen Nevis is also possible, but only for the fit early starter. The climbs are usually approached by descending east from the Aonach Mor-Aonach Beag col, but care should be taken with the large cornice and avalanche prone slopes which occasionally form. The cornice can normally be negotiated by descending snow or mixed slopes at the south end of the col. It is also possible to descend further north, but the slopes there are steeper and more exposed.

Descent

The summit plateau, ringed by giant cornices on the east and north faces, is a serious place in winter. The small summit cairn lies perilously close to the summit rim and is normally buried by snow. After finishing a route, it is best to locate the north ridge of the mountain, and descend this back to the col. Traverse Aonach Mor to return to the Gondola, which will probably be closed by the time you get there! To descend to Glen Nevis, head down from the col into the Allt Coire Giubhsachan and follow the faint path down to Steall.

Layout

The north face has a rock wall and steep buttress nearest the col, a gully area in the centre, and the lower rocky part of the North-East Ridge on the left. The climbs described are concentrated on the rock wall and buttress near the col. Stand and Deliver climbs the prominent icefall which hangs down the steep central section of the nearest wall.

Stand and Deliver   120m   V,5 *
C. Cartwright, R. Clothier   16th April 1989
Start about 100m down from the col, where an easy icefall leads up to and then splits round a steep headwall. **Whiteout** (Grade II) takes the right branch. The imposing icefall directly above the initial gully of Whiteout provides a long and sustained ice pitch which leads to the final snow slopes.

About 100 metres down from and left of Whiteout the rocks steepen into an impressive buttress of compact schist, which provides the finest ice routes on the mountain. **Camilla** (V,5) is a serious ice route which climbs the twin icicles which hang down the overhanging wall at mid-height on the right side of the face. It is not often in condition. Start at the toe of the buttress, about 25 metres right of the prominent icefall taken by Royal Pardon, climb to the foot of the ice walls and weave through them, going first right then back left.

Royal Pardon   220m   VI,6 ***
R.G. Webb, S.M. Richardson   18th February 1987
This tremendous ice climb takes the thin ice smear which hangs down from the shallow depression in the centre of the buttress. A serious route, comparable in difficulty and quality to the steeper ice climbs on the Ben.

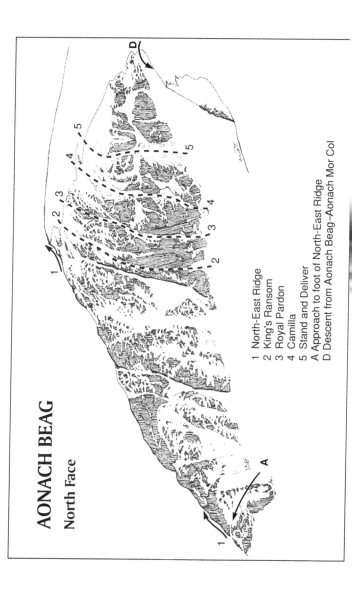

AONACH BEAG
North Face

1 North-East Ridge
2 King's Ransom
3 Royal Pardon
4 Camilla
5 Stand and Deliver
A Approach to foot of North-East Ridge
D Descent from Aonach Beag–Aonach Mor Col

1. 50m   Climb a series of icefalls to a flake belay at the bottom right side of the smear.

2. 40m   Climb the smear, passing two vertical sections, to a poor peg belay on the right.

3. 20m   A short pitch up the final ice wall leads to a snow couloir.

4 to 6. 110m   Follow the couloir for 50m to where it steepens into an icy gully which trends up and left. Two good ice pitches up this lead to the top.

King's Ransom   250m   VI,6 *
S.M. Richardson, R.G. Webb (1PA)   14th February 1987
This varied and exciting route starts up the narrow gully which cuts deeply into the left flank of the buttress, before breaking out right across difficult mixed ground to reach the crest.

1. 20m   Start about 40 metres left of Royal Pardon, beneath the gully, and climb easy-angled ice to its start.

2. 50m   Climb the gully, passing behind a large chockstone, and climb the vertical free-standing ice pillar above. An excellent pitch.

3. 40m   Continue up the gully to its end. Belay on a spike below the impending wall on the left edge of the buttress.

4. 20m   It is possible to escape left from here onto easier ground, but this avoids the challenge of the upper pillar. Instead, follow the ramp line on the right to where it fades, and pull over the steep wall above (1PA) to reach a second ramp. Climb this for 10m (delicate) to reach the crest of the buttress.

5 to 7. 120m   A fine snow arete and easier mixed ground lead to the plateau.

North-East Ridge   460m   III *
J. Maclay, W. Naismith, G. Thomson   April 1895
This classic mountaineering expedition finishes virtually on the summit of the mountain. Although not in the same class as the great Nevis ridges, this route is in a wild and remote setting.

The traditional approach is from Glen Nevis. From Steall, continue along the glen for 2km before heading north up the hillside to bealach 731m (Map Ref 211 705) which lies just west of Sgurr Choinnich Beag. Descend 100m, then head north-north-west, cross three burns (the second and third are small ravines), to reach a fourth stream line. The start of the ridge is now immediately above. Allow 3 hours from Glen Nevis; the final section from the bealach is very rough underfoot and will take at least 1 hour. An easier option from the Gondola is to continue descending below the other routes, then cut up right onto the lower section of the ridge.

The lower part of the ridge is broad, broken and open to much variation, but after 100m the climbing becomes steeper. Turn the pinnacles at half-height on their right, regain the crest of the ridge, and pass an overhung nose on its left. The knife-edge snow ridge above leads to the easier and broader upper section and the summit. The pinnacles can be climbed direct, but this is distinctly harder.

WEST FACE

High on the west face of Aonach Beag, a line of crags runs southwards for about 800 metres from the Aonach Mor-Aonach Beag col. Many icefalls form here, but the best routes have been found on the buttresses where the rock is well suited to mixed climbing, with good turf and protectable cracks. The climbing here is briefly described as an alternative to the North Face, if that should turn out to be in poor condition, but the climbs are worthwhile in their own right, especially for those who wish some isolation.

The best approach is from Glen Nevis (not too bad, especially for Raw Egg Buttress), but the climbs on the northern part of the face are close to the Aonach Mor – Aonach Beag col.

Broken Axe Buttress lies at the northern end of the face, just left of a deep easy gully which slants up from the right. The slopes to its right include several rocky outcrops, and a number of icefalls form down the broken mixed ground between. Some 500 metres from the col, just to the left of a broad snow gully, is the prominent Raw Egg Buttress.

The easiest approach to Broken Axe Buttress is to contour south from the Aonach Mor – Aonach Beag col. The base of the buttress is about 150 metres south of, and approximately 50m below, the level of the col.

BROKEN AXE BUTTRESS   (Map Ref 193 717)

Broken Axe Buttress (no prizes for the reasons behind this name) takes the form of a right-angled triangle set forward from the main face. Its upright left edge is a well defined crest in the upper reaches.

Twinkle (150m IV,5) reaches the crest by a technical but well protected direct line on mixed ground.

Axeless (150m III) takes the line of least resistance, starting right of Twinkle, crossing it at a small col at half-height, and working up to the left of the crest to avoid a steep chimney. A deep slanting snow gully running behind the buttress defines its right side.

Moving some way to the right of Broken Axe Buttress, **Beyond the Call of Duty** (150m III,4) takes the three-tiered icefall, which is the central and most prominent in the series of icefalls between Raw Egg and Broken Axe buttresses.

Immediately left of Raw Egg Buttress is an icy couloir, **Poached Egg** (150m II).

RAW EGG BUTTRESS   (Map Ref 191 711)

The winter routes on this prominent feature all provide technical but well protected mixed climbing, ideal for the Northern Corries enthusiast who's fed up with the crowds.

The impressive wall high up on the left side of the buttress is taken by **Aonach Wall** (150m V,6), a very steep climb with the crux at the top.

Raw Egg Buttress (180m IV,4) takes a line of turfy grooves just right of the arete right of Aonach Wall, again with a tricky final pitch.

Salmonella (125m VII,8) is a strenuous and demanding climb which follows the chimney and crack system between Raw Egg Buttress and the left edge of an impressive steep wall. The stances are good, the protection is mostly excellent, and it provides a good workout for the arms and a challenge to footwork and ingenuity.

The right edge of the steep wall is defined by a deep gully which steepens into a narrow chimney, capped by a bridge formed by three giant chockstones. This is the line of **Ruadh Eigg Chimney** (60m IV,5).

Opposite: Turf Walk, East Face of Aonach Mor   Climber: Colin Grant
Photo: Roger Everett

Next page: The first pitch of Last Post, Creag Meagaidh
Climber: Brian Sprunt
Photo: Andy Nisbet

CREAG MEAGAIDH
1128m   (Map Ref 418 875)

Creag Meagaidh is situated north of Loch Laggan in the Moy Forest. It is a large and sprawling mountain, with an extensive summit plateau and several ridges that enclose a number of deep corries. The finest of these is the north-east facing Coire Ardair, which lies 1km east of the summit. Over 3km long, and nearly 500m high, its mica schist cliffs are among the highest in Britain. The quality and scale of its winter climbing puts many of the climbs in Coire Ardair into the same class as the Ben Nevis classics. Creag Meagaidh is a great ice climbing venue; the turfy buttresses are much inferior.

The rock strata lies horizontally and slopes inwards, which results in a large number of snow-holding ledges. The shattered nature of the rock allows both pegs and nuts to be placed for runners and belays, but don't depend on their frequency. Ice screws are essential for the steeper ice routes, but normally only as runners.

Weather and Conditions
The cliff holds plenty of snow, and the majority of the routes come into condition most winters. With the exception of Pinnacle Buttress, where unusually good conditions are required, the main gullies are very reliable. Since it is centrally placed, Creag Meagaidh can get the best of both worlds, receiving the snow from the west (but avoiding its worst weather) and getting enough thaw to avoid the persistent powder of the east. Together with the benefits of sunshine to promote ice formation, these attributes combine to make Creag Meagaidh a classic gully venue. Although the gullies can also provide good climbing on water ice during a period of cold weather early in the season, the best conditions are likely to be found during a cold and settled spell in February or March following heavy snowfall earlier in the winter. However, it should be noted that, as with any cliff in Scotland with a big and high plateau to its west, the corrie is particularly prone to severe avalanche conditions. Also the cliff has areas on all buttresses where windslab is able to collect. The wind also builds up big cornices, so the corrie should be avoided during thaws.

Previous page: The Wand, Creag Meagaidh   Climber: George Reid
Photo: John Lyall

Opposite: The cliffs of Coire Ardair, Creag Meagaidh   Photo: Donald Bennet

Access

The approach starts from the A86 road at the track to Aberarder Farm, where there is a large carpark. Take the track to the farm, passing through a gate just east of the buildings, and continue by a path on the north side of the Allt Coire Ardair. The path stays well above and parallel to the burn as the glen takes a great curve to the west, at which point the cliffs come into view. The path eventually descends to the floor of the glen, about 500 metres before the Lochan a' Choire, then it continues to the north-east corner of the lochan. The total distance is about 7km and this takes about 2 to 3 hours under normal conditions. In heavy snow the path may be obliterated and progress becomes very laborious and time-consuming.

Descent

The summit plateau of Creag Meagaidh is very flat and featureless, and great care is necessary when navigating in poor visibility. Many climbers, who are notoriously reluctant to get the map and compass out, have been benighted or have inadvertently descended to Glen Roy. In good conditions, descent by Raeburn's Gully from Pinnacle Buttress or Easy Gully from the Post Face is most convenient. The ridge of Sron a' Choire, which leads back to Aberarder, may also be used and this is the easiest descent from the Bellevue Buttress or Pinnacle Buttress areas. Otherwise, descent is best made by the Window, which leads to the Inner Corrie and so to the lochan. There is a line of old fence posts running down to the Window, and a little rock buttress which has to be avoided on the left. These are useful identity features in poor visibility.

Layout

From Lochan a' Choire, there is an excellent panoramic view of the cliffs. High on the left is Bellevue Buttress, which is separated from the magnificent, towering Pinnacle Buttress by the left-trending line of Raeburn's Gully. To the right of Pinnacle Buttress are the gentler slopes of Easy Gully, above which rises the Post Face with its four great gullies, or Posts. A prominent feature of Bellevue Buttress, Pinnacle Buttress and the Post Face is a virtually continuous ledge which crosses their upper half. This gives the line of the unique Creag Meagaidh Girdle Traverse, The Crab Crawl, one of Tom Patey's enduring monuments. Right of the Post Face, the crags turn in towards the Inner Corrie, whose features are not clearly distinguished when viewed from the lochan. The Inner Corrie terminates at the Window, the name given to the very prominent bealach between Creag Meagaidh on the left and Stob Poite Coire Ardair, 1055m (Map Ref 426 886 - unnamed on the O.S. map), to the right.

The climbs are described from left to right.

BELLEVUE BUTTRESS

At the left end of the cliffs to the left of Raeburn's Gully, there are two buttresses. The larger one, which tapers towards the plateau on the left, is called Bellevue Buttress (with a huge roof in its lower section), and the narrower one to the right is Raeburn's Gully Buttress.

Eastern Corner   300m   III *
C.G.M. Slesser, K. Bryan   28th January 1961
The deep corner which separates Bellevue Buttress from Raeburn's Gully Buttress is the most accessible route in the corrie and passes through some fine rock scenery. The first 150m provides some steep ice climbing, followed by 150m of steep snow which leads to the plateau and possible cornice difficulties.

Raeburn's Gully   360m   I ***
H. Raeburn, C. Walker, H. Walker   31st October 1903
The gully which slants up left beneath the impressive left side of Pinnacle Buttress gives a straightforward snow ascent. The gully is long, continuously steep and the Pinnacle Buttress face provides exciting scenery. The cornice is not normally a problem. If the snow is deep but still safe, the upper section of Raeburn's Gully Buttress can be taken after the first 150m. The gully is sometimes used in descent and it also gives access to Ritchie's and Smith's gullies.

PINNACLE BUTTRESS

The great buttress between Raeburn's Gully and Easy Gully is nearly 500m high and at least as far across. The broad, triangular frontal face, which tapers towards Easy Gully on the right, is bounded on the left by a steep wall which towers above Raeburn's Gully. This is one of the highest continuously steep cliffs in the British Isles, and exposure on the upper part of the face is both bewildering and Dolomitic. The routes do not come into condition as quickly as the Post Face.

The summit tower of the buttress is bounded on its right by the prominent exit gully of 1959 Face Route which rises from the central snow patches. The Raeburn's Gully wall has three parallel slits rising from the middle section of the gully. From left to right these are the lines of Ritchie's Gully, Smith's Gully and The Fly. There are three ledge lines which cross this section of the face. The upper ledge is unnamed and unclimbed. The middle line is taken by the exposed **Appolyon Ledge** (Grade II), and the lower line, which is gained by a difficult 30 metres traverse from 15m up Smith's Gully, is **Vanishing Ledge** (IV,5). Lower down, starting from the foot of Raeburn's Gully, is the diagonal line of Raeburn's Ledge which is taken by the initial pitches of **Nordwander** (IV,4).

Ritchie's Gully   165m   IV,4 *
J.R. Marshall, G.J. Ritchie   February 1957
G.N. Hunter, N. Quinn (Direct, as described)   March 1969
The shortest and furthest left of the three parallel slits on the Raeburn's Gully face gives a fine and varied route, although snow build-up can affect the length of the lower part of the climb. Climb a steep icefall, turning an overhang by a right traverse, and continue up to Appolyon Ledge. The initial icefall can be avoided by traversing right along Appolyon Ledge. Continue up the gully to the cornice which can sometimes be difficult.

Smith's Gully   180m   VI,5 ***
J.R. Marshall, G. Tiso   8th February 1959
The central gully on the Raeburn's Gully face gives a tremendous climb of great character, continuously steep and sustained. This was a step cutting *tour de force* by Marshall and the name was a jibe at Robin Smith who had failed on the route two years earlier. Despite the passage of time, it is still considered to be one of the hardest traditional Scottish gullies. The route takes a while to come into condition and the crux fourth pitch can be particularly difficult if unconsolidated.

Climb the gully and exit left at the top chockstone to belay on the left above a snow bay (35m). Continue up the gully to where Appolyon Ledge crosses. Climb the vertical ice wall above (crux) to easier ground. Snow slopes lead to the cornice, which can normally be avoided on the right.

The Fly Direct   250m   VII,6 ***
M. Fowler, A. Saunders   19th February 1983
The narrow gully to the right of Smith's Gully is one of Scotland's most sought-after ice climbs. The route is serious and very sustained, and

although it is not often in condition there have been a number of repeats. The third pitch is probably the crux and can be very intimidating if thinly iced.

1. 20m   Start about 7 metres left of the gully line and climb steep mixed ground trending up and right to reach the base of the gully proper, which is guarded by a bulge split by a wide crack. This point can also be reached by starting in a niche 10 metres right of the gully line, climbing up, then left under a roof to gain the foot of the gully.

2. 30m   Bridge the wide crack for 5m, then continue up the depression above to a good block belay.

3. 50m   Climb the steep icefall for 20m to where it eases. Continue straight up and step right into a niche (good peg belay); there is also a belay on the left wall.

4. 40m   Move easily up to Appolyon Ledge. Belay on the right.

5. 30m   Climb the open continuation chimney above and exit right under a big roof to belay below a steep icefall.

6. 50m   Climb the icefall (optional but awkward belay on the left at half-height).

7. 30m   Move left to reach the easy exit snow groove.

The Midge   400m   VI,5 *
G. Harper, A. Nisbet   19th February 1983
This route tackles the huge wall to the right of The Fly. It is long and impressive, but lacks technical interest and is probably climbable quite often, the only critical factors being ice in the initial corner and the presence of the icefall in the upper section of The Fly Direct. Start at the snow fan near the foot of Raeburn's Gully, where Raeburn's Ledge slants up to the right.

1 and 2. 80m   Climb straight up a steep icy corner to reach the left end of a big snow patch.

3 and 4. 60m   Continue up the short groove above, then move left and climb iced slabs to the right of a big right-facing corner (which holds little ice) to reach Vanishing Ledge.

5. 40m   Traverse left and belay below a second right-facing corner which initially leans to the right.

6. 50m   Climb the corner, passing an old peg, and exit left at the top. Move up to belay under a roof.

7. 40m   Pass the roof on its immediate right, then move briefly left before trending right to Appolyon Ledge.

8 to 11. 130m   Traverse left for 30m to join pitch 5 of The Fly Direct, which offers the easiest way through the upper rocks.

Pinnacle Buttress Direct 360m VI,5 *
J. Sylvester, K. Howett *22nd March 1984*

In an exceptional winter an icefall forms down the face below the exit gully of 1959 Face Route to reach the left toe of the buttress at the base of Raeburn's Gully. When the icefall fails to reach the ground it can be reached from a grassy horizontal ledge leading across the face from 45m up Raeburn's Gully.

1. 45m Traverse the ledge to a peg belay below the icefall.
2. 40m Climb the icicle and continue up vertical ice above to a short iced slab. Peg belay.
3. 45m Follow the steepening slab on the left to reach a faint vertical groove which leads to a thread belay.
4. 45m Climb the ice smear above to join 1959 Face Route.
5 to 8. 185m Finish as for 1959 Face Route.

1959 Face Route 450m V,4 *
J.R. Marshall, J. Stenhouse, D. Haston *9th February 1959*

A mixed route with exciting situations which takes an intricate line up the front of Pinnacle Buttress to the prominent gully right of the summit tower. Start at a small bay about 80 metres right of Raeburn's Gully. From the bay a depression leads up to a shallow gully, which develops into a series of icy chimneys higher up. Climb the depression for 60m, then continue up the shallow gully for another 60m to a point 50m below the base of the first chimney. Traverse left for 60m to the foot of a left-slanting chimney-groove with an obvious chockstone. Climb the groove for 90m to large snow patches in the centre of the face. Go up left to the foot of the prominent exit gully with its 30m barrier icefall, then climb this to the buttress crest. Easy climbing leads to the top.

THE POST FACE

The Post Face stretches from Easy Gully on the left to Staghorn Gully on the right where the cliffs turn in to the Inner Corrie. Its most prominent features are the four parallel slits of the Posts, separated by well defined buttresses, known as the Pillars. As Easy Gully rises leftwards, the Post Face diminishes in height. Last Post is the leftmost and North Post the furthest right of the four gullies. From the foot of Great Buttress, which lies right of North Post, two parallel shelves slant up right to the foot of two smaller gullies, known as the Pipes. The face is very prone to avalanche, with big slopes below the plateau, and it should be avoided when collecting snow or after heavy snowfall.

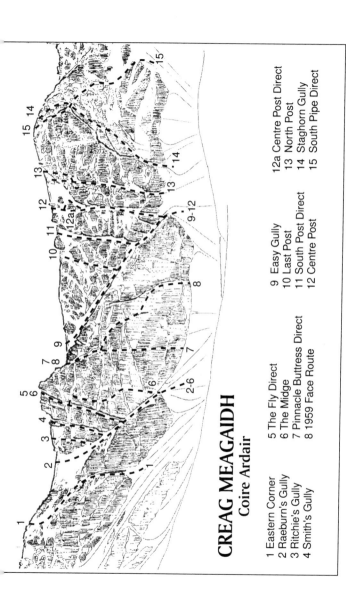

CREAG MEAGAIDH
Coire Ardair

1 Eastern Corner
2 Raeburn's Gully
3 Ritchie's Gully
4 Smith's Gully

5 The Fly Direct
6 The Midge
7 Pinnacle Buttress Direct
8 1959 Face Route

9 Easy Gully
10 Last Post
11 South Post Direct
12 Centre Post

12a Centre Post Direct
13 North Post
14 Staghorn Gully
15 South Pipe Direct

Easy Gully   450m   I
W. Tough, W. Douglas, H. Raeburn   *April 1896*
This is the easiest route in the corrie. It lies right of Pinnacle Buttress
and slants up left under the Post Face. The lower part of the gully is
narrow, but it widens in its upper section. For the easiest line, move out
left from the lower part below its steepest section. In descent, the
reverse; keep well out from the Post Face initially, then cut back in below
it at mid-height.

Last Post   240m   V,5 **
T.W. Patey, R.F. Brooke   *5th March 1962*
This excellent ice climb, the leftmost of the Posts, starts as an impressive icefall (crux) halfway up Easy Gully. Above, a snowfield steepens
to a second icefall, which is climbed in two pitches. Easy snow then
leads to another 30m icefall, which is followed by easy ground to the
plateau. For maximum value, all the icefalls should be climbed direct.
The route is Grade IV if the left side of the first icefall and the right side
of the second are climbed. The third icefall can also be avoided on the
left.

South Post Direct   400m   V,4 **
N.S. Tennent, C.G.M. Slesser   *10th February 1956*
T.W. Patey, R.F. Brooke (1st pitch direct)   *5th March 1962*
I.A. MacEacheran, J. Knight (3rd pitch direct)   *March 1964*
An excellent climb, often in condition and low in the grade. This is the
second Post from the left, and it has two steep and exposed ice pitches
linked by an easier section. The first pitch is a steep tapering icefall,
although it can bank out substantially in a year of heavy snow. Continue
up the couloir above to the foot of the long second ice pitch. Climb this
from left to right (crux) and follow the gully, with one more ice pitch, to
the plateau. The route is Grade III if the initial steep icefall is avoided
by traversing up and left from the foot of Centre Post and the crux pitch
is avoided on the left.

Centre Post   400m   III **
C.M. Allan, J.H.B. Bell   *21st March 1937*
The third Post from the left provides a magnificent climb of Alpine
proportions. The lower 250m is a steep snowfield which leads,
perhaps with one ice pitch, to the foot of the impressive icefall taken
by Centre Post Direct. Turn this on the right by making a steep and airy
traverse up and across the right wall to gain a snowfield, then move

back left around a rock outcrop to rejoin the main gully. Much variation is possible after the traverse. The ordinary route continues up the gully without further difficulty; the **Skidrowe Finish** (Grade III) climbs the narrow gully after the traverse.

Centre Post Direct   400m   V,5 **

B.W. Robertson, F. Harper, E. Cairns   22nd February, 1964

The impressive icefall at just over half-height in Centre Post is a spectacular feature which was recognised as a 'last great problem' for many years. Depending on the build-up of snow, the pitch may vary from 45m to 60m, with the first half being the steepest. It eases only slightly in the upper half. The start and finish, by the Centre Post normal route, are easy by comparison.

North Post   400m   V,5 **

T.W. Patey, J.H. Deacon, G.R. McLeod, P. Danelet   6th February 1960

This is the rightmost and narrowest of the Posts. It is an excellent climb, but variable, and rarely in good condition. When the direct finish is formed (not so common) the normal route is probably Grade IV. Steep snow leads to a narrow chute and a chockstone pitch (crux). Where the gully above widens, a vertical chimney in the left corner gives access to an easy ledge leading to a large platform on the right. Cross back left across the terminal face overlooking the gully by an exposed 25m traverse. A further 30m, first right, then back left, leads to an easy open couloir and the top.

Direct Finish   60m   VI,5 ***

Avoid the vertical chimney by climbing a short steep ice pillar directly above the snow gully to reach the terrace of Post Horn Gallop. An impressive ice sheet on the upper wall leads to the top.

Staghorn Gully   400m   III ***

C.M. Allan, J.H.B. Bell, H.M. Kelly, H. Cooper   29th April 1934

This excellent and popular climb is often in condition. As the cliff bends round from the Post Face into the Upper Corrie, there are two parallel gullies on the upper part of the crag. These are the South and North Pipes, and they can be approached by the long partially hidden shelf which slants up right from near the foot of North Post. The North Pipe, which is better known as Staghorn Gully, is the right-hand and easier of the two gullies, and leads by a series of short ice pitches to a snow bowl below the plateau.

South Pipe Direct   250m   IV,4 **
J.H.B. Bell, V. Roy   January 1935
J.H. Deacon, T.W. Patey (Direct)   7th February 1960
A fine sustained climb, but less often in condition than Staghorn Gully.
Start well up and right of the shelf of Staghorn Gully and climb the
shallow gully to the foot of the Pipes. Cross Staghorn and climb the
South Pipe.

THE INNER CORRIE

The Inner Corrie stretches from Staghorn Gully to the Window. The
climbs here are mostly shorter and less serious than those on the other
faces, but their higher altitude and more northerly aspect means they
stay in condition until late in the season. The main features from left to
right are: the well defined Trespasser Buttress; the deep ice corner of
The Pumpkin; then a narrow gully leading to the twin icefalls of The
Wand and Diadem. Right of this lie broken rocks with a central
snowfield, bounding the left side of the gully taken by Cinderella. Two
further gullies cut the rocks between Cinderella and the Window.

The Pumpkin   300m   V,4 ***
R. McMillan, G.S. Peet, N. Quinn   14th April 1968
A classic - the longest and most popular of the Inner Corrie ice routes.
It climbs the long ice corner right of Trespasser Buttress and is in
condition for long periods most winters. The belays are good but the
ice pitches are long and sustained, although never too steep. They
require ice screw runners, perhaps placed in awkward positions.
Confident parties may find the route easy, but continuous ice is tiring.
   Climb the corner in two long pitches to easier ground. Snow leads
to a steep left-slanting chimney, usually ice-filled and with an awkward
bulge at 20m. An easier mix of snow, ice and turf leads to a sometimes
difficult cornice. An easier finish (really an escape) traverses left from
below the foot of the left-slanting chimney and climbs the deep gully to
the right of the final tower of Trespasser Buttress.

The Sash   240m   II
T.W. Patey, R.W. Barclay, M. Laverty, E. Attfield   March 1963
A pleasant but uninspiring route which is often in condition. Start in the
narrow ice gully which leads up to the two parallel icefalls of The Wand
and Diadem. From below the icefalls follow a line of shelves up and left
to reach the plateau.

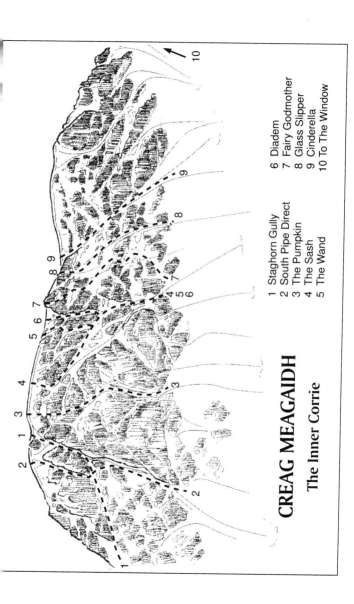

CREAG MEAGAIDH
The Inner Corrie

1 Staghorn Gully
2 South Pipe Direct
3 The Pumpkin
4 The Sash
5 The Wand
6 Diadem
7 Fairy Godmother
8 Glass Slipper
9 Cinderella
10 To The Window

The Wand   210m   V,5 **
Q.T. Crichton, D.F. Lang, G.N. Hunter, N. Quinn   2nd February 1969
The left-hand of the prominent twin icefalls provides a sustained ice
route that is often in condition. Climb the snow gully of The Sash to the
foot of the icefall. The next section varies in height between 45m and
60m, depending on conditions, and is best climbed by keeping close to
the right wall. A good cave belay is available early in the season when
the icefall is more than one pitch. Above, the angle eases and the line
of least resistance is followed to the plateau.

Diadem   210m   IV,4
J. Brown, T.W. Patey   19th February 1964
Another fine ice climb which follows the right-hand icefall. It is easier
than its twin to the left, but is less often in good condition as it forms a
funnel which collects fresh snow. Approach as for The Wand and climb
the icefall and easy ground above to the foot of a long ice corner. Follow
this to easy snow and the top.

Fairy Godmother   210m   III *
M.G. Geddes, N.G. Rayner   27th December 1970
A good varied route - probably the best on this section of the cliff. Start
midway between The Sash and the narrow chimney of Glass Slipper at
a right-sloping ramp. Follow the ramp for one pitch, then trend up and
left by a series of ramps and walls to reach the central snowfield. Climb
the obvious short gully someway left of the three exit gullies above the
snowfield, then go left up a ramp to an airy perch overlooking Diadem.
Finish by the steep tower above.

Glass Slipper   210m   III *
I.A. MacEacheran, J. Knight   March 1964
The steep narrow chimney just left of Cinderella leads to the central
snowfield in two pitches. Above, climb the central break to the top.

Cinderella   210m   II *
W. Tout, T.W. Patey   February 1963
The prominent snow gully in the centre of the corrie gives a pleasant
climb, often straightforward to a big cornice. There may be one or two
short ice pitches early in the season.

Glen Coe

As one of Scotlands premier winter venues, Glen Coe offers a huge variety of rewarding climbs of all grades and on all types of terrain. The topography of the surrounding hills with their distinctive peaks and narrow ridges gives Glen Coe a certain Alpine grandeur. The backdrop to the climbing is superb and on a clear winter's day the scenery is breathtaking. Added to this is the fact that the 'Coe' is richly steeped in climbing history with a past stretching back over 100 years.

The main A82 road passes through the Glen on the way to Fort William some 19 miles distant and it therefore acts as a convenient base for those also wishing to climb on Ben Nevis. There is plenty of accommodation on offer and the two main climber's hostelries at opposite ends of the glen, The Kingshouse and The Clachaig, act as convenient magnets for the thirsty after a hard day's winter toil. The village of Glencoe lies nearby and as well as providing provisions, it also has a climbing shop in the form of Glencoe Guides and Gear.

For these reasons Glen Coe is justly popular. However, this often creates its own problems by increasing the number of people vying for places to park and routes to climb. There are few suitable laybys and on a good day these soon fill up, so please park considerately. It may be necessary to queue for certain routes, especially for one of the Coe's many classics, and it is a good idea to have alternative plans just in case.

Maps

The Ordnance Survey 1:50,000 Landranger Series Sheet 41 and Harveys 1:25,000 Superwalker Map 'Glen Coe' are suitable for the areas described in this chapter.

Conditions and Weather

Glen Coe's proximity to the West Coast means that the weather is at times influenced by the Gulf Stream and conditions can be somewhat fickle. Atlantic fronts can track across the area with monotonous regularity, bringing a rapidly changing and often ferocious weather pattern. Although there should always be some routes in condition, catching snow on the harder routes can sometimes be a problem since the hoar associated with the Cairngorms is not so reliable here. This rapidly changing weather pattern, combined with the complex nature of the terrain, often complicates approach to and descent from the routes. For this reason it is best to be prepared for navigation in poor weather and before venturing onto the hills it is best to familiarise oneself well with the terrain and the descent. On the other hand, polar highs can bring the remarkably cold, clear and still weather that remind you why the winter experience can be such an enjoyable one.

Again, due to the weather and the terrain, there are very few areas that are totally free from potential danger of avalanche. When some routes catch the long awaited snow, the approaches and descents become more prone to avalanche. Frozen melt water on the paths presents another hazard typical of the area - there are many who have injured themselves here after a simple slip on an icy path.

BUACHAILLE ETIVE MOR
1022m   (Map Ref 223 543)

This prominent peak watches over the eastern entrance to Glen Coe and rises gracefully in the angle between Glen Coe and Glen Etive to produce an inspiring sight to those approaching across the wild expanses of Rannoch Moor. A complex array of buttresses, ridges and gullies are thrown down from its summit onto the moor below to form the conical shape that is the main summit peak of Stob Dearg. There are few finer sights in the country than the spectacle of the Buachaille in its full winter raiment. Before setting foot on the mountain it is worth familiarising oneself with its layout during daylight and a quick trip along the road in front of it should enable all of the various facets to be viewed.

Access
Although there are two main starting points for approaches to the frontal faces of the Buachaille, the one used in winter is that from the western side, close to the SMC hut at Lagangarbh, since the descent from the summit brings one back to the starting point. This approach leaves the A82 at Altnafeadh (Map Ref 221 564). Follow the track down to the bridge across the River Coupall, then just beyond the white cottage of Lagangarbh take the left branch of the initially wet path (the other branch goes straight on into Coire na Tulaich and is the simplest way to and from the summit) and follow this diagonally beneath the westerly buttresses. After about 20 minutes the path crosses the great slabby rift of Great Gully, unmistakable even in thick mist. In winter, however, it is sometimes confused with easier gullies further west.

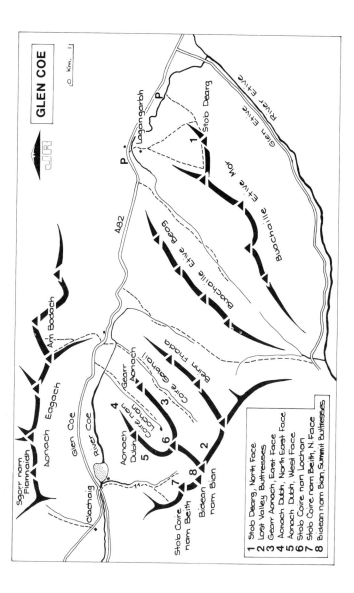

GLEN COE

0 Km. 1

1 Stob Dearg, North Face
2 Lost Valley Buttresses
3 Gearr Aonach, East Face
4 Aonach Dubh, North East Face
5 Aonach Dubh, West Face
6 Stob Coire nan Lochan
7 Stob Coire nam Beith, N. Face
8 Bidean nam Bian, Summit Buttresses

Now there are a number of choices. For the Great Gully amphi-theatre, the route continues up the steep slopes on the left (east) side of Great Gully to go beneath some small walls and contours towards the gully just below Slime Wall. This takes about 50 minutes.

For climbs on the North Buttress and Crowberry Ridge areas, follow the path on the left side of Great Gully until it is possible to break off left and make a rising traverse across the broken lower rocks of North Buttress towards some prominent boulders. The steep rocks of the North Buttress lie up ahead. A little higher and to the left, the broad ledge at the foot of the East Face of North Buttress leads easily into Crowberry Gully, which can be crossed to reach the lowest part of Crowberry Ridge.

From Great Gully it is also possible to continue on the traverse path to join a path which comes straight up the hillside from Jacksonville, the Creag Dubh M.C. hut (Map Ref 235 553). The paths meet below the prominent Waterslide from where the route zigzags up towards the foot of D Gully Buttress. It then makes a rising traverse to the right, staying close under the lowest rocks of Curved Ridge to emerge at the bottom of a gully system below Crowberry Ridge, fed by both Easy Gully above and Crowberry Gully further right. This is Crowberry Basin, the start of Curved Ridge. It is important to note that the whole area leading up to and including Crowberry Basin is subject to avalanche in deep soft snow.

Descent

There is only one reasonable descent route from the summit. Other possibilities will be mentioned in the appropriate sections. From the summit, follow the fairly level ridge south-west on a bearing of 240 grid for about 400 metres, then go due west on a bearing of 270 grid for about 300 metres down uncomplicated slopes to reach a flat, cairned col at 870m (Map Ref 216 542), the head of Coire na Tulaich. Naviga-tion on this section can be difficult in a white-out and it may be necessary to remain roped. The most common mistake is to continue too far south-west and descend into Glen Etive, relatively safe but rather inconvenient. However, great care should be taken not to stray too far north, or west, or to turn west too early, as there are large cliffs at the head of Coire na Tulaich. From the col, turn north (beware of the cornice) and go down the steep narrow gully leading into the corrie. This often icy slope has been the scene of many accidents and crampons may be a necessity, as may be a rope. The lower part of the corrie leads easily down to Lagangarbh. This descent takes one through some potentially avalanche prone areas.

If there is any doubt over snow conditions following heavy snowfall and thaw, then from the col ascend to point 903m (Map Ref 214 542) and descend by the ridge on the west side of Coire na Tulaich. There are some large outcrops here, in particular Dwindle Wall, but these can be avoided by moving left to go round them, then staying on the ridge until below the lower funnel exiting from the corrie.

The climbs are described as they are met from the approach, generally from right to left.

NORTH AND NORTH-WEST FACES

Layout

The North Face of the Buachaille includes all the cliffs to the west of North Buttress. The cliffs fall naturally into two regions; the Lagangarbh Group, the first rock met on the approach, and the Great Gully Group.

The Lagangarbh Group consists of, from right to left: Lagangarbh Buttress; the distinctive, stepped Staircase Buttress; Broad Gully; Broad Buttress (split by a deep groove higher up) and finally, Narrow Gully (an obvious, trench-like gully). Narrow and Broad Gullies provide pleasant Grade I/II climbs, but they tend to be avalanche prone.

The Great Gully group consists of, from right to left: Great Gully Buttress and Great Gully Upper Buttress; Great Gully; Cuneiform Buttress; the obvious gash of Raven's Gully and last but not least Slime Wall. In a good winter the Great Gully area is transformed into a magnificent amphitheatre of high standard ice and mixed climbing. Despite its low altitude, good conditions, although not so long lasting as in other areas in Glen Coe, are more frequent than people think.

Descent

It is possible to descend from above the Slime Wall area by traversing right immediately above the finish of Raven's Gully into Great Gully, then to descend this, keeping close under Cuneiform Buttress, to join the traverse path which comes in from North Buttress below Slime Wall. In potential avalanche conditions Great Gully should be avoided at all costs. If in doubt, go to the top of the mountain *via* North Buttress and descend by Coire na Tulaich as described earlier.

Lagangarbh Chimney   60m   III *
This route lies on Lagangarbh Buttress, the most westerly of the North Face buttresses. Approach by leaving the path about 700 metres (10 minutes) from Lagangarbh and climbing directly uphill. A prominent feature on the front face of the buttress is a chimney line on the right, which often contains ice and gives a good route for a short day. The last 15m is the crux. Descend by gullies on either side of the buttress, or into Coire na Tulaich.

Ephemeron Gully   340m   IV,4 *
K.V. Crocket, A. Walker, P. Craig   28th December 1985
This lies on Broad Buttress, the next buttress west of Great Gully Buttress. Approach by turning uphill from the path before reaching the outflow from Great Gully. Hard under the west face of the buttress, left of Broad Gully, is a sinuous line of icy grooves. Under icy conditions this gives five ice and three mixed pitches. From the top, either descend Broad Gully, or go up and over the top of Lagangarbh Buttress.

Great Gully   360m   II
N. Collie   1894
This massive gully dominates the north side of the Buachaille and can provide a scenic route to the summit. Early in the season several pitches of water ice may provide sport, but these generally bank out later to give a straightforward snow climb. There is usually a pitch where the gully kinks right under Cuneiform Buttress. Great Gully is a notorious avalanche trap and it should only be climbed after a settled spell. It should be avoided at all costs should there be any chance of unstable snow.

Cuneiform Buttress, Ordinary Route   135m   IV,5
J.R. Marshall, D.N. Mill, G.J. Ritchie   15th December 1957
Start at the lowest rocks near the foot of Raven's Gully. Follow the line of least resistance to a broad grassy terrace. From its right end climb a short but steep pitch to grassy grooves which lead to another broad ledge under the vertical upper third of the buttress. Traverse right round an exposed edge onto the west face. Climb an obvious shelf, then turn towards the centre of the cliff and climb to the top.

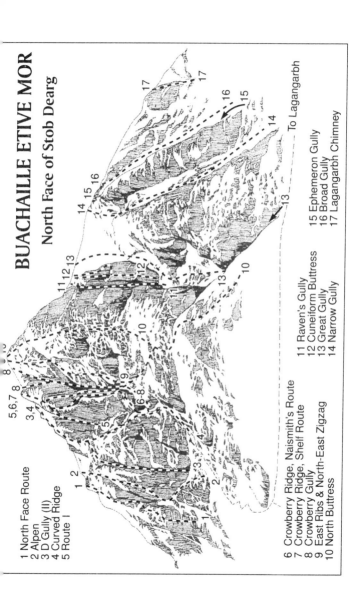

BUACHAILLE ETIVE MOR
North Face of Stob Dearg

1 North Face Route
2 Alpen
3 D Gully (II)
4 Curved Ridge
5 Route I

6 Crowberry Ridge, Naismith's Route
7 Crowberry Ridge, Shelf Route
8 Crowberry Gully
9 East Ribs & North-East Zigzag
10 North Buttress

11 Raven's Gully
12 Cuneiform Buttress
13 Great Gully
14 Narrow Gully

15 Ephemeron Gully
16 Broad Gully
17 Lagangarbh Chimney

To Lagangarbh

Cuneiform Buttress, The Long Chimney   135m   IV,5
R. Smith, D. Leaver   15th December 1957
Follow Ordinary Route to the broad grassy terrace, traverse hard right and climb the obvious, long shallow chimney.

Raven's Gully   135m   V,6 ***
H. MacInnes, C. Bonington   14th February 1953
A magnificent climb up the dark and compelling cleft formed between Slime Wall and Cuneiform Buttress. Normally there is an easy pitch leading to a cave belay beneath a huge chockstone whose left wall provides considerable entertainment. Snow leads to a narrowing of the gully with a chockstone above. Another two difficult pitches lead to the gully fork. Now move left round a rib and climb snow and ice grooves to a platform on the gully edge. Climb the chimney on the right (sometimes hard), or traverse left and finish up icy grooves.
Direct Finish: 50m   VI,6 ***
Y. Chouinard, D. Tompkins   February 1970
A stunning finish if caught in condition. From the fork continue straight up with much interest and bridging.

Misty High   150m   V,5 *
A. Paul, D. Sanderson   17th March 1979
A fine route up the icefall at the extreme left side of Slime Wall, not often in full condition. Climb the icefall and the ensuing right-hand chimney to easier ground which leads to a short chimney. Exit under a chockstone to reach North Buttress. Follow the icefall on the right for 90m to easier ground.

NORTH-EAST FACE

Layout
This aspect of the Buachaille is most apparent from the Jacksonville carpark, and comprises from right to left: the broad and massive North Buttress, with the East Face on its left; Crowberry Gully; Crowberry Ridge and the Rannoch Wall; Curved Ridge and Easy Gully; and finally D Gully Buttress.

North Buttress   300m   III ***
This splendid route can be climbed under almost any conditions and will always provide plenty of interest. The outlook is superb. Scramble

up the path on the east side of Great Gully, with a few steeper steps, to the foot of the prominent, continuous line of shallow chimneys which splits the middle section of the buttress. These provide steep and intersting climbing, which may be Grade IV in unhelpful conditions. After about 150m the chimneys end on High Ledge where easier-angled ground, with the occasional awkward step, leads to the summit.

Crowberry Gully   300m   IV,4 ***
H. Raeburn, E.W. Green   April 1909
The continuous gully incised into the mountainside between North Buttress and Crowberry Ridge provides a magnificent climb of great character and beauty. Conditions vary enormously depending on the build-up of snow. There are seldom more than five distinct pitches, most of which can be obliterated by heavy snow. Ideal conditions are not frequent and the gully can be very dangerous due to avalanche. From Crowberry Basin, easy snow leads to the narrows. A short pitch may be encountered here. More snow then leads to the first hard pitch, the Thincrack Chimney. This may give 10m of steep climbing but often forms no more than a few awkward steps. The junction is now reached where a steep rib divides the two forks. From a stance at the foot of the left fork make a rising right traverse, which may be hard if the ice is thin, below the rib into the right fork. Another pitch leads to the Cave Pitch which is nearly always the crux and is climbed by an impressive curtain of ice on the right wall. Snow leads to the final slopes.

Left Fork   35m   IV,5 **
C.M.G. Smith, R.J. Taunton, I.C. Robertson   March 1949
From the top of the Thincrack Chimney a narrow iced-chimney leads to a great chockstone. This is hard but short and well protected. Easy snow leads to Crowberry Gap.

Should Crowberry Gully be in dangerous condition or fully occupied, both quite common, then alternatives exist. Naismith's Route is on Crowberry Ridge to the left, and North Buttress can be gained by a traverse to the right.

Another two interesting alternatives lie on the east flank of North Buttress beside Crowberry Gully. **East Ribs** and **North- East Zigzag** both follow lines of least resistance and both are open to much variation at Grade III/IV.

To the left of the gully, the right flank of Crowberry Ridge is cut by two long parallel ribs with shallow gullies on their left. Shelf Route follows the lower line and Naismith's Route the upper.

Shelf Route   210m   IV,6 **
W.M. Mackenzie, W.H. Murray   March 1937
The obvious line running parallel to and left of Crowberry Gully provides a superb and exposed outing. When in condition it is a difficult mixed climb with the crux high on the route. Start from the narrows at the foot of Crowberry Gully by a traverse of steeply shelving snow to reach a cave. If there is not enough snow, this point can be reached from the platform at the foot of Crowberry Ridge. Climb the right wall and rib of the middle of three chimneys and follow the trough in the shelf for several pitches. The trough steepens to a scoop in the angle between its left wall and a small pinnacle on the right. Climb to a point where the scoop merges into the face beneath a small rectangular tower and move right to gain a square recess under the pinnacle. The pinnacle is usually climbed on the right by an awkward traverse. Above, a long groove leads to the crest below Crowberry Tower. Either climb around the Tower and descend its right side to Crowberry Gap or traverse its left side towards the top of Curved Ridge.

Naismith's Route   210m   IV,4 *
This route is harder than North Buttress, but it is the easiest line up the ridge. Start from the right side of the platform at the foot of Crowberry Ridge and follow a groove up the left side of a 15m pinnacle to a ledge. Move right along this to the left-most of the three chimneys. This point can also be gained from the narrows at the foot of Crowberry Gully, but this depends on the amount of snow. Climb the chimney, which becomes a long shallow gully with a series of short pitches. In the upper section continue up a gully until it ends on a wide sloping slab. From the top of the slab climb the short left wall, which overhangs and is hard, to gain the crest of Crowberry Ridge. Failing this, traverse onto the crest from the bottom of the slab. Follow the ridge and continue up to Crowberry Tower.

The crest of Crowberry Ridge is taken by the famous **Direct Route** (Grade V) which continues above Pinnacle Ledge to Abraham's Ledge then goes left and up the crest with difficulty. Around to the left of the crest is The Rannoch Wall, with Curved Ridge and Easy Gully on its left running up to meet the termination of Crowberry Ridge.

Curved Ridge   240m   II ***
G. T. Glover, R. G. Napier   11th April 1898
Gracefully curving up and under the Rannoch Wall through some impressive rock scenery, Curved Ridge provides one of the finest 'Alpine' type routes in Glen Coe. It is technically hard for the grade but the hard sections are short. It can be climbed under most conditions, but if any avalanche hazard exists great care should be taken around the Crowberry Basin and the exposed slopes under Crowberry Tower. Curved Ridge is not a good descent in winter. The ridge starts at around the 630m contour. From Crowberry Basin, climb a short steep ice pitch in Easy Gully and gain the ridge. The crest provides the most difficult line but the gully on its right is an easier alternative, although it can be avalanche prone under heavy snow. The crest provides several interesting sections. Turn the final narrow part on the left to emerge on a flat rib beneath a cairn. Make an exposed traverse left under Crowberry Tower to the gully which goes up to Crowberry Tower Gap. A good little pitch leads out of the Gap to the summit slopes. A quicker alternative from the cairn continues left to a gully which curves up towards the summit, although this too can be avalanche prone.

Route I   70m   IV,5 *
H. MacInnes and partner   February 1972
This fine exposed mixed climb on the upper left part of Rannoch Wall takes a vegetatious line of weakness which slants left and develops into an obvious groove. Start some 15m above the cave pitch in Easy Gully at a short vegetated chimney with a large red slab to its left. Climb the chimney to belay at some more open rocks (15m). Trend right, then take a long slant up a narrow shelf, which ends at an awkward stance where two sloping slabs are topped by a 4m wall. Climb the wall, crux, and finish by the long upper groove.

EAST AND SOUTH-EAST FACES

Layout
Left of and below Curved Ridge and Rannoch Wall is D Gully Buttress. It is bounded on its right by D Gully and on the left by Central Buttress, from which it is separated by a wide bay backed by a line of chimneys and little gullies. It forms a right-angle with Central Buttress, the two merging at the top. The right flank of Central Buttress juts out somewhat, producing a narrow but distinctive north face which overlooks Jacksonville.

Access and Descent
Traverse left below the rocks of D Gully Buttress from a point approximately 60m above the Waterslide.

From the tops of the climbs it is possible to traverse right to Curved Ridge. Either continue up this to the top of the mountain or, in favourable conditions, gain the cairn at the top of the ridge and descend Easy Gully.

Alpen   255m   IV,4 *
K.V. Crocket, C. Stead, S. Belk, I. Fulton   March 1972
This route takes the line of chimneys and gullies on the left flank of D Gully Buttress. It trends left to a big snow bay, then zigzags rightwards. Between Central Buttress and D Gully Buttress an easy open gully leads up then left. Start halfway up this easy gully at the foot of a wall.
1. 45m   Climb steep turf ledges to the start of a corner.
2. 20m   Continue up the corner to belay in a cave.
3. 10m   Climb the right wall of the cave to the upper chimney.
4. 40m   Climb the chimney, then trend more easily left to a small spike belay.
5. 15m   Move left to belay below the right-hand of two parallel chimneys (the left-hand one is North Face Route).
6. 40m   Climb the chimney, then follow a ramp right to a belay.
7. 40m   Go up left in the open gully.
8. 45m   Finish up right on the buttress top.

North Face Route   220m   V,6 **
J.R. Marshall, J. Stenhouse   January 1958
A mixed route which offers an entertaining variety of climbing up the narrow but distinctive north face of Central Buttress. Start from the base of the north-east edge of the buttress, at a spike just left of a rock niche, then climb a series of corners and walls. Easier ground leads to Heather Ledge at the extreme right of the south-east face. Go around the edge and follow an obvious traverse line to a recess. Now descend rightwards to a ledge and climb an awkward 3m wall to a ledge slanting right. Follow the ledge, then climb a chimney and traverse left to climb a short steep crack near the buttress edge. Follow the edge to the top.

On the left-hand side of Central Buttress is **Waterslide Gully** (IV,5). On its right, **The Veil** (V,5) takes an impressive icefall which unfortunately is rarely formed thick enough for comfort. Down to the left is

Lady's Gully, then the Blackmount Buttresses and finally the deep gully of The Chasm. **Lady's Gully** (Grade IV) provides a first rate climb, and it is usually in condition after a heavy snowfall. A number of short pitches lead to a big pitch, often of thin ice on rock. An exit can be made by either fork, then continue either right to Curved Ridge (usually more conveniemt) or left above The Chasm to descend slopes towards Glen Etive.

The Chasm (V,5) provides an excellent long climb given a rare extended freeze. Even in the best conditions, water may be lurking not far beneath the ice! The best line will depend on build-up, but expect to have to weave around the walls (usually on the left) to avoid some steep and poorly formed sections. In the upper section the gully narrows to an impressive slit, and a winter ascent will depend on the formation of a substantial ice pitch in the direct line. This is steep and bold, but above it easy slopes lead to the summit ridge. Descent is possible, with care, on the slopes to the left (south-west) of the gully. It is possible to escape from the gully at a number of places should conditions in the upper part prove unsuitable.

THE BIDEAN NAM BIAN MASSIF

Bidean nam Bian (1150m) is the highest point of a large and complex massif. Proceeding from east to west, the major peaks are: Stob Coire Sgreamhach; Bidean itself with Stob Coire nan Lochan jutting out in front of it to the north; Stob Coire nam Beith; and finally An t-Sron. Projecting northwards from these peaks are three long ridges which terminate abruptly in steep blunt faces overlooking the glen. These are the Three Sisters: Beinn Fhada, Gearr Aonach and Aonach Dubh.

Three principal corries are formed between these ridges and the various peaks. From east to west these are Coire Gabhail (The Lost Valley), Coire nan Lochan and Coire nam Beitheach. With the exception of one route, Sron na Lairig, all climbs are on the faces and hillsides around these three corries and this is how they will be described.

The ridges and peaks of the Bidean massif offer some rewarding high level winter mountaineering. Suggested starting routes to some of the ridges can also be used as approaches to other climbs. These are Sron na Lairig (Grade II) on Stob Coire Sgreamhach, The Zigzags (Grade I) on Gearr Aonach, Dinnertime Buttress (Grade II) on Aonach Dubh and Summit Gully (Grade II) on Stob Coire nam Beith.

Sron na Lairig   300m   II ***
P.D. Baird, Coulson, Allberry, Kendall, T.M. Wedderburn
March 1934

The prominent subsidiary ridge of Stob Coire Sgreamhach which descends north-east into the Lairig Eilde gives an excellent outing with a remote and Alpine feel. Start from the Glen Coe side of the Lairig Eilde at a signposted footpath to Glen Etive (Map Ref 188 563). A long but easy walk of about 4km leads to the corrie. The broad lower part of the ridge, with a central gully with a spur on each side, is open to much variation. Higher, the route takes a well defined crest, similar in parts to the Aonach Eagach. This is usually gained by a line on the left side; harder variations on ice exist to the right.

To descend from the top of the ridge, go south-east to a col (Map Ref 164 528) and return into the Lairig Eilde. Alternatively, continue over the summit of Stob Coire Sgreamhach to the col at the head of the Lost Valley, but note that the broad gully descending north-east from this col can be corniced and is prone to avalanche.

COIRE GABHAIL (THE LOST VALLEY)

The entrance to the Lost Valley is sharply defined by the steep frontal noses of Beinn Fhada on the left and Gearr Aonach on the right. A large jumbled mass of boulders and trees blocks the entrance to the flat section of the valley and it is beyond this that most of the climbs lie, either on the main East Face of Gearr Aonach, or on the two Lost Valley Buttresses on the summit ridge of Bidean.

Cross the River Coe by a footbridge (Map Ref 173 564) just below The Meeting of the Three Waters and follow a good path up the right side of the wooded gorge of the Allt Coire Gabhail. Just beyond a stile the path levels out at the deep-cut entrance to the main gorge. Here, a path breaks off right up a rocky bluff towards the nose of Gearr Aonach. Continue through the gorge to a large boulder opposite the slabby Sentry Crag (which can form vast sheets of climbable ice). Ahead is a formidable barrier of jumbled boulders and trees formed by a huge landslip from Gearr Aonach. Cross the stream and bypass the boulder field easily around its left side to a magnificent viewpoint of the Lost Valley. A short descent gains the flat valley floor.

If the best path is missed, one is plunged into the midst of the boulder field. Entertaining though this may be, especially when breaking trail through deep snow in the dark, the chance of dropping down a hole is best avoided! However, it may be necessary if the stream is in spate.

LOST VALLEY MINOR BUTTRESS
(Map Ref 149 538)

This is the smaller and left-hand of the two conspicuous buttresses lying just right of the col at the head of the Lost Valley. Facing north-east at an altitude of about 900m, this crag readily comes into winter condition and provides a good, reliable venue for middle grade routes.

Access
From the far end of the flat section of the Lost Valley, follow the higher of two paths rising up the side of the Upper Gorge to where the paths converge at a deeply-cut stream flowing down from the right. Great care should be taken at this point as a slip might lead to a fall into the deep, vertical-sided gorge of the Allt Coire Gabhail. Cross the stream, continue towards the obvious col at the head of the Lost Valley, then bear right to the buttress (allow 2 hours).

Descent
This is possible by either of the gullies on the left of the crag (Grade I), which are separated by a rocky rib, or the gully to the right of the crag (Grade I), which may have a large cornice. Alternatively descend the ridge south-east to the col, the Bealach Dearg, at the head of the Lost Valley (Map Ref 151 537). There is likely to be a small cornice. If the slope is doubtful due to avalanche danger, continue over Stob Coire Sgreamhach and down its south-east ridge to a col (Map Ref 164 528), then descend into the Lairig Eilde.

Chimney Route   80m   IV,4
J.R. Marshall, J. Moriarty   January 1959
The obvious chimney on the left side of the buttress provides several interesting chockstone problems.

Minor Issue   80m   IV,6
R. Anderson, G. Taylor   10th January 1988
This climb follows the corner-groove line left of the buttress edge, between Chimney Route and the chimney-corner of **Central Scoop** (Grade IV).
1. 15m   Climb the corner-groove to a ledge.
2. 20m   Move left and climb a corner to a small block, step right and follow a groove to easy ground.
3. 45m   Continue more easily to near the top.

Right Edge   130m   IV,4 **
J.R. Marshall, J. Stenhouse, D. Haston   February 1959
The main central corner and ramp line leading up right beneath the headwall gives a fine varied route with some good situations.
1. 40m   Ascend the chimney past a chockstone, then go up an icy groove to a belay in the corner.
2. 45m   Move up to the headwall, either *via* the corner or by its slabby right wall, then traverse awkwardly up right to the edge. Care should be taken in arranging protection.
3. 45m   A shallow gully leads to easy snow slopes and the top.

Minor Adjustment   115m   IV,5 *
R. Anderson, C. Greaves   19th February 1989
This is the obvious groove and corner just up the gully from Right Edge, a direct line joining that route after its upper traverse.
1. 45m   Climb the steep groove to a small ledge and spike, then follow a ramp steeply up left around the edge to ledges. A short traverse right leads back to the corner; belay 3m higher.
2. 25m   Continue up the corner, then move right and climb a short groove to step right below a small roof. Follow the snow ramp to a short, wide crack and climb this to a belay.
3. 45m   Easier ground leads to the top.

LOST VALLEY BUTTRESS   (Map Ref 148 540)

This, the larger and right-hand of the two buttresses, is divided by a great central groove into an easier angled left half and, set back at a higher level, the steeper right half.

Access
Either traverse rightwards from the Minor Buttress or, from the top of the Upper Gorge, follow the right bank of the deeply-cut stream which descends from the col between Bidean and Stob Coire nan Lochan. This leads over two steepenings to a level section which continues to the slopes (possibly avalanche prone) beneath the crag (allow 2½ hours). The buttress can also be reached from the col between Bidean nam Bian and Stob Coire nan Lochan, or *via* the Zigzags on Gearr Aonach followed by skirting Stob Coire nan Lochan.

THE LOST VALLEY BUTTRESSES

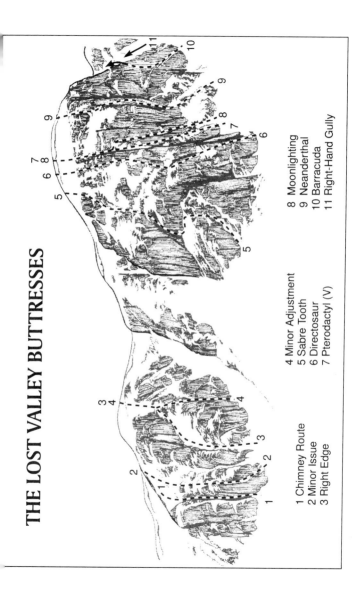

1 Chimney Route
2 Minor Issue
3 Right Edge

4 Minor Adjustment
5 Sabre Tooth
6 Directosaur
7 Pterodactyl (V)

8 Moonlighting
9 Neanderthal
10 Barracuda
11 Right-Hand Gully

Descent

From the top of the buttress head west along the ridge a short way, passing the corniced top of Right-Hand Gully to reach Descent Gully (Grade I) (Map Ref 146 540). There is a convenient boulder which can be used if an abseil is required to break through the cornice. This gully can be prone to avalanche.

The alternative is to descend the ridge south-east to the col at the head of the Lost Valley; see above.

Sabre Tooth   120m   IV,4 *
I. Clough, H. MacInnes   9th February 1969
Towards the right side of the left half of the buttress there is a prominent vertical corner (the alternative start, Grade IV). Start up left from this corner. Climb to a snow bay, break out right, gain the terrace, then traverse left to a steep, shallow corner (also approachable by a traverse from the left). Climb the corner to a line of grooves which lead to the top.

Directosaur   160m   VI,7 *
G. Ettle, R. Anderson, R. Milne   March 1989
A good route taking a direct line up the right edge of the left half of the buttress. Start at the lowest rocks below the edge.
1. 45m   Climb the shallow groove just left of the edge, step left and move up to a ledge leading back right to the edge. Ascend a steep flake crack on the left, then follow easier ground to below a steep corner.
2. 30m   Climb the corner, then follow grooves up the right side of a huge block-like feature and continue to its top.
3. 35m   Move across right and climb a short groove to regain the crest. Snow grooves now lead to the upper rocks.
4. 50m   Continue up the snow grooves to the final slopes.

Moonlighting   120m   V,6 *
R. Anderson, G. Taylor, N. West   27th January 1988
Pterodactyl (Grade V) is the obvious line splitting the buttress into its two distinct halves. Start just right of this, at the top of a bay beneath a groove.
1. 35m   Climb the groove to a ledge at the foot of a wall.
2. 35m   The steep flake line up on the left leads to the edge overlook-

ing Pterodactyl. Go up and right to a shallow groove leading to a short wall.
3. 50m   The gully of Pterodactyl now leads to the top.

Neanderthal   120m   VII,7 ***
R. Anderson, G. Nicoll   14th February 1987
An improbable line up the huge corner some 30 metres right of Pterodactyl. Superb climbing in an impressive situation.
1. 20m   Move easily up a gully, then climb its left wall to a ledge.
2. 15m   Traverse right and climb a chute to belay at the *cul-de-sac.*
3. 20m   Move out right, then go up to the roof and gain the base of the corner. Climb the corner to a small ledge.
4. 25m   Continue up the corner to the right side of a square roof, then move left beneath this to cracks in a recessed wall. Climb the cracks over a small roof and go through the final eaves by the narrow slot which is clearly visible from below, lurking on the skyline. Belay by large blocks a short way above.
5. 40m   Climb the short corner to easy snow slopes and the top.

Barracuda   80m   V,7
R. Anderson, R. Milne   16th January 1988
An obvious steep crack springs from the ramp which runs up leftwards from the right edge of the frontal face. This gives a very short hard section followed by much easier climbing.
1. 10m   Follow the ramp past a groove to belay beneath a crack.
2. 20m   Climb the crack to the buttress edge and belay 5m higher in a shallow gully.
3. 50m   Follow the gully directly over a steepening to the top.

Trilobite   60m   III
I. Clough, H. MacInnes   9th February 1969
This climb follows the steep groove which runs up the face from where Right-Hand Gully narrows, opposite a ramp going up right (**The Ramp**, Grade II).

Right-Hand Gully   90m   II
The steep gully bounding the right side of the buttress often contains a small pitch and has a big cornice.

EAST FACE OF GEARR AONACH
(Map Ref 163 555)

This face overlooks the flat section of the Lost Valley. The upper half is formed by a steep continuous wall, rising over 100m from a broad snow ledge to meet the summit ridge. This is the Mome Rath Face, which is defined by the long, left-trending gullies of Lost Leeper on the left, and Rev Ted's on the right.

The lower parts of these two gullies allow access to the face, which does not come into condition often due to its sunny south-easterly aspect and its altitude of some 600m. The sun, however, provides a thaw-freeze cycle and when routes have built up, a number of excellent ice lines form, all of which have a tremendous outlook.

Descent

The recommended descent is to head south along the ridge into Coire nan Lochan and to come down the east side of the waterfall issuing from the corrie. It is also possible to descend easy snow slopes into the Lost Valley at the south-west end of the face.

At the extreme left end of the face are four main gullies, the leftmost three being hidden until almost directly beneath them. Approach from the path rising up the hillside beyond the flat section of the Lost Valley.

Gully A (Right Fork)   245m   IV,4 *
H. MacInnes, D. Crabbe   January 1964

This is the first gully encountered once the path starts to rise at the southern end of the Lost Valley. **Gully B** (Grade II), then **Gully C** (Grade I) lie to the left. A steep initial pitch leads to the bifurcation where the steep ice scoop on the right leads to easier climbing up the gully. An alternative from the bifurcation is the **Central Branch** (Grade IV), which continues directly up a steep ice scoop. **The Left Branch** (also Grade IV) starts as a steep ice pitch slightly left of the main gully.

Opposite: Raven's Gully, Buachaille Etive Mor   Climber: James Grossett
Photo: John Lyall

Next page: Crowberry Gully, Buachaille Etive Mor   Climber: Charlie Milton
Photo: Roger Wild

Lost Leeper Gully   300m   III
*H. MacInnes, A. Gilbert, P. Debbage, D. Layne-Joynt, D. Allwright
13th February 1969*
Rising from the end of the flat section of the Lost Valley, this shallow, indefinite gully bounds the left side of the Mome Rath Face. It provides interesting route finding with, higher up, the possibility of some ice pitches. Belays in the main part of the gully are poor. Beware of avalanches.

THE MOME RATH FACE

The face high up between Lost Leeper and Rev Ted's Gullies has a broad snow ledge beneath it which does not quite extend to the left end of the face. The left edge of the face is defined by a prominent deeply recessed diedre, the line of Rainmaker. A prominent icicle fringe, visible from the road, forms on the upper overhangs of the face. Also visible from the road and providing an indicator of conditions is a long thin ribbon of ice falling down the face to the right.

Snowstormer   VI,6 *
D. Cuthbertson, A. Paul, C. McLean   31st January 1984
Rainmaker (VI,6) follows the deeply recessed diedre; this route closely follows the exposed edge on the right. In its lower part it is mixed, with ice climbing above. Climb a short corner and continue to a belay on a small pedestal above an obvious V-notch (25m). Icy corners directly above lead to a belay under a small overlap overlooking Rainmaker. Easier climbing leads to the top.

Outgrabe Route   115m   V,5 **
R. Anderson, R. Milne   January 1980
A more direct and virtually independent line from that of the original Mome Rath Face Route. About 25m right of the left extremity of the alp, the Mome Rath shelf slants up and left. Start 10 metres left of this, below two obvious crack lines. Climb to a recess, continue up the left-hand crack and belay in the gully-chimney fault above. Follow this in two pitches, keeping left of the icicle fringe on the second.

Previous page: Neanderthal, Lost Valley Buttress
        Climber: Grahame Nicoll   *Photo: Rab Anderson*

Opposite: Central Grooves, Stob Coire nan Lochan
        Climber: Mark Garthwaite   *Photo: Garthwaite Collection*

Mome Rath Face Route   150m   V,5 **
A. Fyffe, J. McArtney   16th February 1969
This is one of the original winter routes on this area of the face, climbed the same day as The Wabe. It takes a left-slanting shelf to break out left about 20m up a steep chimney. Move left into another chimney. Climb this a short way to a bay on the left, then finish up a short steep corner-chimney.

Jabberwock   105m   VI,5 **
A. Paul, D. Cuthbertson   30th January 1984
Climb the icefall between Mome Rath Route and The Wabe, taking in the icicle fringe at the top. The icicle has to be complete!

The Wabe   135m   V,5 ***
H. MacInnes, J. Hardie, I. Clough   16th February 1969
An excellent and exposed route taking the fine icefall which descends the face to the right of the icicle fringe. Climb a wall to a ledge, then head up left to a small stance just below a prominent nose; flake belay. Turn the nose on the left, immediately above an overhang, and go up the corner on the right to a pedestal below the right edge of the icicle fringe. Move right and climb an icefall through a recessed panel to a stance on the rib to the right. Go diagonally right, then move back up left to finish.

Whimsy   120m   IV,5
R. Clothier, D. Hawthorn   January 1984
Climb the icefall which comes down the corner just to the right of The Wabe.

Rev Ted's Gully   300m   III *
H. MacInnes, Rev. Ted   February 1960
This is the long obvious gully which slants left up the full height of the face. The lower reaches are straightforward and it can be used to approach the Mome Rath Face. From the junction in the upper cliffs there are several options. The best are the icy chimney just left of an icefall, or the icefall direct. An easy right branch leads to a bay and another steep chimney, interesting but awkward. From the bay an escape right can be made, thus reducing the entire route to Grade II. Again, beware of avalanches.

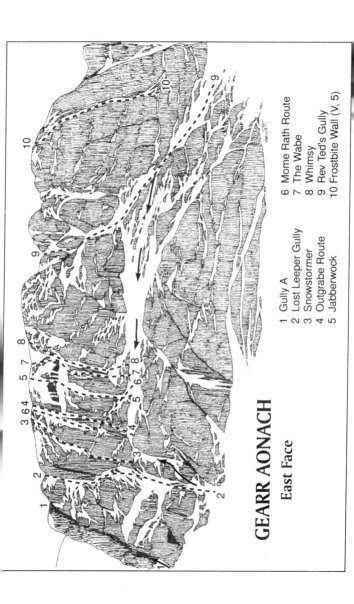

GEARR AONACH

East Face

1 Gully A
2 Lost Leeper Gully
3 Snowstormer
4 Outgrabe Route
5 Jabberwock

6 Mome Rath Route
7 The Wabe
8 Whimsy
9 Rev Ted's Gully
10 Frostbite Wall (V, 5)

Ingrid's Folly/Peregrine Gully   300m   III **
Glencoe School of Winter Climbing Party   *1960*
This long recessed gully system runs the full height of the face and is the first gully encountered on emerging from the boulder field (the second is **McArtney Gully**, Grade III). It gives an entertaining combination of routes. Follow the gully of Ingrid's Folly with some amusement, including a through route, to the easier upper gully. An easy finish can be made up this but further fun can be obtained by traversing up left into the shallow fault of Peregrine Gully. This provides further pitches of caves and chockstones. Avalanche prone.

The Graduate   170m   IV,4 *
D. Knowles, J. Loxham, D. Wilson, A. Wilson   *8th February 1969*
A prominent, large right-facing corner forms the left side of the huge recess which once housed the debris of the Lost Valley landslide. The corner is not often in full condition, but it is useful in lean conditions when it can provide steep, turfy climbing after a hard freeze.

The Zigzags   200m   I *
The easiest approach to the Gearr Aonach ridge is by the broken ground between the nose on the right and the North-East Face on the left. It is a fine start when combined with an ascent of Stob Coire nan Lochan and the ridges beyond. Those of a nervous disposition may require a rope for the upper section. From the entrance to the lower gorge of the Lost Valley, a short distance beyond the stile, a path leads up a rocky bluff. Above this, move up leftwards to the lowest rocks of the North-East Face at the start of the broken ground. Traverse up and right below overhanging rock walls. Go up past a tree, then back up left to the foot of the wall above and climb a short chimney step. Make a long traverse left beneath broken walls, then go up and back right to where the shelf opens out (small cairn). Go up, then left beneath a small wall to the ridge.

If used as a descent, reverse these directions. The way down may be difficult to locate. A small cairn marks the start, on the right when heading down, at the termination of the ridge. Due to the sheer nature of the terrain there are no other alternatives here. Care should be taken, especially under heavy snow when the ledges can form wind-slab. Conditions may dictate that the descent be pitched. It is not a recommended descent in heavy snow or for those without prior knowledge; it will always be safer to descend *via* Coire nan Lochan.

STOB COIRE NAN LOCHAN
1115m   (Map Ref 148 549)

Sitting at the inner end of the long ridges of Gearr Aonach and Aonach Dubh, this high peak presents a north-east facing corrie which provides a tremendous cliff with a superb outlook. The corrie is an idyllic spot, with several tiny lochans backed by tall columnar cliffs and deeply cut gullies. The height of the corrie floor (780m), coupled with its northerly aspect, makes it the most reliable winter face in Glen Coe. Accordingly there is a variety of excellent routes of all grades. Since the cliffs take little drainage there is not much ice, but there are a number of fine snowed-up rock routes. There are few routes that require a lengthy build-up and there are a number that can be done after a cold snap and a dump of snow. Some of the harder mixed routes hold little snow and it is best to catch them in hoared-up condition after they have been in the cloud and wind. Due to the rock type and its formation, the frost shattering of the winter has created a fair amount of loose rock, particularly on terraces and ledges, so take care.

COIRE NAN LOCHAIN   *(Map Ref 150 553)*

The topography of the corrie is straightforward. On the left, Summit Buttress lies beneath the summit. To its right is the uncomplicated slope of Broad Gully, then further right in turn are Forked Gully, Twisting Gully, South, Central and North buttresses and finally Pinnacle Buttress. The buttresses are divided by narrow gullies, the most prominent being SC Gully between South and Central buttresses.

Access

Start from either of two large laybys on the main road opposite the entrance to the corrie. Cross the bridge over the River Coe at Map Ref 166 566 and follow the well trodden path up the side of Gearr Aonach. There are two paths; after some 30 minutes the lower path reaches the burn tumbling down the valley floor just above a waterfall. A crossing here leads to the East Face of Aonach Dubh. Continuing up on the Gearr Aonach side, the two paths converge and continue beneath a series of rocky outcrops to cross the burn just before a small ravine into which a waterfall plummets from the floor of the corrie. Go right then up around a rocky outcrop to gain the corrie (1½ to 2 hours). The steep slopes below the crags accumulate large amounts of fresh snow after a south-westerly blizzard, so beware of avalanche danger.

Descent
The quickest descent from the top of the climb is by Broad Gully. However, a good, safe alternative is to follow the rim of the corrie northwards, taking care of the deeply cut gullies, to easy ground on Aonach Dubh where a short easy slope leads back into the corrie.

The routes are described from left to right.

Boomerang Gully   210m   II *
W.H. Murray, J. Black, R.G. Donaldson   January 1949
This pleasant route follows the obvious curving gully immediately left of the steepest rocks of Summit Buttress. There is often an ice pitch where it turns to the right. At that point the left branch (Grade II) moves onto the face.

Scabbard Chimney   120m   V,6 ***
L.S. Lovat, J.R. Marshall, A.H. Hendry   12th February 1956
Although an excellent natural winter line, this superb climb is not likely to hold much ice. Start beneath the most obvious feature of the buttress, a chimney slanting up right under the steep right flank.
1. 50m   Climb a short chimney to easier ground, then climb the steep crack and corner line with interest to a stance beneath a sentry box.
2. 40m   The right-hand side of the sentry box has a crack which leads with some difficulty to the rib on the right. Climb this, then return back left to easier ground which leads to a shoulder overlooking Broad Gully.
3. 30m   Climb the narrow gully on the left.

From the belay below the easy gully, a long abseil into Broad Gully gives a quick approach to the following route. The abseil sling can be collected on the way past. Those going well should also be able to include Innuendo for an energetic day.

Spectre   120m   IV,5 *
K. Bryan, J. Simpson   12th January 1958
This fine companion to Scabbard Chimney takes the steep shelf about 10 metres to the right. Climb a broken wall to a point directly below the first true chimney section of Scabbard (20m). Above and to the right, a 10m slab leads to a ledge. Follow this to the right for 5 metres to where an awkward descent leads to the long shelf. Above, climb an icy bulge and an icy groove. Climb a steep slab and a bulge to an easing and continue to a broad ledge leading to the narrow gully of Scabbard Chimney.

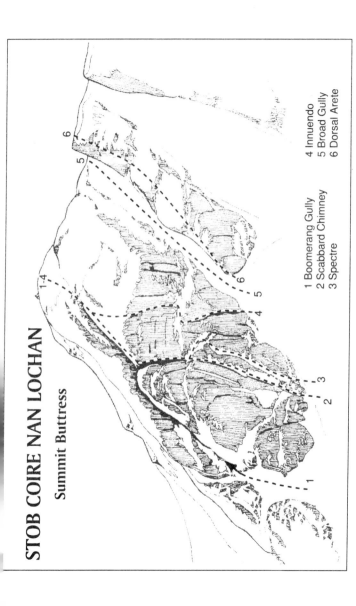

STOB COIRE NAN LOCHAN
Summit Buttress

1 Boomerang Gully
2 Scabbard Chimney
3 Spectre
4 Innuendo
5 Broad Gully
6 Dorsal Arete

Innuendo   150m   IV,5 *
H. MacInnes, R. Birch, P. Judge, R. O'Shea   1969
This is the obvious chimney-groove on the side wall overlooking Broad
Gully, right of and below the final gully of Scabbard Chimney. Start level
with the foot of Dorsal Arete. Climb the chimney-groove to a ledge on
the left (35m). Continue to a belay in an overhung bay. Exit from the
bay by an awkward chimney on the right and climb easily up rightwards
to below the upper wall. Finally, traverse right beneath a hanging
chimney until steep cracks lead back left into the chimney above the
overhang. The chimney leads to easier ground.

Broad Gully   150m   I *
This is an easy access and descent route, but it should be avoided in
avalanche conditions. An alternative, safer descent takes the ridge
down to the north, as described above.

Dorsal Arete   120m   II ***
J. Black, T. Shepherd, J. Allingham, J. Bradburn   28th January 1951
Starting from Broad Gully, this excellent and popular route takes the
rib between it and Forked Gully. Climb a groove in two pitches to a good
ledge. Above, the arete becomes more defined and very narrow, with
steep sides falling away on both flanks. This section is often avoided
by a rising traverse on the left flank, leading to the final wall. The belays
are good.

Twisting Gully   150m   III,4 **
W.H. Murray, D. Scott, J. Cortland-Simpson   December 1946
This is one of the classic Scottish winter routes, taking the gully running
up the left side of South Buttress. Climb to a deep recess where the
gully forks, belay on the left wall. Climb the chimney on the left to where
it steepens, gain a ledge on the vertical left wall (crux), then traverse
left along this to the crest. Above, an awkward mantelshelf is followed
by some 30m of snow and a small pitch, then easy ground leads to the
final snow fan and a choice of steep exits.

Moonshadow   150m   IV,4 *
J.R. Marshall, I.D. Haig   January 1958
K.V. Crocket, C. Stead   30th January 1972
The first section of this good and sustained combination is the Right
Fork of Twisting Gully. The prominent right-trending corner on the left
flank of the buttress provides a fitting finish. The Right Fork can be
continued to rejoin Twisting Gully.

1. 30m   Climb Twisting Gully to where it forks.
2. 40m   Move right and climb the chimney on steep ice to belay 10m above an ice bulge.
3. 35m   The corner starts on the right wall. Climb the wall to a thread belay in the corner.
4. 45m   Continue up the groove past a chockstone to the top.

Chimney Route   125m   VI,6 **
The steep chimney overlooking the start of Twisting Gully gives a first rate climb. It is often mistaken for Direct Route or Tilt, both of which start further right.
1. 25m   Climb steeply up the chimney
2. 45m   Continue up, then move slightly right on turfy ground to the left end of the upper terrace and a junction with Tilt. On this pitch it would also be possible to head straight up into the wide chimney of Inclination. This is separated from the upper terrace by a huge fin of rock.
3 and 4. 55m   Now follow Tilt to the top.

Tilt   140m   VI, 7 **
M. Hamilton, K. Spence, A. Taylor   20th January 1980
Excellent sustained climbing. Start immediately left of the buttress crest at a line leading to a chimney some 20m up.
1. 40m   Climb cracks and ledges to the foot of the chimney, then climb this to the crest.
2. 25m   Follow the groove above and once above an overhang move right onto the wall and climb to a huge flake.
3. 20m   Climb grooves to the upper terrace.
4. 25m   Move left along the terrace. Climb a wall to make an awkward entry into a V-groove and finish up this.
5. 30m   Easy climbing leads to the top.

SC Gully   150m   III ***
P.D. Baird, E. Leslie, H. Fynes-Clinton   March 1934
Cleaving a line through impressive rock scenery between the tallest cliffs of South and Central Buttresses, this is one of the classic gully climbs of Glen Coe. Normally there is a short ice pitch near the start. A second pitch continues up steep snow in the narrowing gully to a *cul-de-sac*. The next pitch, the crux, takes the icefall curving its way up the right-hand corner. Reach this by an awkward right traverse to a

ramp, then climb the icefall, which may be some 20m high, to the easy upper section of the gully. A long runout may be required to reach a belay. More snow leads to a corniced exit. The route can be much harder in lean conditions.

East Face Route   130m   V,7 *
M. Hamilton, R. Anderson   20th March 1982
Overlooking the entrance to SC Gully on the side wall of Central Buttress are two steep, staggered, parallel, shallow chimney systems. This route climbs part way up the left-hand one before moving into the right-hand one.
1. 20m   Climb the chimney, then move left to a pedestal.
2. 15m   Move back right and climb past the left end of a roof in the corner to good belays in a shallow recess.
3. 30m   Move across the wall on the right, make a hard swing around the arete, then go up right to enter another gully system.
4. 45m   Climb the gully past a steepening to belay on its left wall.
5. 20m   Move right to the snow crest. Finish up Ordinary Route.

Central Grooves   130m   VII,7 ***
K. Spence, J. McKenzie   February 1983
A magnificent climb up the obvious diedre which springs from the toe of the buttress.
1. 30m   Climb the corner to small ledges.
2. 25m   Continue up the corner to ledges on the crest.
3. 50m   Follow the grooves above, passing left of a conspicuous overhang, to finish on a broad terrace.
4. 25m   Easy climbing leads to the top.

Ordinary Route   150m   IV,4 **
H. Raeburn, Dr and Mrs C. Inglis Clark   April 1907
An excellent, open route with fine situations. Start in the small bay some 10 metres right of the crest where an angle is formed between the main face and the projecting spur on the right. Climb mixed ground, then a groove, moving right at its top to gain the edge overlooking NC Gully. Follow the edge to a tower, visible from below, and turn this on the right by a short chimney. Continue by a series of short awkward walls. It can be technically easier but more difficult to protect under icy conditions.

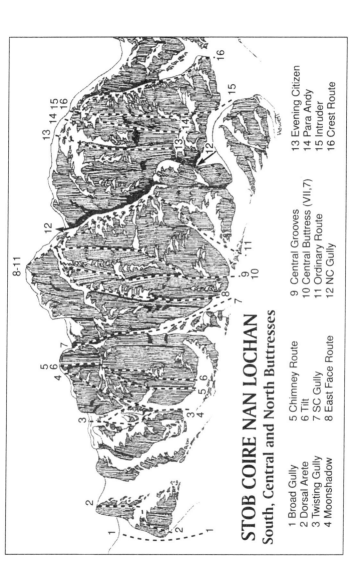

STOB COIRE NAN LOCHAN
South, Central and North Buttresses

1 Broad Gully
2 Dorsal Arete
3 Twisting Gully
4 Moonshadow

5 Chimney Route
6 Tilt
7 SC Gully
8 East Face Route

9 Central Grooves
10 Central Buttress (VII,7)
11 Ordinary Route
12 NC Gully

13 Evening Citizen
14 Para Andy
15 Intruder
16 Crest Route

NC Gully   180m   II *

This gully splits Central and North buttresses. It is normally a straight-forward snow climb with a small cornice, but it can sometimes form a short pitch. A good introduction to gully climbing.

Evening Citizen   95m   IV,5 *

K. Spence, H. MacInnes, A. Thomson   1971

This route takes the obvious corner line left of a prominent roofed pillar, overlooking NC Gully. Start in NC Gully then climb the corner-chimney and go up steeply to the crest.

Para Andy   90m   VI,7 *

A. Cunningham, A. Nisbet, A. Newton   8th January 1988

The large corner-groove right of the roofed pillar is notable for some sensational exposure above the big roof. Climb directly up to the groove (35m). Climb the groove until squeezed against a roof (some dangerous blocks), then traverse left and mantelshelf. Belay on the ledge on the front face above the big roof. Pass the short wall immediately above by going left and back right to a crack line in the centre of the face. Climb this until moves left lead to a ledge and a blocky arete leading to the top of the tower.

Intruder   100m   VI,7 *

R. Anderson, G. Nicoll   14th February 1988

This climb follows the slimmer, right-hand groove right of the roofed pillar. Start at the lowest rocks.

1. 15m   Move up left and climb to the base of the groove.

2. 25m   Climb the groove to a flake, then continue to a ledge at the foot of a large flake.

3. 35m   Gain the groove up on the left and climb this to the top of a pinnacle. Move up, then go right to climb a short groove and traverse right to belay by an obvious perched block.

4. 25m   Easy climbing leads to the top.

Crest Route   110m   V,6 **

M. Hamilton, R. Anderson   24th November 1985

This fine route takes the crest between the east and north faces. It is a good introduction to modern snowed-up rock climbing. Start at the lowest rocks.

1. 35m   Move right, climb broken stepped ground to a short wall, then climb a crack to a pedestal.

2. 30m   Climb the flake crack above, then go right across a slab and climb a groove to the crest. Step left at a large spike to a ledge level with a pinnacle.

3. 20m   Regain the groove-crack and follow this directly up the crest to belay by an obvious perched block.

4. 25m   Finish more easily.

NORTH-WEST FACE OF GEARR AONACH

The hillside just west of the nose on Gearr Aonach is marked by a prominent gully running virtually the full height of the face. The stream flowing from this gully crosses the approach path some 5 minutes walk from the bridge over the River Coe, on the approach to Stob Coire nan Lochan.

Avalanche Gully   600m   IV,4 **
H. MacInnes and party   1960
The gully slants right; where it forks, in both the lower and upper reaches, the right branch should be taken. There are some steep pitches which can be turned. Higher up, the gully runs out into broken ground overlooking Farewell Gully and a choice of finishes. Although it takes time to come into full condition, all that is required is a good freeze. Given a hard freeze the lower stream can provide some 6 or 7 pitches on water ice, starting from just above the path. The climb is graded for these conditions and would be easier under snow.

The **Lower Left Fork** (Grade IV) gives a short climb to finish on an open ledge exiting left. The **Upper Left Fork** (Grade IV), when combined with the normal route, provides a first rate climb. It has a short pitch to start, then it goes under a big chockstone to a steep pitch, rarely in condition. Above, a further pitch is usually climbed on the left to easier snow. It is possible to escape on either side.

EAST FACE OF AONACH DUBH
(Map Ref 157 558)

This face has a number of walls which can be reached by crossing the burn where the path meets it just above the waterfall after some 30 minutes walk on the approach to Stob Coire nan Lochan. A number of routes have had ascents, but they require a lot of snow and a good low freeze. However, they may be useful when higher ground is under very heavy snow and/or avalanche prone.

Immediately above the stream crossing are the Lower Walls. The first corner encountered can form an impressive ice streak, **Excellerator** (V,5) whilst to the right around the edge are **Paul Rodger's Wake** (IV,4) and then **Heart of Glass** (IV,5), an ice line up an obvious chimney. Going back uphill is a stepped icefall (Grade III), then an obvious corner on the buttress, **Drain Pipe Corner** (IV,5). Under deep snow the summer line of the **Long Crack** (VI,7) up the face to the left provides a technical outing. Further ice forms up left and on the Terrace Face above.

Further up the hillside, opposite the stream crossing, is The Far East Buttress. **Orient Express** (IV,5) takes an obvious line up the initial corner to climb a thin iced chimney.

NORTH FACE OF AONACH DUBH
(Map Ref 156 563)

The most obvious feature of the massive face lying above Loch Achtriochtan is the great black slot of Ossian's Cave. Left of this, a prominent gully slants leftwards through the lower part of the face. Further left again is the Lower Cliff. After a good freeze and a dump of snow this face provides a number of good long routes with a short approach.

Slanting across the face from left to right is a prominent ledge system. Its upper half, right of Ossian's Cave, is known as Sloping Shelf. Although no routes here are described in this guide, it is worth knowing that its slabby nature and easily accumulated snow tends to make it a very high avalanche risk.

Access
Cross the footbridge across the River Coe at Map Ref 166 566, as for Stob Coire nan Lochan, then cross the boulders at the outflow of the burn descending from the corrie and head up and right to the base of the routes.

Descent
From the top of the Lower Cliff, head downhill towards Coire nan Lochan and drop down steeply between the cliffs of the East Face and the Lower North-East Nose, to pass beneath the latter and go down on the Aonach Dubh side of the burn. If in doubt, head up then along into Coire nan Lochan before descending.

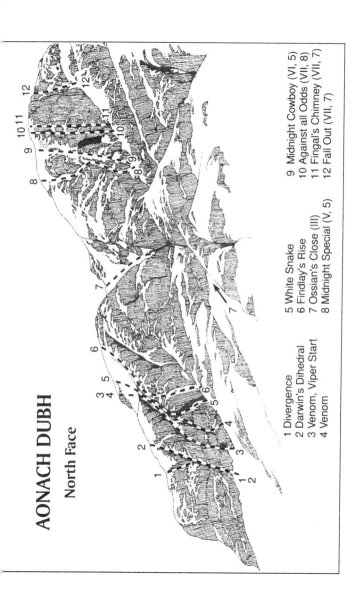

AONACH DUBH

North Face

1 Divergence
2 Darwin's Dihedral
3 Venom, Viper Start
4 Venom

5 White Snake
6 Findlay's Rise
7 Ossian's Close (III)
8 Midnight Special (V, 5)

9 Midnight Cowboy (VI, 5)
10 Against all Odds (VII, 8)
11 Fingal's Chimney (VII, 7)
12 Fall Out (VII, 7)

Darwin's Dihedral   240m   VI,6 **
D. Cuthbertson, M. Lawrence   28th December 1981
This climb takes the right branch of the obvious Y-shaped feature. Climb
an icefall and then the large, right-facing corner. **Divergence** (Grade
IV) follows the left branch.

Venom   300m   IV,6 *
A. McAllister, M. Duff, R. Anderson, D. Brown   January 1979
A short way to the right, twin gullies start about 100m up the face; this
climb takes the left-hand one. Start towards the right side of the initial
wall and climb an icicle to a shallow chimney. This leads through trees
to a tree-covered ledge. Traverse left to another chimney, which leads
to the gully. Continue up, turning two large roofs on the right.

Venom, Viper Start   120m   IV,5 *
R. Anderson, D. Brown   February 1979
This climbs the icefall and less obvious chimney left of the original start.
The chimney leads more directly to the left-hand gully, avoiding the
traverse of the arboreal ledge. For the energetic, an abseil descent can
be made through the trees, followed by an ascent of the normal line.

White Snake   360m   IV,5
A. McAllister, M. Duff, R. Anderson, D. Brown   January 1979
The right-hand of the two gullies. Climb an obvious icefall up a slanting
corner to a huge roof, go left and continue up the right-hand gully.

Findlay's Rise   150m   IV,5 *
I. Nicolson   1978
The obvious icefall on the buttress just right of White Snake usually
forms by mid-winter, given sufficient freezing. Climb the ice direct and
continue up the buttress, usually awkward, sometimes desperate.

COIRE NAM BEITHACH

This is the great north corrie of Bidean nam Bian, the entrance to which
is flanked on the left by the West Face of Aonach Dubh, and on the right
by An t-Sron. Framed between the two is the great pyramidal cone of

No.6 Gully, West Face of Aonach Dubh   *Photo: Steve Kennedy*

Stob Coire nam Beith, left of which lies the West Top of Bidean, then further left at the head of the corrie are the two distinctive summit buttresses of Bidean nam Bian.

WEST FACE OF AONACH DUBH
(Map Ref 145 555)

This face flanks the entrance to Coire nam Beithach and dominates the lower reaches of the Glen. The majority of the climbs require a build-up of snow and ice and the face can take time to come into ideal condition.

The face is best seen from the old Glencoe road near the Clachaig Inn. It is divided vertically by six gullies, forming distinct buttresses, and cut horizontally by two ledges. The lower, narrow ledge is called Middle Ledge, while the upper, broader ledge is known as The Rake.

The gullies are numbered 1 to 6 from left to right, with the main mass of the middle tier between Gullies 3 and 4 further split by two scoops. The most prominent gully is No.2, which runs up to the col between Aonach Dubh and Stob Coire nan Lochan. To its left are Dinnertime Buttress (originally A Buttress), then No.1 Gully. To its right the buttresses continue from B to F, divided by the gullies from No.3 (with C-D Scoop and Amphitheatre Scoop on its right) to No.6.

Access

Begin where the main road crosses the River Coe (Map Ref 137 566) at the junction of the main road and the old road leading to the Clachaig Inn. Parking is at a premium here so be considerate. Walk across the bridge, taking care for fast moving traffic, go through a small gate and follow the path which gradually steepens as the prominent waterfalls are approached. The well constructed footpath zigzags its way up the right side of the falls heading towards Stob Coire nam Beith.

Strike off left below the lowest waterfall, cross the stream and gain the lower slopes of Dinnertime Buttress. No.2 Gully is easily crossed at this point, giving access to the grassy lower tier of B Buttress, or any of the gullies further right. Middle Ledge is most easily gained *via* the lower tier of B Buttress, from where it runs rightwards. Climbs on the right side of the face can be gained more directly from where the path to Stob Coire nam Beith levels out above the waterfalls.

On the Aonach Eagach ridge   *Climber: John Bennet*

Photo: Donald Bennet

Descent

(i) The safest descent from the top of the face, particularly in bad weather, is to head east and descend *via* Coire nan Lochan.

(ii) From the col between Aonach Dubh and Stob Coire nan Lochan, go down the easy upper section of No.2 Gully. Even in bad weather it is difficult to miss the gully since it has a wide re-entrant. When it steepens below Middle Ledge, traverse onto Dinnertime Buttress. The rocks of both gully and buttress are thereby avoided. The Rake provides an easy way left into No.2 Gully from some routes.

(iii) Traverse towards Stob Coire nam Beith and descend into the corrie below its north face. Do not descend too early as there are crags below.

Dinnertime Buttress   335m   II *

The leftmost buttress between No.1 and No.2 Gullies provides a good poor weather route and an alternative approach to Stob Coire nan Lochan. Various options exist on reaching the final rocky section.

No.3 Gully   300m   III

The gully right of B Buttress is shallow and indefinite where it starts, but it can give a good ice pitch. It is much more defined above Middle Ledge.

The Screen   75m   IV,5 **

D. Bathgate, J. Brumfitt   February 1965

The icefall which forms over the lowest tier right of No.3 Gully gives a good outing when combined with C-D Scoop or The Smear. Climb to an icicle recess, traverse right, then move left above the icicles to the final steep runnel.

The Smear   75m   IV,4 *

I. Clough, I. Duckworth, F. Wells, R. York   26th March 1969

On C Buttress, just right of No.3 Gully where it cuts the middle tier, this icefall provides a continuation to The Screen.

C-D Scoop   150m   II *

D. Bathgate, J. Brumfitt   February 1965

The gully right of No.3 Gully, rising above Middle Ledge, can be climbed on its own, or following an ascent of The Screen. From Middle Ledge, two short ice pitches lead to The Rake. A good finish, giving one further pitch, is by the hidden right branch of the gully on the left, the continuation of No.3 Gully.

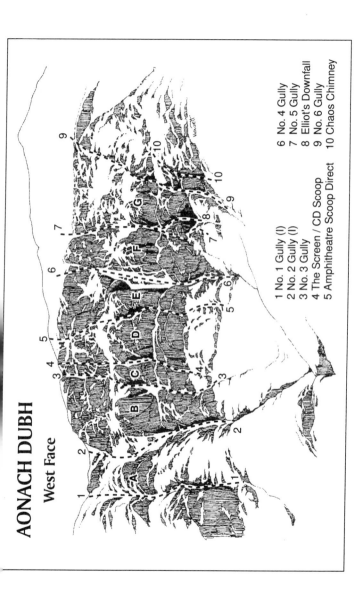

AONACH DUBH
West Face

1 No. 1 Gully (I)
2 No. 2 Gully (I)
3 No. 3 Gully
4 The Screen / CD Scoop
5 Amphitheatre Scoop Direct

6 No. 4 Gully
7 No. 5 Gully
8 Elliot's Downfall
9 No. 6 Gully
10 Chaos Chimney

The Flute   75m   IV,5 **
D. Cuthbertson, W. Todd   30th January 1979
The narrow, icy chimney line right of The Screen leads to Middle Ledge.

Amphitheatre Scoop Direct   240m   V,5 ***
I. Clough, G. Lowe, J. Hardie   18th February 1966
R. Bruce, A. McAllister, R. Anderson   January 1979
This is one of the best routes on the face. Above Middle Ledge a scoop
divides D and E Buttresses. Start beneath the lower tier in line with the
scoop and climb an icefall in two pitches to Middle Ledge. Above, climb
steep ice up a corner *via* a pedestal belay on the left wall to easier
ground; this leads to The Rake where an easy continuation slants left
to the top. The upper section can easily be reached by a traverse along
Middle Ledge.

No.4 Gully   300m   IV,4
J. Brown, D. Whillans   26th December 1952
The prominent broad gully in the centre of the face can give several
ice pitches below Middle Ledge. Higher, the gully trifurcates with the
main central branch rarely being in condition. Exit out left, or climb
Christmas Couloir.

Christmas Couloir   240m   IV,4 *
I. Clough, D.G. Roberts   25th December 1965
Approach by No.4 Gully or Middle Ledge. The route takes an obvious
rake above and right of the bed of No.4 Gully, just left of F Buttress. At
the crag splitting the gully, climb a steep section right of the buttress;
this is right of the unclimbed right fork of No.4 Gully. This is the crux
and is often heavily iced. Above, the route continues up the right side
of The Amphitheatre, leading to three obvious finishes, the direct one
being the most difficult.

No.5 Gully   300m   III *
A. Fyffe, C. MacInnes, N. Clough   18th February 1969
Climb an obvious short, shallow, slanting gully to the left of the hanging
icicle of Elliot's Downfall. Where the gully steepens, move up right to a
ridge left of the gully bed. Traverse right into the gully and climb an ice
pitch to the easier upper section. There may be an easy-angled 45m
ice pitch here.

Elliot's Downfall   105m   VI,6 ***
D. Cuthbertson   February 1979
This spectacular pillar of ice occasionally forms the Direct Start to No.5 Gully. One long very steep pitch leads to two easier pitches and a junction with No.5 Gully. It is prone to collapse, especially when the extra weight of a climber is added and it is being stressed by enthusiastic tool placements!

No.6 Gully   240m   IV,4 ***
D. Munro, P. Smith   30th March 1951
The rightmost gully on the face comes into condition most winters. Normally, two ice pitches lead to the crux, a large icefall at the level of Middle Ledge. There is a small stance about 15m up the icefall, otherwise a long pitch ensues. At the top of the gully there is a small bay and a choice of finishes. A traverse off right above steep ground leads to the corrie beneath Stob Coire nam Beith.

Chaos Chimney   135m   III *
A. Fyffe, E. Viveash, B. Jenkins, P. Hardman, J. Snodgrass   February 1969
The chimney-gully right of No.6 Gully can be difficult if it is not well filled with snow and ice.

STOB COIRE NAM BEITH
1107m   (Map Ref 139 546)

This shapely peak, the north-west top of Bidean, dominates the view from Glen Coe over Loch Achtriochtan. It is a huge, conical mass some 350m high, riven with buttresses and gullies.

Approaching up the Allt Coire nam Beithach, the most obvious feature is Summit Gully, running up left of the right-hand skyline. On its right is West Buttress and on its left is a buttress formed by The Pyramid and The Sphinx. Left of these, the shallow North-West Gully wanders up and left. Then comes No.4 Buttress, with the prominent Deep-Cut Chimney running up its left side. Left of this is No.3 Buttress, the highest and broadest on the mountain whose principal feature is the shallow but continuous Central Gully. Beyond this and hidden from view is Arch Gully.

Access

Begin as for the West Face of Aonach Dubh at the junction of the main road and the old road leading to the Clachaig Inn. Go through a gate on the other side of the bridge and follow the well constructed path which zigzags up right of the waterfalls. Above these the path levels out and crosses a slabby section (if iced, it may be easier to descend to stream level) to reach a fork in the streams. Cross the right branch, head up the side of the vague central branch, then go around the top of a rocky bluff and left to the corrie floor (1½ hours). The vague central branch of the stream leads to Summit Gully.

The path following the right branch continues to the Bealach An t-Sron, a col on the ridge between Stob Coire nam Beith and An t-Sron; this is the surest descent route. Lying at a height of some 630m the main corrie floor is occupied by some large boulders and old fence posts, a useful reference point in poor visibility.

Descent

The easiest route is to go down the cairned west ridge to the col between Stob Coire nam Beith and An t-Sron. In poor visibility this descent can be confusing, especially when approached from Bidean nam Bian. From the summit cairn of Stob Coire nam Beith a ridge drops gently northwards, appearing to offer a descent. However, this actually heads off down the north face of the mountain. Instead, go west from the cairn around the broad head of Summit Gully (which is only some 5 metres from the summit) and descend. The ridge levels off and becomes sharply defined where it curves around the head of the subsidiary corrie. Continue to the Bealach An t-Sron, where a small hump separates the two lowest points (Map Ref 135 547). From the col, head eastwards into the subsidiary corrie and go down to the main path.

Descent can also be made from the convergence of Buttresses 2 to 4 by traversing south-east towards Bidean nam Bian, contouring the upper easy part of Arch Gully, then crossing easy ground above No.1 Buttress and Zero Buttress, to drop into the basin which runs up beneath the West Top of Bidean nam Bian. Easy slopes lead down to the corrie. This is useful if time is pressing.

Arch Gully   III
J.H.B. Bell, C.M. Allan   *December 1933*
This gully runs up the left side of the main mass of rock. It is set back and hidden until the lowest rocks have been turned.

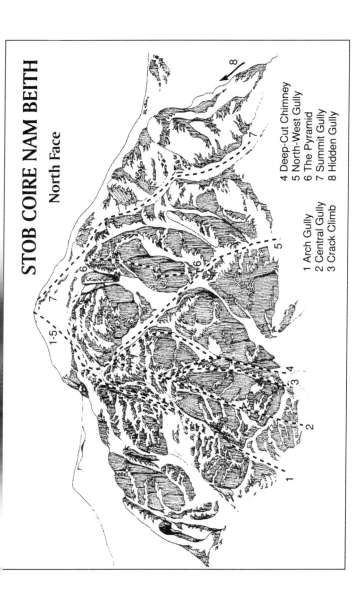

STOB COIRE NAM BEITH

North Face

1 Arch Gully
2 Central Gully
3 Crack Climb
4 Deep-Cut Chimney
5 North-West Gully
6 The Pyramid
7 Summit Gully
8 Hidden Gully

Central Gully   450m   IV,4 **
J. Clarkson, J. Waddell   12th January 1958
One of the best winter climbs on the mountain, this route takes the shallow gully up the centre of No.3 Buttress. It is a natural ice trap, and a large icefall can form at the start. From just left of the lowest rocks climb the left side of the icefall (the right side is an optional start) to gain the gully. Follow this with continuous interest up several steep pitches to easier ground.

Crack Climb   450m   III *
L.S. Lovat, N.G. Harthill   12th January 1958
The crack and groove at the right edge of No.3 Buttress, overlooking Deep-Cut Chimney. Start at the apex of a cone of scree at the foot of the buttress. Climb the crack for two pitches to a grass ledge, continue up, then traverse 10 metres right towards Deep-Cut Chimney, and a possible escape. The vertical wall above leads with difficulty to easier ground.

Deep-Cut Chimney   450m   IV,4 ***
W.M. Mackenzie, W.H. Murray   7th April 1939
The prominent narrow chimney-gully dividing Buttresses 3 and 4 provides a classic climb. In its time, it was one of the hardest winter routes in the Central Highlands. The chimney ends 120m up in a small amphitheatre, normally reached in three or four short ice pitches. The true line is then by the left fork, which will be difficult if thinly iced. The right fork allows an escape to easier ground. To finish, either climb 200m of easier ground to the summit or contour south-east across the upper part of Arch Gully and traverse off left.

North-West Gully   450m   III **
G.T. Glover, Wordsell   April 1906
Sometimes mistaken for Summit Gully, this is the shallow gully which starts right of No.4 Buttress and just left of the ridge formed by The Pyramid. It wanders up and left to the convergence of the main buttresses well below the summit. The scenery is good and there is usually at least one pitch, even by the easiest line. If the ice pitches left of the normal start are included, the gully can attain Grade IV. From below The Pyramid go up and left into the gully where easy snow leads up past The Sphinx to a fork. The left fork continues without difficulty to the convergence of the buttresses. The right fork leads in 80m to a

second fork (the buttress splitting the gully here is taken by **The Mummy**, Grade IV). At this junction the left fork is better and may give a short pitch leading to the shoulder. A steep wall left of the shoulder gives the crux of the climb. Easier climbing above leads to the summit. There is a risk of avalanche on this climb.

The Sphinx   135m   IV,4 *
J.R. Marshall, I. Douglas   12th January 1958
North-West Gully's right side is formed by two buttresses set one above the other, forming the ridge left of Summit Gully. The lower, wedge-like buttress is **The Pyramid** (Grade III) and this, or the gully can be used to gain the upper buttress, The Sphinx. About halfway up this buttress, there is a cave. Start below and slightly left of it by a shattered wall. Climb to a small basin under the cave and traverse right to a platform under the steep upper rocks. Climb walls for 20m to reach a chimney, then gain a little recess 3m up to the right where a pinnacle-flake on the right-hand edge leads to easier ground.

Summit Gully   450m   II *
This is the big gully which runs up left of the right-hand skyline and trends up left to a point just right of the summit cairn. It starts to the right of the ridge formed by The Pyramid and should not be (though it often is) confused with North-West Gully on the left. From below, Summit Gully appears to be the only deep and obvious gully on the mountain. The vague central branch of the approach stream leads directly to it. The gully combines length with good scenery. There may be a short ice pitch near the foot and despite occasional forks the route is fairly obvious. High up, a cave pitch seems to bar the way and often provides a reasonable pitch, otherwise turn it on the right. Much higher, a prominent rock rib forms an island in the gully. Another avalanche-prone route in poor conditions.

Hidden Gully   350m   IV,4 *
L.S. Lovat, W.J.R. Greaves   13th February 1955
A fine route taking the narrow, twisting gully well up right from the lowest rocks, above a large rock island at the entrance to the subsidiary corrie on the right. The gully remains hidden until one is above the rock island. A 20m snow cone leads to a cave, then climb the icy left wall. Easy snow for 30m leads to another cave; avoid this on the left by a very short ice pitch. Snow with occasional ice and a gradual increase in angle lead in 90m to a saddle above a rock rib in the middle of the

gully. Beyond, the gully steepens and narrows, and 25m of snow leads to an overhang and a short chimney. A short distance above, a rock rib divides the very narrow gully into two narrower exits. Take the left-hand option, a long, slanting open chimney with a steep exit (35m). Finish in 150m or so by the right bounding ridge of Summit Gully.

BIDEAN NAM BIAN
1150m   (Map Ref 143 542)

This majestic mountain has two distinctive buttresses just below its summit. Diamond Buttress (Map Ref 144 544), the left-hand of the two, is bounded on its right by Central Gully, at the foot of which sits Collie's Pinnacle. Church Door Buttress (Map Ref 143 544) is the impressive right-hand buttress. To the right lie the cliffs below the West Top.

Access
From the corrie floor beneath Stob Coire nam Beith, follow the right side of the stream, go around a rocky spur to a shallow basin, then continue up slopes to another shallow basin. Diamond and Church Door Buttresses are directly ahead up the slope whilst up on the right, through a gateway formed by a rock sentinel and the shoulder of Stob Coire nam Beith, lie the slopes beneath the West Top. These highest buttresses are about 2½ hours from the road.

Descent
(i) From the col between Bidean nam Bian and its West Top go down beneath Church Door Buttress.
(ii) Follow the north-east ridge to the col (Map Ref 146 545) between Bidean nam Bian and Stob Coire nan Lochan, then down into Coire nam Beith (beware of avalanches).
(iii) Go over the West Top to the col (Map Ref 140 543) between this and Stob Coire nam Beith, then descend beneath the cliffs of the West Top into the corrie.
(iv) Continue over Stob Coire nam Beith and go down its west ridge to the col at the Bealach An t-Sron (Map Ref 135 547) where easy slopes lead into the corrie. In dangerous snow conditions this alternative is by far the safest. In poor visibility, refer to the more detailed description given in the Stob Coire nam Beith section.
    The cliffs and their routes are described from left to right.

DIAMOND BUTTRESS

North Route Direct   210m   III
L.S. Lovat, W. Harrison   13th March 1955
This climb follows the left edge of Diamond Buttress. Start below an obvious scoop at the lowest rocks at the left end of the face. The scoop swings up right onto the face and eventually overhangs where it splits a projecting spur. Climb the arete on the right, then make a short steep horizontal traverse round an edge into another scoop. Snow covered slabs and an awkward crack lead to a platform above the overhang of the first scoop. A long traverse left leads back to the crest, then follow this to the top. The original route (Grade II) skirts around the left edge of the buttress by chimneys and scoops.

Direct Route   150m   V,6 **
J. McLean, M. Noon   January 1959
This route takes the obvious winter line on the right side of Diamond Buttress, a system of grooves leading up and right to the right end of the central girdling ledge. Continue by more grooves going up and right to emerge on the right-hand edge not far below the summit.

Central Gully   180m   I/II **
N. Collie, G.A. Solly, J. Collier   March 1894
This gully separates Diamond and Church Door Buttresses, and is divided at its foot by Collie's Pinnacle. It gives an interesting and scenic approach to the summit of the mountain. There are two routes: the first (Grade I) starts right of the Pinnacle and continues directly to the top. There should be no complications given enough snow; the second (Grade II) starts left of the Pinnacle, where there can be a short pitch. About 75m above the Pinnacle, take the right fork. Beware of avalanches in poor conditions.

CHURCH DOOR BUTTRESS

Crypt Route   135m   IV,6 **
H. MacInnes and party   1960
This unique route finds a way up the chimney in the alcove formed by the gothic face of Church Door Buttress, overlooking Central Gully above Collie's Pinnacle. It is atmospheric and entertaining, and don't forget your headtorch! The difficulties are mainly on rock. Climb the

chimney for 20m to a rock corridor cutting into the buttress. Go to the dark end of the corridor where a choice of three routes leads to the Arch and a finish up Flake Route.

The Tunnel Route

A narrow passage in the left wall leads to a chamber. Another tunnel leads to a second chamber, from where a long very narrow tunnel runs up to a 45cm hole. Exit and climb through a hole in the lower right end of the Arch.

The Through Route

Climb up the cave-like end of the corridor to a second smaller cave and make a direct exit to gain the Arch.

The Gallery Variation

From the second cave of The Through Route, climb into another chimney in the same fault leading to a third and smaller cave. Enter the Gallery above, step down from the Gallery floor then, facing out, traverse 15 metres right to where it is possible to climb up into the floor of the Arch.

Flake Route   130m   IV,6 *
G.R. Scott, F.W. Cope   18th March 1942

Just right of Crypt route an enormous flake is split from the buttress by a crack. Climb to a col *via* the crack, or climb the other side of the flake having traversed around it lower down the gully. Step awkwardly up and right, then go straight up broken ground until a left traverse can be made to the Arch. Cross the Arch to climb the shallow chimney (crux). Grooves and walls lead to the top. Care required if thinly iced.

West Chimney   180m   V,6 ***
A. Fyffe, H. MacInnes   8th February 1969

A classic, entertaining outing. Start in the bay formed on the right of the spur projecting from the base of the buttress.
1. 45m   Gain a ramp-chimney line and follow it under a Damoclean chockstone, then climb over two more chockstones into a bay at a *cul-de-sac*.
2. 15m   There is a tunnel up on the left; find it, then burrow into and through it to emerge mole-like onto a ledge. This may expend considerable time and effort.
3. 40m   Move back to the chimney line, then follow it up and under a chockstone to its top. Traverse left across ledges and boulders, then step down to a fine belay on the Arch - don't fall down the hole!
4. and 5. 80m   Finish up Flake Route.

BIDEAN NAM BIAN

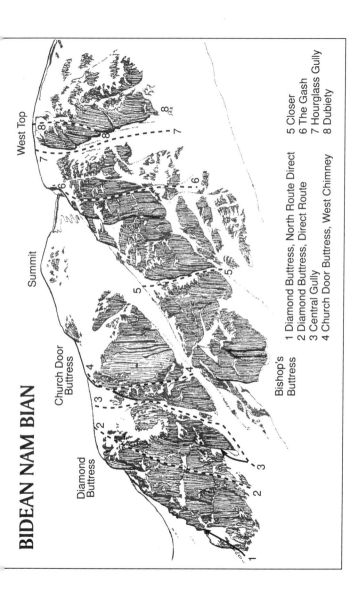

West Top   Summit   Church Door Buttress   Diamond Buttress

Bishop's Buttress

1 Diamond Buttress, North Route Direct
2 Diamond Buttress, Direct Route
3 Central Gully
4 Church Door Buttress, West Chimney
5 Closer
6 The Gash
7 Hourglass Gully
8 Dubiety

WEST TOP
1141m (Map Ref 141 543)

To the left of the West Top, the rocks merge with the slopes below Church Door Buttress. On the right a small basin can be gained from the main ridge, or by heading up right from the foot of the boulder slope leading to Church Door Buttress. Entry to the slopes running up below the face is guarded by Zero Buttress on Stob Coire nam Beith to the right and a small sentinel of rock some 20m high on the left. The lowest rocks form a prominent compact buttress, Bishop's Buttress, and extend up rightwards to the obvious feature of Hourglass Gully.

Closer 75m IV,5 *
C. Dale, A. Kassyk, D. Talbot 18th February 1982
Right of Bishop's Buttress is a deep cleft (Grade V). This route takes the prominent steep chimney around to the right, with an icefall at its base. Climb the icefall to gain the chimney, then follow this over bulges and chockstones to a cave recess. Continue over bulges and chockstones to the top.

The Gash 120m IV,4 *
I. Clough, M. Hadley, M. Large 22th March 1959
Further up, left of Hourglass Gully, is an obvious V-shape formed by two gullies. The right-hand one is **The Hash** (Grade III). Gain the more prominent left-hand gully by a rising traverse from Hourglass Gully, or more directly from below. A ledge on the right provides a good stance. Climb the steep runnel over several bulges to a large overhanging chockstone, then turn this on the left to reach a cave below a second chockstone. A right traverse leads to easier ground or, if you are of a burrowing nature, find an intriguing through route in the back of the cave to a squeeze exit.

Hourglass Gully 120m I *
I. Clough and party February 1966
The gully splitting the cliffs below the top gives a steep but straightforward snow climb with perhaps one or two steps.

Dubiety   110m   IV,5 *
F. Yeoman, J. Mathie   23th February 1987
This lies on the right retaining wall of Hourglass Gully. Start some 30m up the gully. A steep iced corner-chimney on the right leads awkwardly to a poor stance and good thread belay on the right. Climb the iced corner directly to finish at the summit.

AONACH EAGACH

The distinctive notched ridge opposite the Bidean Massif offers a superb traverse of Alpine proportions. It is useful to arrange it so that there are two vehicles involved, one being left at each end of the ridge, unless the additional exercise of walking along the road is required!

Aonach Eagach Ridge   4km   II/III ***
In good conditions and fine weather a traverse of the ridge provides an exhilarating expedition in majestic surroundings. Speed is of the essence if a party is to avoid benightment; 5-8 hours seems fairly typical for an average party in good conditions. Where a competent party might happily solo, many would prefer to rope up and should certainly not feel embarrassed to do so. This is not a route for the winter hillwalker, a large number of them have finished the route by helicopter. Start from a car park (Map Ref 174 567) about 300 metres west of the white cottage of Allt-na-reigh. Either follow the path up the broad ridge of Am Bodach directly, or go up and right into the corrie to the east, where easy slopes go up and left to the top of Am Bodach. The descent from that top involves some tricky down-climbing on the north side of the ridge followed by a move back south and down a short chimney-crack. Meall Dearg (951m) is ahead and beyond this there is a narrow pinnacled section which has an awkward slabby descent. The ridge carries on to Stob Coire Leith and then to the final summit, Sgorr nam Fiannaidh (967m).

Descent
It must be emphasised that there are no safe descent routes on the Glen Coe side of the ridge between the peaks of Am Bodach and Stob Coire Leith. If a party has run out of daylight it is better to complete or

reverse the traverse. The first reasonable descent route encountered on the traverse is due south down to Loch Achtriochtan from Sgorr nam Fiannaidh. The slopes are steep and there is a risk of avalanche in soft snow conditions. However, in good conditions this is the most straightforward descent. Do not go down the shallow corrie on the west side of these slopes where a stream flows down a rather rocky gully.

The path down the west side of Clachaig Gully is now badly eroded, with loose boulders and nasty scree, and it is best avoided.

In difficult conditions, the safest way down is to go 700 metres west from Sgurr nam Fiannaidh to a minor top, then 1½km north-west to the col below the Pap of Glencoe. From there descend south-west on a path to reach the road 1km north-west of the Youth Hostel. It is important that climbers descending from the ridge by this route should avoid the fenced-off area above the Youth Hostel. This is private land, used for livestock grazing. If climbers refuse to do so, future access could be put at risk.

Menage à Trois, North-East Corrie of Beinn an Dothaidh
Climber: Chris Cartwright   *Photo: Bruce Goodlad*

The Southern Highlands

There are two main areas of interest to the winter climber in the Southern Highlands. Both are approached by the A82 Glasgow to Fort William road. The Arrochar Alps lie some 36 miles (58km) beyond Glasgow and The Bridge of Orchy hills some 29 miles (46km) further north. For those coming from the south and passing through Glasgow on the way, the quickest approach is to stay on the M8 motorway until past Glasgow Airport, then to cross the Erskine Bridge (toll) to pick up the A82 road which runs alongside Loch Lomond.

Most of the climbing in this area has a comparatively recent history, which is surprising considering the quality of the routes and the accessibility of the cliffs. The main guide which covers this area is the SMC Climbers' Guide to *Arran, Arrochar and the Southern Highlands*. Information on winter climbing on the island of Arran has not been included within this selected guide since the area is remote from the rest of the climbing areas. Those wishing to visit this fickle venue, with its awkward approach for weekend visits, will no doubt not mind having to acquire the comprehensive guide.

Conditions and Weather

Due to their southerly latitude, these areas can often escape the worst effects of frontal systems ravaging across the hills further north. This southerly latitude, however, when combined with the relatively low altitude of the cliffs means that they are severely affected by mid-season thaws and are often stripped bare. Despite this, the cliffs are in condition much more often than one might think since the long slow thaw-freeze cycle required to bring many other cliffs into condition is not a necessity here.

Another factor is that if the weather is poor in Fort William or Glen Coe, it is only a short drive south to the cliffs of the Southern Highlands. It is also worth knowing that when the cliffs in the areas further north are under threat of avalanche, it should be possible, with a bit of due care and attention, to find safe climbs in the Southern Highlands. For those facing a long weekend return drive south of the border, the cliffs of this area can offer a convenient second day's climbing fairly close to the road.

Quartzvein Scoop, Coire Daimh, Beinn Udlaidh   Climber: Grahame Nicoll
Photo: Rab Anderson

The climbing in the Southern Highlands is on metamorphic rock, usually schist. This tends to be vegetated, with frozen turf and moss an important factor on many of the climbs. Since the rock is fairly soft in nature, care should be taken with axes, crampons and pegs, especially on The Cobbler which is also a popular rock climbing venue. The cliffs in the Bridge of Orchy hills offer a mix of climbing on all of the different mediums, which means that as long as there is some snow and the freezing level is fairly low, there should always be some routes in condition. The pure ice routes of Beinn Udlaidh are created by frozen spring waters which readily form icefalls and frozen gullies given a good freeze. The Arrochar area generally provides climbing on turf and snowed-up rock, only requiring a freeze with a dump of snow.

Two other climbs are described. One is the Central Gully of Ben Lui, possibly the most classic of all Scottish winter climbs, and the other is the Eas Anie icefall on nearby Beinn Chuirn; a pure ice climb in contrast to the snows of Central Gully. Both are within easy reach of Tyndrum.

Maps
The maps that cover the areas in this chapter are the Ordnance Survey 1:50,000 Landranger Series Sheet 50 for the Bridge of Orchy hills and Sheet 56 for the Arrochar Alps.

THE BRIDGE OF ORCHY HILLS

The cliffs described in this section are close to Bridge of Orchy on the A82 Glasgow to Fort William road between Tyndrum and Glen Coe. The main climbs are on the easily accessible cliffs of Beinn an Dothaidh and Beinn Dorain. Stob Ghabhar, to the north of Loch Tulla, is briefly included and a short way down Glen Orchy itself is the pure ice climbing offered by Beinn Udlaidh's Coire Daimh. Bridge of Orchy has a roadside hotel, normally passed at speed in the dark, a railway station and very little else.

STOB GHABHAR
1087m   (Map Ref 230 455)

Access
Leave the A82 at Bridge of Orchy and follow the A8005 round Loch Tulla to Victoria Bridge (5½ km, parking just before the bridge). From Forest Lodge take the track west along the river as far as the small,

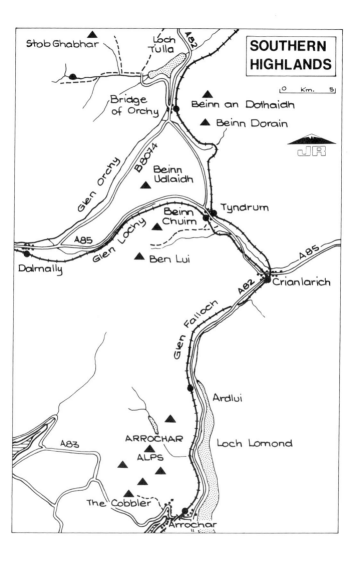

SOUTHERN HIGHLANDS

Stob Ghabhar
Loch Tulla
A82
Bridge of Orchy
Beinn an Dothaidh
Beinn Dorain
Glen Orchy
B8074
Beinn Udlaidh
Tyndrum
Beinn Chuirn
Glen Lochy
A85
Dalmally
Ben Lui
Crianlarich
A85
A82
Glen Falloch
Ardlui
Loch Lomond
ARROCHAR ALPS
A83
The Cobbler
Arrochar

Km.

corrugated metal hut belonging to Glasgow University M.C. At the hut turn right to follow the good stalker's path north into Coire Toaig, following the Allt Toaig to reach the col between Stob Ghabhar and Stob a' Choire Odhair. Contour west over rough ground, rising gently to enter Coirein Lochain, the small north-east corrie of Stob Ghabhar, with the cliffs and the Upper Couloir ahead. Avoid a lower tier of easy rock on the left and go up and right to the upper buttress. The final section of the approach is avalanche-prone and careful recognition of the prevailing conditions should be made before making the traverse towards the routes (6km, 2½ hours).

Descent
From the summit follow the south-east ridge, descending to reach easy ground west of the Allt Toaig. Cross this to regain the approach path. If the burn is in spate, continue along its bank to gain the track from Clashgour Farm.

The Upper Couloir   90m   II ***
A.E. Maylard, Professor and Mrs Adamson, Miss Weiss   May 1897
This veritable classic up the obvious couloir is normally a straightforward snow gully, with one ice pitch in the middle of up to 10m in height and 70 degrees angle. In very lean conditions there may be an impassable chockstone pitch.

Hircine Rib   130m   VI,6 **
S. Richardson, G. Dudley   30th December 1989
A fine mixed route up the buttress left of the couloir. Start just right of the lowest rocks below a left-slanting groove.
1. 10m   A steep, bold wall leads to a ledge.
2. 20m   Climb the groove, stepping left after a vertical section to gain an icy runnel leading to a belay on the right arete.
3. 25m   A steep friable rib is bounded on its left by a slabby groove. Climb this to half-height, then traverse across the slab to gain a ledge on the left arete. Continue right up the vertical continuation corner to an exposed stance.
4. and 5. 75m   Follow a groove for 5m, then step left to easier ground leading to the plateau.

BEINN AN DOTHAIDH
1002m   (Map Ref 332 408)

Climbing on this fine hill is in two corries, Coire Achaladair on its north-east, and Coire an Dothaidh to its south-west, gained from Achallader Farm and Bridge of Orchy Station respectively. The North-East Corrie normally gives more reliable climbing conditions and since there is little ice it comes into condition fairly quickly following a fall of snow. Some climbs in the Coire an Dothaidh are fed by springs and require a good freeze. The rock is compact schist with protection commonly in the form of rock pegs and drive-in ice screws in frozen turf.

NORTH-EAST CORRIE

Access
From the Achallader Farm carpark (Map Ref 321 443) walk past the farm and cross the railway by a bridge. Follow a path high above the west bank of the Allt Coire Achaladair, then head diagonally right to pass under the end of the north ridge, aiming for a small cone-shaped hillock, and so enter the subsidiary corrie under the cliffs (4km, 90 min).

Layout
To the left of the corrie entrance are several easy gullies (Grade I) on the north face leading to the plateau close to the col between the summit and the West Top. The obvious, wide gully above and just inside the subsidiary corrie is the West Gully, a useful landmark in misty conditions. Most of the climbing, and certainly all of the steeper and more technical routes, are found in the right-hand, or subsidiary corrie. The two large buttresses here are North Buttress on the left and the West Buttresses further right, separated by the obvious West Gully (Grade I).

Descent
This can be by the West Gully, given safe snow, although it is often corniced. A more reliable descent goes west then north-west for a short distance along the top of the West Buttress to a level part of the north ridge. From there descend north-east back into the corrie, or continue easily down the north ridge to Coire Achaladair.

Taxus   240m   IV,4 ***
Original Route *A.W. Ewing, A.J. Trees*   *8th March 1969*
Icefall Finish *J. Crawford, D. Dawson, J. Madden, W. Skidmore*
25th January 1976
The steep gully branching left out of West Gully is best climbed *via* the
Icefall Finish. The initial steep section provides one or two pitches,
which can be of ice or steep snow. Above, snow leads to the bifurcation.
The Icefall Finish goes up the mixed buttress above directly to the
plateau *via* an obvious recess belay. If this is not fully formed, follow
the original line *via* the left-hand branch (this reduces the climb to
Grade III). Climb to a snow ridge and follow it until an easy leftward
traverse gains a narrow gully leading to the plateau close to the West
Top.

The Upper Circle   200m   III *
S. Kennedy, N. Morrison, A. Nisbet   *10th January 1981*
On the left wall of West Gully, beyond the start of Taxus, is a prominent
ramp, guarded by a steep wall. Gain the ramp by a short hard corner,
then follow the ramp in three pitches, going right at the top of the third
pitch to gain a platform. To avoid a short vertical wall, traverse down
and left round a corner into a small gully which leads back right to a
saddle. Finish by a choice of lines.

West Gully   300m   I **
Prof. W. Ramsay, W. Ramsay Jnr, F. Campbell, C.C.B. Moss   *26th*
March 1894
The uncomplicated snow gully cutting up between North and West
Buttresses gives and easy climb with good scenery.

THE WEST BUTTRESSES

The rocks lying right of West Gully are divided by fault lines into (from
left to right) the North-West, West, and Far West Buttresses. All the
routes except the first two start from a sloping terrace gained from the
small corrie under the buttresses, which is best approached from the
right. From the normal approach *via* the Allt Coire Achaladair, the most
obvious line apart from the West Gully is the gully of **Haar** (Grade III),
starting up the left corner of a square-cut recess dividing the two
left-hand buttresses.

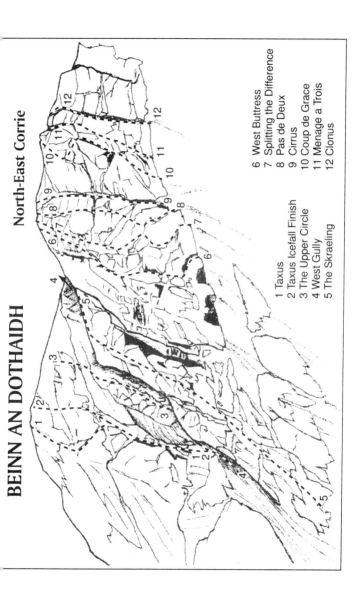

BEINN AN DOTHAIDH

North-East Corrie

1 Taxus
2 Taxus Icefall Finish
3 The Upper Circle
4 West Gully
5 The Skraeling

6 West Buttress
7 Splitting the Difference
8 Pas de Deux
9 Cirrus
10 Coup de Grace
11 Menage a Trois
12 Clonus

The Skraeling   240m   IV,4 *
I. Fulton, J. Hutchinson   February 1976
On North-West Buttress, left of Haar, is an obvious corner in the main buttress. This route gains a broad terrace below the corner by either starting up rocks right of the foot of West Gully, or by a traverse left from the corrie. Climb slabs then make a difficult right traverse to enter the corner. Two steep pitches in the corner lead to easier grooves.

West Buttress   120m   III *
J. Crawford, D. Dawson, W. Skidmore   1st February 1976
A good turf climb, requiring a minimum of snow and a good freeze. Start from the terrace below the main cliff about halfway between the gully of Haar and the next gully right (Cirrus) where a tapering shelf leads left above an undercut section to a series of chimney-grooves. Gain this system using the shelf and zigzag up using the grooves to gain easier ground above.

Splitting the Difference   155m   IV,4
G.E. Little, C.J.S. Bonington   16th March 1989
Start about 5 metres left of the cleft of Cirrus. The first two pitches are as for **Slow March** (Grade IV).
1. and 2. 55m   Go up left to belay in a snow bay, then move up right to an overhanging corner and follow a ramp leftwards to a wide triangular corner.
3. 30m   Slow March goes left to grooves. Instead climb the corner by interesting wide bridging, then continue up the groove above.
4. 35m   Continue up the turfy groove, immediately left of a clean rock tower, to gain easy broken ground.
5. 35m   Climb easy ground to the top.

Pas de Deux   155m   V,6 **
G.E. Little, D. Saddler   17th February 1986
This intimidating climb takes the challenging and unlikely-looking barrel-fronted buttress. If it looks too steep for you from the approach, walk a bit further past it up the corrie to see its true nature! Varied and exciting climbing has ensured that it is rapidly becoming a classic. Start at the foot of Cirrus at an obvious ramp on its left wall.
1. 30m   Climb the ramp with increasing difficulty to gain a good ledge.
2. 45m   Move back right to climb a short awkward corner. Traverse a ledge rightwards until it narrows, then go up a short wall to gain a

right-trending zigzag line leading to a thread belay overlooking Cirrus. This is below and right of a striking tower of clean rock, seen from below.
3. 35m   Climb the left side of a slot, past an icicle fringe, to gain an open corner on the right of the tower. Climb the steep right wall of the corner, then follow a snow ramp trending left above.
4. 45m   Broken ground leads to the top.

Cirrus   135m   IV,4 ***
J. Crawford, J. Gillespie, W. Skidmore   *24th March 1974*
A good line, testing if lean. The obvious deep cleft dividing the West and Far West Buttresses normally provides a steep 10m ice pitch at about mid-height and several other short pitches.

Coup de Grace   120m   V,7 *
S. Richardson, A. Robertson   *28th February 1993*
A good technical mixed route taking the bulging groove line left of Menage à Trois. Start directly below the groove.
1. 40m   Climb a short wall and continue up turf and snow to belay at the top of the first chimney of **Far West Buttress** (Grade III) which takes a zigzag line to the left.
2. 20m   Climb a crack, pull round the bulge and move up a turfy depression to belay below a second bulge.
3. 20m   Make a difficult series of moves up the smooth vertical wall above, step right onto the arete and bridge up the impending corner; a fine pitch.
4. 40m   Traverse left for 10m to the foot of a right-slanting turfy ramp and follow this to the top.

Menage à Trois   105m   V,6 **
G.E. Little, D. Saddler, S. Visser   *14th February 1987*
About 10 metres to the left of the obvious corner of Clonus is a steep parallel corner, facing right at mid-height on the face. Start below this corner. A popular climb.
1. 35m   Climb a steep wall to a snow bay, then go up to gain a ramp leading rightwards into the base of the corner. Belay on the right.
2. 35m   Climb the corner, technical but well protected, then break out right near the top to gain a wide ledge.
3. 35m   Follow a groove to the top.

Clonus   115m   IV,4 *
D. Hodgson, W. Skidmore   26th December 1976
This climb takes the right-facing corner about 30 metres right of Cirrus.
1. 35m   Climb the corner and iced slabs to a good stance above a small slot.
2. 40m   Climb slabs to an overhanging barrier pitch in the corner, continue up the groove right of the corner for 5m with some difficulty, then gain a ledge and traverse left across the top of a corner to easy snow. A rising right traverse leads back into the corner. Escape is possible below the crux *via* a snow shelf to the right.
3. 40m   Continue up the corner, now almost a gully, to the top.

CREAG COIRE AN DOTHAIDH (Map Ref 325 403)

This vegetatious west-facing crag is a prominent landmark above Bridge of Orchy, especially when sheathed in ice. Some of the climbs are fed by springs and require a few days of good freeze to come into condition. On clear days there may be a risk of falling ice from the effects of the thawing sun, particularly on Fahrenheit 451.

Access
From Bridge of Orchy station a path leads directly up the Allt Coire an Dothaidh towards the col between Beinn an Dothaidh and Beinn Dorain. The crag lies to the left of the col at an altitude of about 750m (3km, allow 1 hour).

Layout
The two most obvious lines are Salamander Gully on the left, with an icefall high up, and the icefalls of Fahrenheit 451 on the right.

Descent
Go right (south) and down to the col between Beinn an Dothaidh and Beinn Dorain. The descent from the col is fairly steep at first.

Salamander Gully   150m   IV,4 *
K.V. Crocket, J.A.P. Hutchinson   25th January 1976
Near the left end of the cliff is a gully leading to an icefall. This gives a scenic and enjoyable route, which should be in condition after a 3 to 4 day freeze. Climb the gully to the icefall, which is crossed by a ledge.

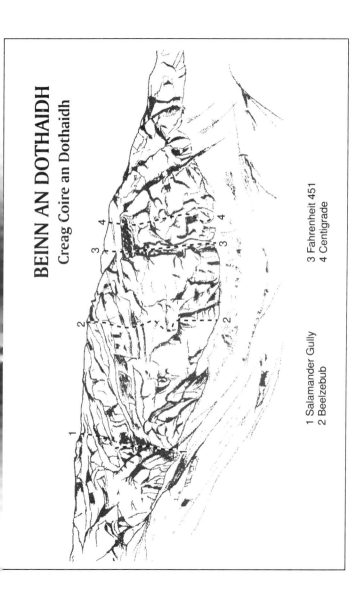

BEINN AN DOTHAIDH
Creag Coire an Dothaidh

1 Salamander Gully
2 Beelzebub

3 Fahrenheit 451
4 Centigrade

The easiest line up the ice takes a groove on the left which leads by a right traverse across the icefall to a belay below a bulging icefall. Climb this up and left to an iced slab which leads to a small ice pitch and so to the top. Escape leftward is possible below the icefall, (Grade III).

Beelzebub   170m   VI,6 *
R. Everett, S. Richardson   16th January 1994
A direct and serious route up the crest of the buttress in the centre of the crag. Start at the lowest rocks directly below a prominent smooth red wall 50m above.
1. 50m   Pull over a small roof and continue directly up the centre of the buttress, following a series of steep turfy grooves with spaced protection to a belay beneath the red wall.
2. 50m   The easiest route through the steep slabs above will depend on the amount of ice present. If thinly iced, a broad snow ledge can be followed left for 10 metres to a below a 10m-high corner lying to the right of a short chimney. From the foot of the corner, a right-slanting ramp leads to easier ground above the belay. Continue up, then go left to a short right-facing corner. Climb this and belay on the snowfield above.
3. 40m   Step left, then climb steep snow and ice to a belay below a prominent roof.
4. 30m   Climb the ice step on the left, then follow icy grooves which lead up and right to the top.

Fahrenheit 451   135m   IV,3 ***
K.V. Crocket, I. Fulton   February 1976
Near the right end of the face a prominent icefall builds up, requiring at least a week of good freeze. An initial gully leads to ice walls, corners, short traverses, and huge sheets of water ice. When in condition it is immensely enjoyable.

Centigrade   105m   III *
D. Baker, R. Howard   30th January 1983
A pleasant, varied route. Start below a large protruding rock, 15 metres right of Fahrenheit 451.
1. 45m   Climb diagonally right under a wall for 20m to an ice groove and climb this to a belay above.
2. 45m   Climb the ramp above to move left on ice, then go up and right to the foot of a scoop.
3. 15m   Climb directly out of the scoop.

BEINN DORAIN
1076m   (Map Ref 326 378)

This steep-sided but otherwise rather monotonous mountain is the home of an impressively steep crag which provides a number of excellent modern mixed climbs. It is very accessible directly above Bridge of Orchy station.

CREAG AN SOCACH   (Map Ref 323 398)

This steep crag on the south side of Coire an Dothaidh is seen from Bridge of Orchy. It has only recently been developed and contains a number of steep mixed routes of a high technical standard. Too much snow is a disadvantage, while there is limited ice. The compact schist can make protection difficult to arrange, but as the routes see more traffic, vegetated cracks are being cleared out.

Access
From the station, follow the path up the burn as for Creag Coire an Dothaidh, but bear up right to the base of the crag (3km, 1hr).

Descent
Go hard left (north), then follow a burn steeply down into the corrie.

The Glass Bead Game   120m   V,5
R. Carchrie, K.V. Crocket, R. Duncan, G. McEwan, A. Walker
13th December 1987
A wide ledge runs out right from below the steep chimney of **False Rumour Gully** (Grade IV) at the left end of the crag. Start at the point where the ledge curves round the toe of the buttress. Climb a corner, pull out left and go up a groove to a ledge and belay. Step left round an exposed edge, then go up and left to a ledge and block belay. Step onto a slabby wall directly above the block and make a rising traverse right, aiming for a small spike right of a steep wall. Gain the slab above the spike and belay above (sustained and technical). Go hard right, passing a corner to gain a ramp and follow this to a short overhanging chimney. Climb the chimney over a roof and continue to a belay above. Easy ground leads to the top.

A worthwhile alternative to the above route is to climb the curving chimney-groove which starts from the lowest point of the cliff and leads directly to the short overhanging chimney. This is the lower section of **Kick Start** (Grade IV,4 overall).

The Sting   120m   V,6 **
G.E. Little, K. Howett   19th January 1991
To the right of the previous route is an area of dark, clean bulging rock low down on the face. A narrow rock ramp cuts across its right flank. Start at a fan of slabs below the clean bulging rock.
1. 30m   Move up, then go left across slabs to a block with a horizontal crack. Take a snow ramp trending right until it is possible to climb up to a small rock bay at the base of the narrow rock ramp.
2. 25m   Climb the ramp, then go directly up steep ground to the right end of the central snow ledge.
3. 10m   Cross to the left end of the ledge to below a slim corner.
4. 15m   Climb the superb corner crack (large hexentrics useful) to its top, then make an interesting move left to a ledge.
5. 40m   Climb to the base of a vague wide rock rib, move slightly left, then surmount a short difficult wall and trend right up steepening ground to the top. A groove on the right of the rib is an alternative.

The Promised Land   120m   VI,6 **
G.E. Little, D. Saddler   29th March 1987
Start about 20m down from Second Coming, well right of the lowest point of the cliff. This route needs a good ice build-up on the second pitch, but this can be assessed from below.
1. 45m   Move up to a snow ledge, then traverse left to its termination at flakes. Ascend very steep rock, then move right into a snow bay below a groove; flake runner. Traverse hard left for 10 metres, then go up to gain a large snow ledge and belay below an ice scoop, right of an obvious corner.
2. 35m   Climb the ice scoop, exiting right by a short awkward wall, then go up to below an ice chimney.
3. 40m   Climb the left wall of the chimney on thin ice to gain an ice groove, then climb directly up to the top by a second ice groove above, common to Second Coming.

Antichrist   120m   VI,7 *
S. Richardson, R. Everett   15th March 1992
A good route taking the groove system between The Promised Land and Second Coming, starting 20 metres left of the latter. It was originally climbed in lean conditions.
1. 15m   Climb easily up to the rake.
2. 25m   Climb the awkward wall 5 metres right of the flakes of The Promised Land and enter the groove which leads to a good stance.

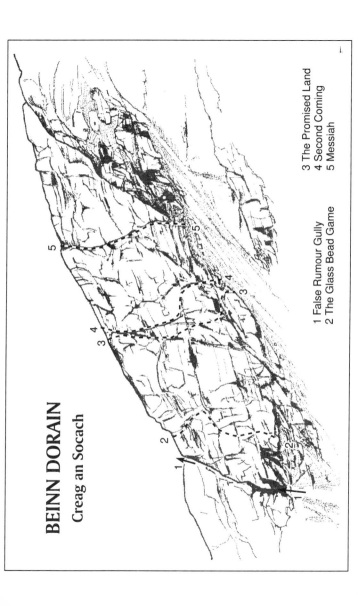

BEINN DORAIN
Creag an Socach

1 False Rumour Gully
2 The Glass Bead Game
3 The Promised Land
4 Second Coming
5 Messiah

3. 40m   Continue up the fault line, trending left to an overhang. Climb this, then traverse right onto the lip of the overhanging wall on the right. Move up in a spectacularly exposed position to reach the terrace 5m up and right of the ice chimney of The Promised Land.
4. 20m   Continue up the impending wall above, starting on the right arete, then moving left to reach a hairline crack. A series of steep moves on widely spaced tufts (not visible from below) leads to a ledge.
5. 20m   The final ice groove of Second Coming leads to the top.

Second Coming   95m   III,4 **
I. Fulton, C.D. Grant   Winter 1978
High in the centre of the cliff is an obvious curving ramp line which forms the demarcation between the very steep clean wall on the right and the more slabby, vegetated face on the left. A steep turfy groove drops from the ramp but does not reach the base of the crag. Start to the right of the turfy groove.
1. 50m   Ascend steepening, then broken ground to a ledge. Hand traverse a sharp flake leftwards to gain ledges which lead to the groove. This leads to a corner below steep ice.
2. 45m   Climb the ice or the small chimney on the left, traverse left along a snow ramp, then go up an icy groove to the top.

Messiah   85m   VII,7 ***
G.E. Little, R. Reid   28th January 1988
One of the finest lines in the Southern Highlands. The face right of Second Coming is intimidatingly steep and ledgeless. The only apparent breach is an open corner, low down, leading to a thin groove. This sustained and technical route is becoming easier as the cracks are cleared.
1. 30m   Climb the corner to a niche below overhanging rock. Move up and hand traverse hard left to below a groove. Gain this and go up to a small ledge.
2. 10m   Climb a short corner, then move directly up to the base of a vertical ice-filled groove. (Linking the first two pitches would cause serious rope drag).
3. 45m   Climb the groove into a continuation gully and follow this to the top.

Opposite: Reaching the top of Central Gully at the summit of Ben Lui
Climber: John Bennet   Photo: Donald Bennet

Next page: The frozen icefall of Eas Anie, Beinn Chuirn
Climber: Des Rubens   Photo: Grahame Nicoll

BEINN UDLAIDH
840m   (Map Ref 275 330)

This otherwise unremarkable hill has two unusual features. One is a quartzite dyke which breaks the otherwise grassy slopes on its north side. The other, of more interest to the readers of this guide, is the corrie where streams cascade over a steep cliff to form the highest concentration of easily accessible ice climbs in the country.

COIRE DAIMH

This north-facing, crescent-shaped corrie is backed by two lines of cliff; a 30m lower tier of quartzite and an upper tier of schist. The flat summit of Beinn Udlaidh collects sufficient precipitation to feed a series of springs whose waters flow over the cliff edge. In a good freeze, these quickly build up impressive quantities of ice, giving many high quality pure ice routes. Between the icefalls there are some easier gullies.

Access
Leave the A82 1km south of Bridge of Orchy and take the single track road (the B8074) down Glen Orchy for 5½km to where the stream, the Allt Daimh, issuing from the corrie joins the River Orchy. A path leads up the north-east bank of the stream to gain Coire Daimh (2½km, 1h). Recent forestry work has made the approach very uncomfortable, with the best line possibly lying between the drainage ditches and the burn.

Descent
Go down either flank, taking care during icy conditions when desperate sheets of ice can form on otherwise easy grassy slopes.

Layout
Seen from the entrance to the corrie, the left-hand side is dominated by the Black Wall, bordered on its right by the South Gully of The Black Wall, then a square-cut buttress flanked by Ramshead Gully. To the right, Sunshine Gully appears as a left-sloping ramp, before the prominent left-sloping Central Gully with Central Buttress between it and West Gully further right. The final section of cliff is the West Wall.

Previous page: The first pitch of Deadman's Groove, South Peak of The Cobbler
Climber: Rob Milne   *Photo: Rab Anderson*

Opposite: The summit of The Cobbler   *Photo: Donald Bennet*

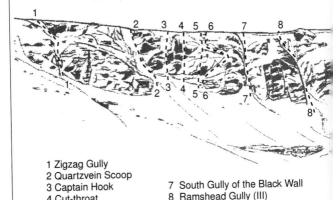

BEINN UDLAIDH

1 Zigzag Gully
2 Quartzvein Scoop
3 Captain Hook
4 Cut-throat
5 Peter Pan Direct
6 Land of Make Believe
7 South Gully of the Black Wall
8 Ramshead Gully (III)
9 Sunshine Gully
10 Central Gully

Zigzag Gully   90m   II *
A. Agnew, J. Jewel   14th November 1970
The gully which starts at the leftmost edge of the corrie may include
one ice pitch of 30m in the centre. From the top of this, traverse left into
a shallow gully which leads to the top.

Quartzvein Scoop   90m   IV,4 ***
D. Evans, A. Gray, A. Shepherd   Winter 1979
The line of icy grooves immediately left of the Black Wall gives an
excellent route amongst impressive scenery. **Ice Crew** (Grade IV)
takes a parallel line to the left.

Captain Hook   75m   VI,6 **
D. Cuthbertson, C. Calow   January 1980
Climb the impressive funnel-shaped icefall on the Black Wall, trending
right. The exit can be corniced and there may be unstable snow.

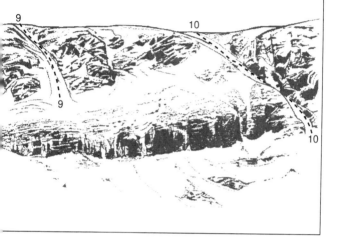

Coire Daimh, East Sector

Cut Throat   75m   VI,6 **
D. Cuthbertson, R. Duncan, R. Young, C. Calow   *January 1980*
This is the obvious icicle right of Captain Hook, but it is rarely in
condition. Climb the lower icefall, then follow the icicle to the top.

Peter Pan Direct   85m   V,5 **
D. Claxton, I. Duckworth, A. Kay, N. Morrison   *1st January 1982*
To the right of the two previous routes are two icefalls. **The Croc** (Grade
V) takes the left-hand one, and this route climbs the one on the right.
Start at its foot and climb directly to the top. It is in condition more readily
than neighbouring routes.

Land of Make Believe   90m   II *
N. Morrison, M. Orr   *29th December 1979*
An easy route through impressive scenery. Start below and right of
Peter Pan Direct. Climb up, trending right to a belay. Continue right to

a small gully, then move up and left to belay at its top. Traverse hard right to a block, step up and continue directly to the top.

South Gully of The Black Wall   120m   IV,4 *
R. McGowan, G. Skelton   30th November 1969
The gully right of the Black Wall gives a good route which often has a large cornice. A narrow chimney leads to easy ground, then climb a steep icefall which can be taken direct.

Sunshine Gully   90m   III **
E. Fowler, F. Jack, R. McGowan, G. Skelton   14th November 1970
To the right of **Ramshead Gully** (Grade III), midway between South Gully of the Black Wall and Central Gully, this gully looks like a left-slanting ramp when seen from the entrance to the corrie. It gives an interesting climb with much ice.

Central Gully   180m   II
J. Buchanan, J. Forbes, G. Skelton   29th December 1968
The left-slanting gully in the centre of the corrie may have four pitches, the second one being the hardest. It banks out later in the season. **Junior's Jaunt** (Grade IV) climbs the icefall on the right some 45m up the gully.

Doctor's Dilemma   180m   IV,4 *
I. Duckworth, M. Firth   Winter 1978
This very good route takes the obvious wide central line of icefalls running the height of Central Buttress.

West Gully   180m   III *
The obvious right-slanting gully can contain two enjoyable pitches, both short, leading to an easy-angled groove and finish. **White Caterpillar** (Grade III) breaks out left halfway up.

Organ Pipe Wall   75m   V,5 *
R. Duncan, J.G. Fraser   27th January 1979
Gain the obvious icefall high on the cliff to the right of West Gully *via* an easy, deep-cut chimney, then climb the icefall directly, following a groove and wall up the middle.

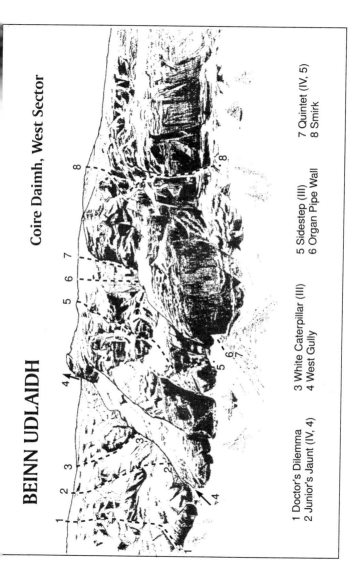

BEINN UDLAIDH

Coire Daimh, West Sector

1 Doctor's Dilemma
2 Junior's Jaunt (IV, 4)
3 White Caterpillar (III)
4 West Gully
5 Sidestep (III)
6 Organ Pipe Wall
7 Quintet (IV, 5)
8 Smirk

The Smirk   90m   V,5 **
R. Duncan, J.G. Fraser   27th January 1979
The very steep and obvious chimney-gully towards the right-hand side of the West Wall gives a superb climb, but it is slow to come into condition. The left fork is the normal route, but a more direct finish is possible.

BEN LUI
1130m (Map Ref 265 263)

The classical shape of this fine mountain, with its two tops linked by the short summit ridge, is an obvious challenge to climbers travelling north along the A82 road between Crianlarich and Tyndrum, particularly when the great north-east corrie is filled with snow in winter and spring. The fact that Tyndrum has had, since the early days of the railways in Scotland, two stations and used to be accessible by the early morning trains from Edinburgh as well as Glasgow, made Ben Lui one of the most popular mountains with the Scottish mountaineering pioneers.

Access
From Tyndrum, a private road goes from Tyndrum Lower station south then west up the River Cononish to Cononish Farm. Alternatively start at Dalrigh (344 290) and follow the private road from there to Cononish, only slightly longer. A path continues west for a further 2km to the foot of the north-east corrie of Ben Lui, at which point the whole face of the mountain rises directly to the summit. Climb up into the corrie by a path on the north-west side of the stream to reach the foot of Central Gully, the classic winter climb on Ben Lui.

Central Gully   200m   I**
W.W.Naismith, W.R.Lester, T.F.S.Campbell April 1891 (descent)
A.E.Maylard, W.Brunskill, W.Douglas, J.Maclay
December 1892 (ascent)
Climb directly up the centre-line of the corrie. Initially the gully is enclosed and quite narrow, but higher up it opens into a wide steep snowfield below the summit ridge. The top of the gully may be heavily corniced, in which case the best finish is to bear left and climb directly up to the summit cairn.

There are variations to Central Gully on its left and right, all of the same character and standard. The exception is the crescent-shaped ridge on the left which gives a good winter scramble, with possibly some difficulty at the start. It ends on the east ridge of Ben Lui some distance below the summit (Grade II).

In mild spring weather there is an avalanche hazard if a large cornice is still hanging over the top of the gully.

The most direct descent from the summit is either down the east or the north-east ridge (the two bounding ridges of the corrie), or if conditions are suitable, Central Gully itself gives a fine glissade once the cornice and steep upper slope have been negotiated.

BEINN CHUIRN
877m (Map Ref 281 292)

This hill, rising just north-west of Cononish, looks like a smaller version of Ben Lui, with its prominent east-facing corrie. There is a gold mine 1km west of Cononish at the foot of the hill, and just above the mine is the prominent waterfall of Eas Anie, which gives a good low-level, bad weather ice climb when it is well frozen.

Eas Anie   150m   (Right Finish) III**
                               (Left Finish) IV*
The frozen waterfall gives continuous ice. The lower part is slightly easier, with some interesting variations on the left side, to a basin. Above there the left fork is steeper, possibly with a short rock section. The right fork often has unusual wind-sculptured ice flutings and includes an ascent through an ice cave, climbing an icicle to reach the upper gully.

It would be quite possible to climb both Eas Anie and Central Gully in one day, as a short descent from the top of the former leads down the hillside to rejoin the path to Ben Lui.

THE ARROCHAR ALPS

These rather romantically named hills are situated around the head of Loch Long, overlooking the village of Arrochar. There are a number of crags of interest, but despite their accessibility it is only in recent winters that the full potential of the area has been explored. As an introduction to the district, only the main climbing area of The Cobbler is covered.

THE COBBLER
881m (Map Ref 259 058)

The centrepiece of the Arrochar Alps, this superb trio of jagged peaks, South, Centre and North, forms a fine corrie. Although lower than many of the surrounding hills, The Cobbler is instantly recognisable straight ahead just before entering Arrochar, a short distance along the A83 after leaving the A82 at Tarbet on Loch Lomond. Although the name is applied to the whole hill, it is really to the central summit peak to which it should refer. On a sunny winter's day the summit block stands out and the reasons behind the name become clear. Due to its proximity to Glasgow, The Cobbler is a very popular hill with winter walkers.

Access
The most scenic approach, recommended for first-time visitors on a clear day, is also the longest and starts from the shores of Loch Long a short way beyond Arrochar village. Just past the head of the loch, laybys on either side of the road mark the start of the path (Map Ref 294 049). The path goes steeply through the trees to join a concrete-slabbed ramp which leads steeply in less than 30 minutes to a path which contours leftwards to a small dam, then follows the Allt a' Bhalachain (Buttermilk Burn) past the two Narnain Boulders to cross the burn higher up. Head up under the rocks of the North Peak towards the col between the North and Centre Peaks.

A more direct route starts from Map Ref 287 042 and follows a path on the south side of the burn to join the main path at the dam. This can be rather boggy, but it is slightly quicker. This approach can be soul destroying if you are the first to arrive after a heavy dump of snow, however, since it is the main path for walkers, a well-trodden trail usually leads through the snow to the hill (3½km, 2h).

The quickest approach starts from a small layby on the Rest and be Thankful road, at a bridge at Map Ref 243 061. There is also another layby a short distance further up the road. Follow the burn which descends from the col between Beinn Ime and Beinn Narnain to reach a small dam at Map Ref 253 067. The main path goes up the left side of the burn to reach the dam, but depending on snow conditions, either side can be followed to the dam. Here a path may be found leading up to the col between the North and Centre Peaks. Under deep snow this latter part of the approach can take an eternity but is good for building up the thigh muscles (about 2½ km, 1hr 15mins). There are two points of descent from the col. For climbs on the North Peak, go a short distance north from the lowest point to the other side of a knoll and

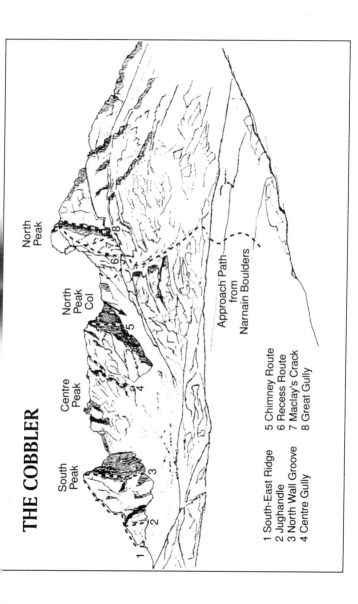

THE COBBLER

South Peak

Centre Peak

North Peak Col

North Peak

Approach Path from Narnain Boulders

1 South-East Ridge
2 Jughandle
3 North Wall Groove
4 Centre Gully
5 Chimney Route
6 Recess Route
7 Maclay's Crack
8 Great Gully

drop down under the North Peak on the main approach path from the corrie. For climbs on the Centre and South Peaks, drop down a gully from the lowest point of the col and descend beneath the rocks of the Centre Peak. In heavy snow it may be better to approach the South Peak from the top of the Centre Peak, descending from the col between them.

Descent
From the North Peak a short descent (possibly a little scrambling) leads to the col between it and the Centre Peak. From the South Peak, climb down or abseil two or three short pitches on the north-west side of the peak to the col between it and the Centre Peak.

Layout
Approaching up the corrie from the Loch Long path, the South Peak lies to the left with its North Face overlooking the corrie. A ridge runs up the left skyline forming a prominent edge between the North and South faces. The Centre Peak lies in the middle with easy slopes leading to the summit block and a steeper more continuous face running up a shallow gully which leads to a col. On the right lies the North Peak with impressive prows jutting out towards the corrie. The climbs are described from left to right.

NORTH FACE OF THE SOUTH PEAK

South-East Ridge   105m   III
This route follows the prominent edge between the South and North Faces, with good exposure for the grade. Several variations are possible, and these become harder to the right, towards the corrie edge. Start from a ledge just left of the lowest rocks of the ridge and take the easiest line. **Jughandle** (Grade IV) starts some 20 metres around from the lower part of the ridge and climbs a corner crack to gain the ridge.

North Wall Groove   105m   V,6 ***
N. Muir, A. Paul   16th February 1977
The conspicuous groove which cleaves the upper part of the North Face gives a first-rate outing, only requiring a sprinkling of snow and a decent freeze. Start where a ledge leads up left to the foot of an obvious groove in the lower section.
1. 45m   Move easily up left to the foot of the groove (10m; possible belay). Climb the groove to its end under very steep rock, then make a hard pull out right to easier ground. Turfy steps lead to a belay at the

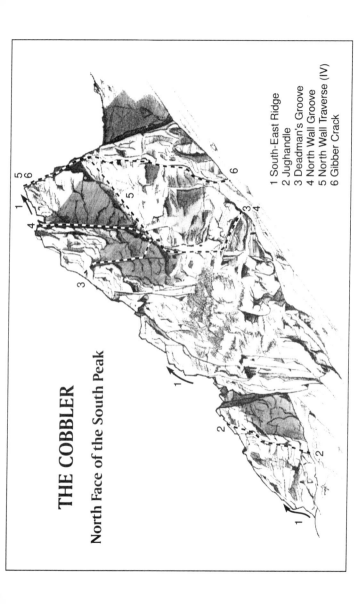

THE COBBLER

North Face of the South Peak

1 South-East Ridge
2 Jughandle
3 Deadman's Groove
4 North Wall Groove
5 North Wall Traverse (IV)
6 Gibber Crack

foot of the main groove. A direct alternative follows the edge just right of the rib (V,6).

2. 20m   Climb the groove on good turf to a belay below the harder upper section.

3. 40m   Continue up the groove until delicate moves right across a thin slab gain clumps of turf in an exposed position. Steep moves lead up and left to a final easy chimney and the top.

Deadman's Groove   130m   VII,7 **
R. Anderson, R. Milne   28th January 1990

A steep and intimidating route up the groove in the wall left of North Wall Groove.

1. 45m   Climb North Wall Groove or its alternative to a stance at the right-hand side of a small roof; thread belay.

2. 20m   Move up right for 3m, then back left above the belay to gain the groove which leads over a steepening (hollow flakes) and onto a fine perch beside the overhanging left arete.

3. 25m   Continue up the groove to its top.

4. 40m   Move left and find easy ground leading to the summit at the top of the South-East Ridge.

Gibber Crack   110m   V,7 *
R. Anderson, R. Milne   25th November 1990

An obvious winter line up the open corner-groove at the right side of the face. Start in a bay at the foot of the groove.

1. 10m   Go up rightwards to a ledge.

2. 20m   Climb the corner-groove to a crack in the right wall and follow this, then move right at a bulge to belay on its top.

3. 40m   Climb a short crack above, then move up right and follow easier ground to belay on a ledge on the crest.

4. 40m   Climb the flake crack directly above, move right, go up a short crack to a ledge, then move right again to climb to a larger ledge. Although it is possible to escape here, it is better to climb to the top *via* the second corner crack right of the arete.

CENTRE PEAK BUTTRESS

This buttress is a large but very broken east-facing crag on the east side of the ridge between the Centre and North peaks. At its south end, directly below the Centre Peak, a wide easy-angled gully goes up from the corrie to the summit rocks. A short distance north there is an obvious narrow gully, **Centre Gully** (Grade II/III). At the north end of Centre Peak Buttress near the North Peak col is the following route:

Chimney Route   70m   V,7 *
T. Prentice, P. Beaumont   2nd January 1994
This is the obvious corner system above and right of the cave-like recess at the north end of Centre Peak Buttress. Start in the gully just down from the North Peak col where turfy ledges lead to the corner. It holds snow longer than most routes.
1. 10m   Follow turf up left to the base of the first corner.
2. 20m   Climb the short, technical corner to a large ledge and continue up the easier corner above to another ledge.
3. 15m   Ascend to a higher grass ledge and traverse right, then step down to beneath a chimney.
4. 25m   Climb the chimney and walls above, taking a large jutting block on the left.

SOUTH FACE OF THE NORTH PEAK

The walls and overhangs of this peak provide impressive surroundings in winter. Unfortunately, due to the southerly aspect, on a fine day routes can strip off pretty fast. The routes all start a short distance above the path from the Narnain Boulders up to the North Peak col.

Right-Angled Gully Direct   80m   V,6 **
Reliable climbing folklore records that Hamish Hamilton made the first winter ascent of this route in the 1930s. A short way below the top he swung his long-shafted ice axe into the turf at the lip of the pitch, and climbed up the shaft. This is one of the earliest reported examples of modern frozen turf technique. Bill Murray (with J.Brown) also made a winter ascent in the 1930s.
   Start up right of the lowest rocks of Ramshead Ridge and climb this to the terrace. Climb the obvious corner of Right-Angled Gully and continue straight up where the ledge of the Ordinary Route goes off right.

Ramshead Gully   60m   IV,5 *
This is the obvious narrow chimney-gully rising from the back of the snow bay right of Ramshead Ridge.

Recess Route   110m   V,6 ***
A Cobbler classic taking the left-hand chimney line up the buttress right of the bay leading to Ramshead Gully. Either start at the lowest rocks at a cracked slab just left of a small overhung recess, or up to its left at a groove. The grade assumes verglas and cloud cover!
1. 30m   Climb from either start to reach a belay in the chimney.
2. 35m   Continue up the chimney to a terrace.
3. 30m   Move right, step into a steep groove and climb this to a cave belay.
4. 15m   Climb the overhang above and continue to the top by a final chimney.

Maclay's Crack   80m   III **
A good route with fine positions. Start round the edge of the buttress just within the lower reaches of Great Gully below an obvious groove.
1. 20m   Climb the crack-groove.
2. 10m   Continue up the left branch to a ledge on the left edge.
3. 40m   A short corner leads to a wider ledge. Follow this for 3m, then climb a shallow groove in the wall above to easy ground.

Great Gully   60m   II
The obvious gully near the right-hand end of the peak, left of Great Gully Buttress. Although the gully can bank out, there will often be an initial tricky section through and around some large chockstones and an awkward rock step at mid-height. A short climb gains the very exposed summit of North Peak, take care in misty conditions!

Great Gully Groove   95m   IV,6
R. Milne, R. Anderson   27th December 1994
There are a number of routes with interchangeable pitches on Great Gully Buttress, of which this is the most obvious line (the obvious groove running up the outside face just right of Great Gully). Start some 10 metres right of a steep shallow recess (**North Rib Route**; V,7) just right of the entrance to Great Gully.
1. 20m   Climb up and slightly left to the right side of a bay.
2. 35m   Enter the bay and climb the groove on the left (North Rib Route goes out left onto the arete and **Lulu** (IV,6) goes out right). Near the top of the groove swing out left around a roof and continue up a crack to a ledge.
3. 40m   Move left, climb a crack at the back of a huge block to a ledge and finish up a shallow groove in the upper rocks. The right side of the huge block is an alternative.

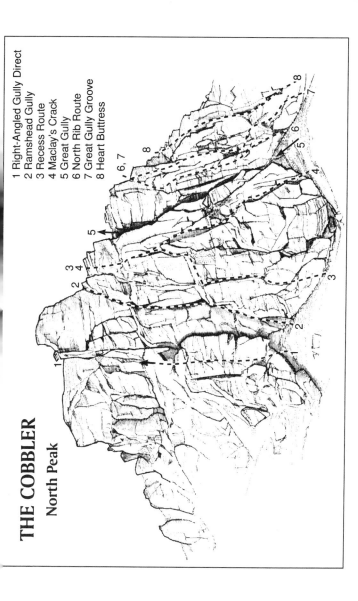

THE COBBLER
North Peak

1 Right-Angled Gully Direct
2 Ramshead Gully
3 Recess Route
4 Maclay's Crack
5 Great Gully
6 North Rib Route
7 Great Gully Groove
8 Heart Buttress

Heart Buttress (Grade III) takes walls and snow grooves to the right to finish up a short gully, whilst left of the boulders to the right is **Soul Groove** (Grade III). These routes are perhaps best combined with the following climb, to give a long continuous climb to the summit.

Chockstone Gully   100m   II *
K.V. Crocket, A. Walker   December 1983
This lies well right of Great Gully and lower down, round on the north face of the North Peak, facing Beinn Narnain. Leave the last steep section of the corrie approach path at about one-third height and traverse easy ledges right and up for about 200 metres to gain the gully edge. Two or three pitches lead to an impressive arch formed by a giant chockstone, exit by a narrow squeeze on the left or a thin slab on the right. The route finishes below Great Gully Buttress.

The Cobbler Traverse   II **
A classic day out using the Loch Long approach up the corrie and traversing all three of The Cobbler's peaks. Start up Great Gully, traverse the North Peak, climb the summit block on the Centre Peak and descend to the col. Climb to the top of the South Peak, abseil back to the col and descend beneath the South Face to finish. At the start, the expedition can be lengthened by climbing Chockstone Gully. It is possible to do this traverse the opposite way round by starting up South-East Ridge and after the Centre Peak descending under the South Face of North Peak to climb Great Gully to the top.

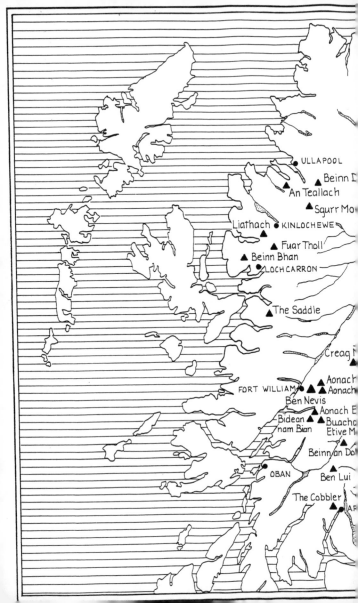